FUNCTIONAL ANALYSIS IN CLINICAL PSYCHOLOGY

Peter Sturmey
Texas Department of Mental Health & Mental Retardation
San Antonio State School, USA

JOHN WILEY & SONS

Chichester · New York · Brisbane · Toronto · Singapore

Copyright © 1996 by John Wiley & Sons Ltd,
Baffins Lane, Chichester,
West Sussex PO19 1UD, England

National   01243 779777
International   (+44) 1243 779777

Other Wiley Editorial Offices

John Wiley & Sons, Inc., 605 Third Avenue,
New York, NY 10158-0012, USA

Jacaranda Wiley Ltd, 33 Park Road, Milton,
Queensland 4064, Australia

John Wiley & Sons (Canada) Ltd, 22 Worcester Road,
Rexdale, Ontario M9W 1L1, Canada

John Wiley & Sons (Asia) Pte Ltd, 2 Clementi Loop #01-01,
Jin Xing Distripark, Singapore 0512

Library of Congress Cataloging-in-Publication Data

Sturmey, Peter.
    Functional analysis in clinical psychology / Peter Sturmey.
       p. cm. — (The Wiley series in clinical psychology)
    Includes bibliographical references and index.
    ISBN 0-471-95848-4 (cased : alk. paper). — ISBN 0-471-96170-1
(paper : alk. paper)
    1. Clinical psychology—Methodology. 2. Functionalism
(Psychology) I. Title. II. Series.
    [DNLM: 1. Psychology, Clinical—Methods. 2. Mental Disorders—
diagnosis.   WM 195 S93f 1996]
    RC467.S85   1996
    616.89—dc20
    DNLM/DLC
    for Library of Congress   95-31822
                                                                    CIP

British Library Cataloguing in Publication Data

A catalogue record for this book is available from the British Library

ISBN 0-471-95848-4 (cased)
ISBN 0-471-96170-1 (paper)

Typeset in 10/12pt Palatino by Acorn Bookwork, Salisbury, Wilts
Printed and bound in Great Britain by Biddles Ltd, Guildford
This book is printed on acid-free paper responsibly manufactured from sustainable
forestation, for which at least two trees are planted for each one used for paper
production.

TO MY PARENTS

CONTENTS

PART IV CRITICAL ISSUES

ABOUT THE AUTHOR

Peter Sturmey received a research doctorate (PhD) from the University of Liverpool for his work on active treatment in people with intellectual disabilities. He has taught at the University of the South West, Plymouth, UK, and the University of Birmingham, UK, and was a visiting professor at Louisiana State University, Baton Rouge, USA. He was Chief Psychologist at Abilene State School, Texas, and is currently Chief Psychologist at San Antonio State School, Texas. He has published widely on many topics related to intellectual disability.

SERIES PREFACE

The Wiley series in Clinical Psychology aims to provide a comprehensive set of texts covering the application of psychological science to the problems of mental health and disability. Fundamental to this work is the skill that psychologists bring to bear in their functional analysis of the problems they deal with. This is true whether they are treating an adult with agoraphobia or an eating disorder, a child who refuses to go to school, or a person who shows stereotyped behaviour associated with a learning disability.

In this book, Peter Sturmey describes carefully each aspect of a full functional analysis, from the hypothesis generation stage through the design of treatment to its evaluation. Taking his examples from the entire range of a psychologist's work with adults and children, he points out that unless interventions are based on awareness of the functions of the target behaviours they will not be fully effective. This is an extremely important message when mental health workers are increasingly needing to treat people with the most severe and apparently intractable problems.

Of particular interest to readers will be the helpful guide to how to communicate the results of a functional analysis to others. Peter Sturmey aims to teach the skills involved in such an approach, rather than merely the knowledge about it. As with all good manuals, he includes both good and poor examples so the reader may learn from both. Finally, he includes a critical review of the available literature and examines what further clinical research work needs to be done.

With a wealth of case examples throughout, this book will benefit all mental health students and practitioners.

PREFACE

Functional Analysis in Clinical Psychology was written to provide for the practicing psychologist, behavior analyst, and student clinician an overview of developments in functional analysis over the last fifteen years. This book arose principally from teaching a course to clinical psychology students who were working with a wide range of different clinical populations including adult out-patients with a wide range of clinical problems, children and adolescents and their families, persons with developmental disabilities, older adults, persons with long-term mental health disabilities, and behavioral medicine. I hope that this book will be a suitable text for others to use in similar courses. My own interest in developmental disabilities will doubtlessly be apparent at times. Work in the field of developmental disabilities has been a fertile area for functional analysis. However, I hope that my efforts to make this a book applicable to clinical work with any population or problem have been successful and helpful to clinical psychologists working in any field.

One particular objective has been to point out the implications of research for day to day clinical practice and vice versa. As someone who has moved from clinical practice, to academia, and back again, who has been actively involved in research, teaching and practice, I have been aware of the frustrations that clinicians and students can experience in accessing and using research in practice, as well as the frustrations that researchers have in attempting to influence practice.

The roots of functional analysis go back a long way. They can be found in Darwin's account of evolution which influenced Skinner's work (Skinner, 1989, Ch. 5). Many of the beginnings of its application to clinical psychology can be seen in the early work of behavior therapists in the late 1950s and 1960s. For example, in re-reading Ayllon and Azrin's (1968) classic text on the token economy many examples of functional analysis can be discerned. These include analyzing baseline behavior to identify reinforcers and the use of constructional tactics to establish functional, alternate behaviors to replace undesirable, maladaptive behaviors indirectly.

Although functional analysis has been with us for a long time there have been major changes over the last fifteen years. These have included both technological changes, such as better and more explicit methods of assessment of the functions of behavior, as well as some conceptual refinements. Since the early 1980s we have had new questionnaires, interview formats, observational methods, and strategies for the practitioner and researcher to use. The development of this new technology has been rapid and its impact continues to be evaluated. Encouraging examples of cross-fertilization from one area of clinical practice to another are beginning to appear. For example, Kearney and Silverman (1990) developed earlier research on self-injury in persons with developmental disabilities as the basis for developing a technology to assess the functions of school refusal in children and adolescents without developmental disabilities.

Developments in functional analysis have taken place in many different fields from criminological psychology (Gresswell & Hollin, 1992) to designing life environments in spacecraft (Brady, 1990). It is difficult for the practicing clinician and the researcher to keep up with developments in their own field as well as those in outer space. One of the purposes of this book is to bring together this diverse literature, to point out some of the commonalities which can be found in many different contexts, and to draw together the range of technologies that are now available for use.

As well as providing a compendium of assessment tools and procedures for use in functional analysis this book also reviews the literature on functional analysis in many different areas. An important distinction is that between the methods and process of functional analysis (Mash, 1985). There have been major developments in methods of functional analysis. Many of these remain to be fully validated as to their robustness, reliability, and validity in influencing the design of effective treatments. Nevertheless, important strides have clearly been made here. The process of functional analysis has been, in comparison, relatively neglected. This gives rise to important questions for both practice and research. Clinicians, and, indeed, technical assistants, can be trained fairly quickly to use the methods of functional analysis. However, the processes of developing and using a functional analysis have remained relatively neglected. Allied to these process questions are matters of efficiency, economy and cost. Services, both publicly and privately funded, continue to be more and more cost-conscious and sensitive to issues of accountability. These matters are intimately bound up with the application of functional analysis in clinical practice. These issues, also, need to be addressed by future research.

ACKNOWLEDGMENTS

Much of the material in this book derives directly from teaching at the University of Birmingham between 1987 and 1991. I own a debt to my colleagues, whose ideas I have undoubtedly freely used. In particular I should like to thank Professor Kevin Howells, Dr Clive Eastman and Dr Delia Cushway who taught much of these courses with me. I learned a great deal from all of them. I should also like to thank the trainees who participated in these courses. A special thanks is due to Mary McCann, Thelma Sargee, and Deb Olvera who have patiently helped me with the preparation of the manuscript at various times. Lastly, thanks to Johnny and Max Matson: sources of inspiration and models of excellence during the summer of 1991.

Part I

INTRODUCTION AND LITERATURE REVIEW

Chapter 1

FUNCTIONAL ANALYSIS: AN INTRODUCTION

A common task facing any therapist is the assessment of a clinical problem in order to determine the appropriate intervention to modify the problematic behaviors, thoughts or feelings. A clinical problem might be related to an individual, group or organization. In any of these cases the clinician faces the same procedure: deciding what information to collect, delineating the problem, deciding what action to take, and evaluating change. This problem and functional analysis as a framework to solving such problems form the theme of this book.

In this chapter the conceptual basis of functional analysis is reviewed. A historical background to the field is provided. The shifting definitions and connotations are illustrated by reviewing alternative accounts of functional analysis. Finally, in the last section of the chapter an overview of the book is provided.

STRUCTURALIST AND FUNCTIONALIST APPROACHES

A number of different approaches have often been taken to this problem. A commonly made distinction between different approaches to the problem has been between structuralist and functionalist approaches (Haynes & O'Brien, 1990). Structuralist approaches are exemplified by diagnostic, personality, and psychodynamic approaches to human behavior. Here, emphasis is placed upon correct classification of the form of the behavior. Examples include psychiatric classifications such as DSM-IV (American Psychiatric Association, 1994), assessment of personality type, or fixation at a certain stage of psychological development. All of these approaches attempt to look at the form of a person's behavior and assign it into a number of predetermined types.

Structuralist approaches have had considerable success in acute physical

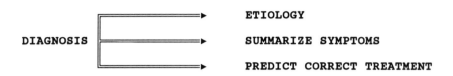

Figure 1.1   A Simplified Structuralist/Diagnostic Model

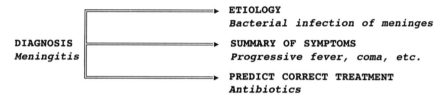

Figure 1.2   A Simplified Structuralist/Diagnostic Model Applied to a Simple Illness

medicine. In acute illnesses the structure of a presenting problem, the cause of the problem, and the implied treatment all closely map onto each other (see Figure 1.1).

Structuralist diagnostic models have been highly successful in acute medicine. Acute illnesses, such as bacterial infections or fractures, lend themselves readily to this simple model where a correct diagnosis and a powerful understanding of the disease process satisfactorily predicts treatment (see Figures 1.2 and 1.3). However, even within medicine, chronic problems with multiple, additive risks, and with important bio-behavioral components such as obesity, hypertension, or coronary heart disease do not lend themselves readily to such a model. With complex psychiatric and behavioral disorders there has been little success in using this model. There is still considerable controversy on the reliability of psychiatric classification (Zwick, 1983). Further, single, discrete causes have not been determined or related to treatment and prognosis in any simple way. Thus, the appropriateness of structuralist approaches to determine treatment has often been questioned.

Functionalist approaches to behavior emphasize the purposes that behavior serves for the person (Goldiamond 1974, 1975a). Functionalist approaches place importance, and often preeminence, on the part environmental events play in causing, controlling, and maintaining behavior. Functionalist approaches emphasize an idiographic approach to the assessment of each problem. That is, they are interested in the analysis and treatment of the behavior of the individual organism,

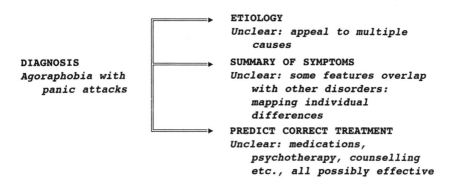

Figure 1.3 A Simplified Structuralist/Diagnostic Model Applied to a Psychological/Psychiatric Problem

rather than with a diagnostic group. Functionalist approaches to behavior de-emphasize the form that the problem takes and shift attention to the purposes that the behavior might serve for the individual. Functionalist approaches emphasize mapping the function, rather than the form, of the problem onto treatment. Thus, presenting problems of very different form could be seen as conceptually similar and imply similar interventions. For example, functional analysis of an elderly person with Alzheimer's disease who deliberately falls and of a child who whines and clings to its parent may show both to be behavior maintained by inappropriate attention. Both might require very similar forms of treatment even though the diagnoses that are implied are very different.

Case Example

An example of this approach is illustrated by a brief case study reported by Bergman (1976). A 7-year-old boy was referred with a diagnosis of Hyperactivity. He was about to be placed on methylphenidate for this hyperactivity. During the assessment his parents reported that they had always had problems with him getting to sleep. His mother regarded him as a 'nervous child'. Previously, his physician had recommended that he be allowed to stay up as long as he liked as he would eventually tire out and fall asleep. This had failed and so he had recommended a trial of methylphenidate.

Interview with his parents revealed that the parents allowed him to sleep with them every night. Thus, his 'hyperactivity' was actually a social operant behavior. The initial intervention was an extinction procedure. His parents were instructed to return him to his bed immediately with minimum interaction every time he came into their room, no matter how many times it took. Within two weeks his night-time hyperactivity had ceased. Day-time 'hyperactivity' was similarly treated with an extinction procedure. His mother was instructed not to think of him as a 'nervous' child any more and to attend to him for independent play. At six month follow-up there had been no recurrence of the night-time hyperactivity and the boy now preferred to play independently with his peers rather than be around his mother all day.

In this study the structuralist approach of the physician can be contrasted with the functionalist approach of the behavior therapist. The physician is concerned to make a correct diagnosis as the basis for selecting a pharmacological treatment indicated by that diagnosis. The behavior analyst is not too concerned about the diagnosis. Rather, emphasis is placed on understanding the environmental determinants of the behavior. The environment is then modified based on the best hypothesis of the nature of the behavior.

HISTORICAL ROOTS

The idea of functionalism has a long history in science and philosophy stretching back over 2000 years (Haynes & O'Brien, 1990). Examples of functionalism may be found in such diverse fields as sociology, anthropology and biology. It is no coincidence that Skinner borrowed heavily from Darwin. Darwin asked 'Why do Galapagos Finches have different beak lengths on different islands?' meaning what is the function or evolutionary advantage to having different beak lengths on different islands. In the same way, a behavioral scientist might ask 'What functions do these apparently pathological behaviors serve for this person? What is the advantage in these behaviors being selected out by the environment?' Skinner repeatedly refers to the parallels between natural selection and operant psychology (Skinner, 1989). Thus he writes:

> Behavior . . . is the product of three kinds of selection, the first of which, natural selection, is the field of ethology. The second, operant conditioning, is the field of behavior analysis. The third, the evolution of the social contingencies of reinforcement we call cultures . . . (p. 27)

The vocabulary and metaphors of operant psychology are clearly borrowed from evolution. Thus, the environment selects behavior. The removal of a reinforcer leads to extinction of the behavior. Operants are selected, split, and are extinguished. More complex forms of behavior gradually evolve. A more detailed discussion of the evolution of behavior during the organism's lifetime can be found in Glenn, Ellis and Greenspoon (1992) and Glenn and Field (1994). The work of Skinnerian psychologists in the 1950s and 1960s forms the basis of much of the current interest in functional analysis.

In Great Britain an important contribution was made by Monty Shapiro. Shapiro developed a series of methodologies which permit repeated assessment of a client's problem (Shapiro, 1966, 1970). Shapiro developed a series of measurement methods that enables a number of target behaviors to be tracked on a daily or weekly basis. This notion of repeated measurement, analyzing the day to day variations in the behavior and the possible causes was an important contribution. The notion of intensively studying the variations in the behavior of one client over time was a key contribution from Shapiro which parallels the intensive study of a single rat or pigeon during learning as conducted by the experimental behavior analysts.

Finally, Israel Goldiamond's work on constructional tactics is another major contribution to functional analysis (Goldiamond, 1974, 1975a, b). Constructional tactics are those methods of intervention which focus upon the notion that problematic behavior is behavior which, although distressful to the client or significant others, successfully produces desirable and logical consequences which the person's adaptive behavior does not. Goldiamond was concerned with both the ecology of a person's multiple behaviors, rather than focusing on a single response or problem, and the social ecology in which the person's behavior occurs. The most well known facet of the constructional approach is the focus upon extending current repertoires of adaptive behaviors and developing new ones. Thus, the focus of the constructional approach is not to treat the target behavior directly, but to support and increase functionally equivalent alternate behaviors.

Goldiamond also identified the role of insight into the contingencies controlling a client's behavior as a key component of treatment. Thus, the notion of sharing a client's functional analysis as a form of treatment can be traced back to Goldiamond's writings.

CONCEPTUAL ISSUES

Although there is a relatively large empirical literature on functional analysis in clinical psychology, theoretical development and conceptual analysis of the term have received surprisingly little explicit attention and are not well known. There have been few reviews of these issues. The reader is referred to Haynes and O'Brien (1990) for the most recent and comprehensive review. An earlier position statement can be found in Owens and Ashcroft (1982). A concise review is presented by Jones (1983). An interesting debate on the nature of functional analysis can be found in a series of articles by Samson and McDonnell (1990), McDonnell and Samson (1992), Owens and Jones (1992) and Jones and Owens (1992).

One problem which has dogged the literature has been the use of several different terms used as more or less equivalent to 'functional analysis'. At other times the same term has been used with somewhat different connotations by different authors. Haynes and O'Brien (1990) list 'functional behavioral analysis', 'behavioral assessment', and 'behavioral case formulation' as some of the terms used. To add to the confusion few explicit definitions of the term 'functional analysis', other than Haynes and O'Brien's own, have been made. These definitions have included: (a) statements concerning the mathematical form of the relationship between different variables; (b) statements relating to the function or purpose of the behavior; (c) a generic, atheoretical approach to assessment and case formulation; (d) descriptive, eclectic functional analyses; (e) descriptive, behavioral functional analyses; (f) using the term exclusively for experimental manipulations of variables in order to show functional relationships between behavior and the environment; and (g) functional analysis as a treatment method or component of treatment. These seven connotations of the term 'functional analysis' will be reviewed below in some detail.

Mathematical Relationship Between Variables

Functional analysis is a term used to describe an abstract branch of mathematics. This branch of mathematics describes the relationship between variables by removing inessential details from the content of the problem. Thus, there are math journals such as *Functional Analysis* and *Journal of Functional Analysis* which have nothing to do with clinical psychology. Within this context a functional analysis is simply descriptive. Causation is not necessarily implied.

Clinical analogs of this kind of functional analysis are readily apparent. Typical assessment questions such as 'Where does the problem occur?' or 'When is the problem worse?' will yield information about the way variables are related to the problem behavior(s). Consider the statement 'during weekdays binge eating rarely occurs before 4 p.m. and is progressively more likely to occur from 4 p.m. to 9 p.m.' This statement would constitute this kind of functional analysis. It simply describes the form of the relationship between time of day and binge eating. It makes no inference about the purpose of the behavior for the person or about any possible causation.

This aspect of functional analysis has been developed by Haynes who draws attention to the fact that the functional analysis between variables may take a number of different forms (Haynes, 1988; Haynes & O'Brien, 1990). Simple linear functional analyses are possible, e.g., 'the likelihood of binge eating in this client increases over time of day'. However, functional analyses may be much more complex than this. The shape of a functional analysis may be linear, quadratic, 'U' shaped or whatever. For example, one might say 'the frequency of binge eating increases dramatically (quadratically) from 4 p.m. to 9 p.m. and then reduces dramatically (quadratically) and remains close to zero from 11 p.m. through 3 p.m.'

Behaviors may have multiple causes and causes may vary across individuals and time. For example, a person with Agoraphobia with Panic Attacks might have panic attacks primarily when they are in social situations when they might be criticized and may also panic when they think about such situations. The overall probability of a panic might also increase when they are under additional stress, for example, when they are working to deadlines. Multiple causes may be interactive or additive. For example, a person might react somewhat badly to a meeting with their boss, but if it is a few days before the deadline they might react catastrophically with extremely intense, long panics. Causes may also be bi-directional (Haynes, 1988). Owens and Ashcroft (1982) note the importance of identifying feedback loops within a functional analysis. For example, a person who fears social incompetence and criticism from others might become anxious in the presence of a stranger. This may cause them to act somewhat oddly in the presence of others. The other person might then ask questions of them to see if they are okay. This might then make the person even more socially anxious and incompetent. This is an example of a positive feedback loop (Owens & Ashcroft, 1982).

Haynes and O'Brien (1990) refined these ideas further in order to clarify the nature of variables that can enter into a functional analysis. They note that some functional variables are causal and others are correlational. Some are controllable or modifiable. Others are not. Some variables are important in magnitude whereas others are trivial. Functional analyses are probabilistic rather than deterministic. Functional analyses are also non-exclusory. That is, a relationship between two variables does not preclude relationships between these and other variables.

Functional analyses are transient and may vary over time. For example, the variables relating to the onset of a problem may not be the variables relating to its further development or current maintenance. For example, there is now some empirical evidence that the functions of self-injury in persons with developmental disabilities can change over time (Lerman, Iwata, Smith *et al.*, 1994). This can be associated with relapse since the initial treatment, indicated by the first functional analysis, is no longer appropriate.

Independent variables may be necessary, sufficient, necessary and sufficient for change, or merely correlational. Thus, identifying the variables that actually cause a clinical problem may be very difficult as in the natural environment there may be other variables that are correlated with the true cause. For example, a person with agoraphobia with panic attacks might report panics when they leave the house. However, they can only leave the house when accompanied by their spouse. Further, recently they have only ever tried to leave the house to go visit their sister who lives half an hour's walk away. In this situation it is unclear if the panic attacks are caused by some perceptual aspect of leaving the house, such as seeing the open sky, the possibility of strangers seeing them and evaluating them negatively, the behavior of the spouse when they try to leave, or the thoughts of what might happen if they get to the sister's house. Haynes and O'Brien go on to note that functional relationships may also have boundaries, within which they hold true and beyond which the functional relationships may change or be inapplicable. For example, a person may only react catastrophically to social criticism when they experience depressed mood. When they do not feel depressed they may be able to dismiss social criticism easily.

Functional variables may be macro-level variables, such as ethnicity or social class, or micro-level variables, such as frequency of social criticism. Finally, causal functional relationships require that the causal variable always precedes the caused event. This is a necessary, but not sufficient, condition for causality.

This analysis led Haynes and O'Brien (1990) to define functional analysis as: 'the identification of important, controllable, causal, functional relationships applicable to a specified set of target behaviors for an individual client' (p. 654).

Thus, the clinical application of functional analysis does not attempt to describe all the relationships amongst relevant variables. Those that are of trivial magnitude and which cannot be modified are excluded in order to simplify the picture and to identify those variables which could be modified during treatment. Thus, in this context, functional analysis is an idiographic form of assessment which is oriented to develop an individually tailored treatment.

Purposes of Behavior

A second connotation of functional analysis is that the behaviors under consideration serve a purpose for the individual. Functional analyses within clinical psychology are full of examples of this kind of functionalism. We commonly talk of the secondary gains that clinical problems have. Here the presenting problem (e.g., agoraphobia) is seen as having the function of eliciting help from other family members or avoiding adult responsibilities such as work or family duties. In a similar way a person with poor social skills or with a dominant, punishing spouse might be unable to effect any change in the family through regular social behavior. However, hyperchondriacal complaints may be an effective way of achieving some of their goals within the family, or establishing some social role for themselves within the family other than that of a quiet, unassuming person.

A strong area of research over the last ten years in this area has been the work done on the communicative significance of behavior disorders, both in children and adolescents, and in persons with developmental disabilities (Carr & Durand, 1985). It has been hypothesized that persons with limited behavioral repertoires, who may be in environments which fail to support adaptive, communicative behaviors, have learned other, functionally equivalent behaviors. These other behaviors are topographically very different from regular communicative behaviors, but serve the same functions as communication. Thus, both speech, signing, or screaming or displaying a tantrum can obtain social or tangible consequences or avoid aversive situations. In this sense a maladaptive behavior has become an effective form of asking for a tangible, for attention, or for a demand to be removed.

Generic Case Formation

Owens and Ashcroft (1982) have argued that functional analysis is a generic method of case formulation which transcends the theoretical orientation of the clinician. They suggested that variables in clinical psychology can be classified as (a) whether they serve to change the probability or severity by the behavior, and (b) whether they are antecedents or consequences of the behavior (p. 183). They argue strongly that this kind of functional analysis may be carried out independent of the theoretical orientation of the clinician. They go on to note that feedback loops are often an important part of clinical formulations.

In a reply, Jones (1983) noted that while functional analysis within mathematics can free the observer from the content of the problem this is not the case in psychology. Jones argues that it is not possible to carry out an abstract, bias free method of data collection on a clinical problem. For example, some theoretical orientations lead clinicians to ask about dreams or recollections of childhood routinely and give them special status. Others do not even routinely enquire about such variables.

Since the publication of Owens and Ashcroft's review formulations of this kind have appeared. The book of case formulations by West and Spinks (1988) presents formulations which, if not rigorously behavioral, are broadly cognitive-behavioral on the whole and illustrate the application of functional analysis to a very wide range of problems. However, few if any authors have taken up Owens and Ashcroft's challenge and presented functional analyses from a wide range of other theoretical perspectives such as psychoanalysis or gestalt therapy.

Descriptive, Eclectic Functional Analyses

Many British clinicians describe themselves as 'eclectic' or 'broadly cognitive-behavioral'. Such clinicians often use functional analysis as part of their clinical work. This kind of functional analysis incorporates cognitive and behavioral variables, and typically will make some hypotheses about the relationship between these variables, although often these hypotheses may be implicit, rather than explicitly stated. However, they do not typically test these hypotheses in a rigorous, experimental fashion. Such formulations typically borrow freely from a wide range of cognitive and behavioral theories and treatments as the individual clinician sees fit.

These formulations are believed to be the basis of the treatments that are implemented. For example, a clinician may hypothesize that a person's depression is due to their style of thinking and lack of appropriate assertive skills. These problems include making attributions that their successes are due to luck, and that many of the negative aspects of their life are due to their own incompetence and correctly reflect their own lack of worth and incompetence. Their poor social skills might include lack of assertive behaviors with their spouse, and outbursts of anger and crying over relatively minor disputes with their spouse. On the basis of such a formulation the clinician may attempt to retrain the person's pattern of attributions by teaching them an adaptive pattern of self-talk and to teach them assertive social behaviors for specific, difficult situations.

Descriptive, Behavioral Functional Analyses

Some descriptive functional analyses are made more narrowly from within the perspective of applied behavior analysis. These formulations are based specifically from considering the current contingencies that may be operating to maintain the maladaptive behavior, and that fail to maintain functionally equivalent maladaptive behaviors (e.g., Ayllon, Haughton & Hughes, 1965). They construe the development of the problems from the perspective of maladaptive behaviors being learned over the lifespan (e.g., Bijou, 1963). However, in these functional analyses an experimental analysis which manipulates the variables that may maintain the maladaptive behaviors is not conducted.

In an adequate descriptive, behavioral functional analysis the behavior of the individual must be adequately described in reliable operationalized terms. For example, stating that 'the person shows compulsive behaviors' would not be adequate. Stating that 'the person opens doors with tissues, refuses to open doors with their bare hands, uses alcohol to clean door handles, cutlery and dishes, washes their hands with industrial sanitizer approximately four hours a day, asks others to fetch contaminated items, etc.' is the beginning of a carefully operationalized target behavior. Where relevant, topographically different molecular responses must be grouped into molar response classes of functionally equivalent molecular responses. For example, a child's 'non-compliance' might be defined as including 'turning his head away, whining, saying that he did not hear an instruction, not coming down from his bedroom when called, etc.'. In this example several very different molecular behaviors are grouped together because it hypothesized that they all serve the same function, namely avoiding compliance with requests.

As well as specifying a target behavior an adequate descriptive functional analysis must also specify the replacement behaviors taught during the intervention. These must be functionally related to the target behaviors. That is they must be adaptive behaviors that can serve the same function as the target behavior and be effective in serving that function. Thus, routinely teaching relaxation to persons with phobias would be inappropriate since phobic avoidance could serve a number of functions other than anxiety reduction.

Response definition is a much more complex and subtle matter than is generally acknowledged. Yet, a functional analysis crucially depends upon this stage of analysis of the problem. Some of these problems are discussed in detail in later chapters.

A second feature of a descriptive, behavioral functional analysis is that the consequences maintaining the behavior must be specified in functional terms. These can include both positive and negative reinforcers that might maintain the maladaptive behavior. Positive reinforcers are those consequences that are presented contingent on the target behavior and make the future occurrence of the behavior more likely. Negative reinforcers are those consequences that are removed contingent on the target behavior and make the future occurrence more likely. As well as the contingencies operating on the maladaptive behavior an adequate functional analysis should also specify the contingencies that have failed to maintain adaptive responding. It may be that the person has never learned appropriate behavior, that appropriate behavior has a fragile learning history, or that currently there is little reinforcement or punishment for adaptive responding.

Consider the following example: a teenage girl was referred to a clinical psychologist for numerous conduct problems, one of which involved staying out late at night unsupervised. Initial home visits revealed that her home was unkept, smelled, and was dirty from dog feces. Her mother had a severe psychiatric disorder and was either withdrawn or at times quite bizarre. She felt it impossible to take her friends, let alone a boyfriend, over to her own house in the evening. However, spending time with her friends was fun. They drank, smoked, listened to music, inhaled glue, had occasional sex, and spent endless hours hanging out and having a good time. A causal analysis of the contingencies operating the girl's behavior indicates that her behavior was entirely rational and a function of the contingencies operating in the home and with her friends.

An important limitation on descriptive functional analysis is that it is difficult to verify whether the stimuli hypothesized to be reinforcers or punishers actually are reinforcers or punishers. For example, evaluations as to whether stimuli will be reinforcers to others which are based on third party reports, can be very inaccurate (Green, Reid, White et al., 1988). The clinician must be wary of making simplistic formulations such as describing social attention as the reinforcer for behavior disorders (Cullen, 1983).

A further problem is that many chronic problems may be maintained by relatively thin, intermittent schedules of reinforcement. If the frequency of the behavior is fairly low then it may be very difficult to ascertain the schedules of reinforcement maintaining the behavior. In a similar way, if a person no longer shows a functionally equivalent adaptive response or only does so at a very low frequency, the clinician may have very limited information to use to assess what the contingencies are that have failed to support adaptive, functionally equivalent behaviors.

A third feature of a descriptive, behavioral functional analysis is that a distinction is made between antecedents and Establishing Operations (Michael, 1982). An antecedent is a stimulus which immediately precedes the behavior and changes the probability of the behavior. Antecedents are relatively discrete and temporally close to the behavior. They correlate closely with the availability of reinforcers or punishers. For example, if a colleague said to a socially anxious person 'Are you coming out with us to-night?' and the person immediately became tense the question from the colleague would be an antecedent. An Establishing Operation is the process that establishes a stimulus as a reinforcer, punisher, or changes the value of a reinforcer or punisher (Michael, 1982). For example, if a child is left alone for a long time this might establish social attention as a reinforcer; likewise, if the child has eaten a large meal this might reduce the value of even a favorite candy as a reinforcer.

A fourth feature of descriptive, behavioral functional analyses is that private events (non-observable variables) may enter the analysis in a number of ways. A private event might be a target behavior. Examples here could include chronic pain, mood, or an intrusive, horrible image. A private event might enter into a functional analysis as an antecedent. For example, a suicidal thought might be the antecedent to a suicidal act, or an intrusive image might be an antecedent for ritual hand washing. Finally, a private event could enter into a functional analysis as a consequence. For example, removal of anxiety following avoidance of the phobic object, a feeling of despair following an unsuccessful date could all constitute important consequences in a functional analysis.

A frequent error is that private events such as thoughts, feelings and physiological states are excluded from a behavioral functional analysis. This is incorrect (Skinner, 1989: Ch. 1). Private events give rise to two kinds of problems for a behavioral functional analysis. The first is a methodological problem. Private events can only be measured by self-report. By definition they can not be measured objectively and reliably. Further, they may be reported inaccurately, or not at all. Some people may find it very hard to accurately discriminate and report their private experiences in language that can be understood by others. For example, many people with anxiety disorders need training to discriminate and report varying degrees of anxiety. The main conceptual problem for behavioral functional analysis relating to private events is that of elevating them to a special causal status not given to other variables.

Experimental Functional Analyses

Several authors, sensitive to the problem that functional relationships between variables may be more apparent than real, have explicitly restricted the term functional analysis to the experimental manipulation of variables to demonstrate causal relationships between an independent variable and behavior (Baer, Wolf & Risley, 1968; Iwata, Vollmer & Zarcone, 1990; Skinner, 1953). Thus, Baer, Wolf and Risley (1968) wrote that:

> the analysis of a behavior . . . requires a believable demonstration of the events that can be responsible for the occurrence or non-occurrence of a behavior . . . an ability of an experimenter to turn the behavior on and off . . . (pp. 93–94)

This approach excludes non-experimental attempts to assess the functions of behavior as, at best, only partial assessments. Non-experimental approaches might generate hypotheses, but cannot be said to constitute a functional analysis as such since the hypothesis is not tested. Indeed, Baer, Wolf & Risley (1968) go on to write that: '. . . a non-experimental [functional] analysis is a contradiction in terms . . .' (p. 92).

A good example of this approach is shown in a creative study by Chapman, Fisher, Piazza and Kurtz (1993). In this study they conducted an experimental analysis of the life-threatening drug ingestion in Lyle, a 19-year-old man with mild developmental disabilities. The problem was made more difficult because the man could travel independently and purchase over the counter medications in potentially lethal quantities. This had led to six visits to the emergency room for overdoses. An initial descriptive functional analysis suggested three hypotheses. These were that the behavior was maintained by attention from medical personnel, by his mother, or by escape from work. The function of the behavior was experimentally evaluated by placing Lyle in a simulated classroom with four pill bottles filled with placebos accessible in a simulated medication treatment room. The four bottles were color coded. Lyle was informed that ingestion of a pill from each bottle was followed by different treatments. One was followed by 30 minutes of medical attention, one was followed by 30 minutes of his mother scolding him, one was followed by escape from work by having to lie down for 30 minutes, and one had no consequence following it. Lyle's pill ingestion was observed covertly through a one-way screen. The dependent variable was the number of placebo pills ingested from each bottle in a session.

There were 15 assessment sessions (see Figure 1.4). After the seventh session he consistently selected the pill followed by 30 minutes escape from work. Based on this experimental analysis of his behavior an intervention was designed based on the hypothesis that pill taking was reinforced by escape avoidance. The intervention consisted of earning non-work activities for completing work tasks and for turning in pills he had apparently found. Pill ingestion was followed by requiring him to clean shoes, a non-preferred task. There was also a fading procedure to gradually remove stimuli associated with the treatment environment. Lyle responded well to treatment in the assessment setting. At follow-up 5 months after discharge only 11% drug screens had been positive compared to 85% of drug screen prior to treatment. Also, there had been no emergency room visits.

Functional Analysis as Treatment

When many clients first present for treatment they may be bewildered or perplexed by their problems which may be perceived as random and out of control. When working with third parties such as parents or staff they may also be at a loss to understand why a problem is happening with a family member or person they work with. Indeed, it is not uncommon for the client or third parties to have their own lay theory as to the cause of the problem. These can include unhelpful personalistic views, such as 'He is an alcoholic', or moralistic views such as 'He is doing it to get back at me'.

Several authors have described functional analysis as a treatment in and of itself or have described it as a treatment component. For example, Miller (1978), in a study of problem drinking, incorporated functional analysis as part of the training for clients in the behavioral self-control group. Clients in this group were taught to reduce the rate of drinking,

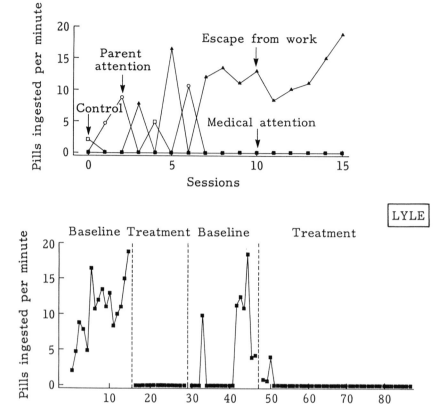

Figure 1.4 The Results of the Functional Analysis of Dangerous Pill-taking by Lyle. Reproduced by permission from Chapman, S., Fisher, W., Piazza, C. C. & Kurtz, P. F. (1993), Functional assessment and treatment of life-threatening drug ingestion in a dually diagnosed youth. *Journal of Applied Behavior Analysis*, **26**, 155–156. Copyright © *Journal of Applied Behavior Analysis*

to identify and modify the antecedents for drinking, and to identify and practice alternative strategies to drinking. Thus, in this approach working with the client to develop a functional analysis of their own behavior and assisting them to use the functional analysis to change their own behavior is viewed as being a part of the treatment process itself. Presenting a functional analysis to a client or working collaboratively with a client to develop a shared functional analysis is often a component of many behavioral treatment packages such as anxiety management and anger management.

The use of a functional analysis as part of treatment has generally been underplayed and it is not known how important having this kind of behavioral insight into one's problems might be in determining the outcome of treatment. However, as noted earlier, Goldiamond (1975a, b) has recommended that clients should be allowed to discover their own functional analysis rather than have it delivered to them by the therapist. From an ideological position, it is generally seen as desirable that the client participates as fully as possible in their own treatment. Thus, having an active consumer who has a full knowledge of their own problem, including the functions of one's maladaptive behavior, should be seen as desirable for several reasons.

Comment

As can be seen from the preceding sections, the term functional analysis has taken on a variety of different connotations in the hands of different authors. Its exact meaning shifts between authors and not all authors are explicit as to how they are using the term.

Functional analyses can be said to vary along at least four dimensions. First, some papers present a functional analysis of a particular diagnostic class of problems such as eating disorders (Slade, 1982), depression (Ferster, 1973), or self-injury (Carr, 1977), whereas others present a functional analysis of an individual case. Second, whereas some authors have emphasized the functional analysis of the outcome of psychopathology, others have used functional analysis to describe processes such as conditioned reinforcement (Schuster, 1969), development in both intellectually average children and children with developmental disabilities (Bijou, 1966) or imitation (McCuller & Salzberg, 1982). Third, authors have varied in the weight placed on current environmental events as opposed to the onset and development of the problem. For example, functional analyses of behavior disorders have generally emphasized current, maintaining events (Iwata, Vollmer & Zarcone, 1990). In other functional analyses of single cases the emphasis can be placed on understanding the onset and development of the problem (Gresswell & Hollin, 1992). For example, Wolpe's analyses of adult neuroses often explore the onset and development of the problems because of the potential importance of conditioning events in adult neuroses in determining the exact content of the desensitization intervention (Wolpe, 1989). Finally, almost all publications in the area of functional analysis have addressed issues related to psychopathology. However, it should be noted that functional analysis can be equally applied to everyday, non-problematic behavior. This is, in fact, hidden within many clinical applications of functional analysis since they may attempt to understand and increase replacement adaptive behaviors. For example, the application of functional analysis to non-clinical problems can be found in the work of Bijou and Baer (1961, 1965) on child development.

OVERVIEW

This book falls into four sections. The first two chapters form an overview of functional analysis. This chapter provides an introduction to the field. Chapter 2 provides a selective review of the literature. The issues covered in these first two chapters cover a broad range of clinical populations and will provide illustrations of clinical practice with a variety of problems and populations. Part II reviews a number of assessment issues and methodologies used in functional analysis. These include interviewing, direct observation, and psychometric measures. Part III discusses issues related to the processes of developing a functional analysis. This includes how to develop and use a functional analysis. In the final section a single chapter reviews critical issues in functional analysis. These include the reliability and validity of functional analysis, the issue of treatment efficacy, and the cost and benefits associated with functional analysis. Finally, areas for future research are discussed.

Chapter 2

FUNCTIONAL ANALYSIS: A SELECTIVE REVIEW OF THE LITERATURE

The literature on functional analysis is very broad and scattered throughout several different literatures. Examples of functional analysis can be found within the literature on the experimental analysis of behavior, where the general laws of learning are studies with one or two rats or pigeons, or in other branches of experimental psychology which attempt to elucidate processes related to learning. Examples of functional analysis can also be found in journals concerned with the application of functional analysis methods to problems of applied significance such as the *Journal of Applied Behavior Analysis, Behaviour, Research and Therapy, Behavioural Psychotherapy*, and *Journal of Behavior Therapy and Experimental Psychiatry*, as well as a number of other clinical and educational journals not specifically concerned with functional analysis. Functional analysis has also been used with a wide range of populations such as children and adolescents in school settings, persons with a wide range of psychiatric disorders including anxiety, depression and psychoses, and behavior disorders, older adults, persons with acquired brain damage, and criminal behavior. It has impacted a wide range of applied problems from self-injury to recycling trash. Although primarily used in the context of psychopathology functional analysis has also been used to understand non-pathological behavior. Furthermore, it has been taken up by psychologists and other professionals in different sub-specialties such as clinical psychology, criminological psychology, special education, gerontology, and business consultancy. Thus, the material on functional analysis is scattered over a fairly wide area of the literature.

In this chapter a selective review of the research literature on functional analysis will be presented. Rather than attempting to discuss each and every paper a small number of illustrative papers will be discussed in detail. A brief summary of various papers will be presented in tabular form for the interested reader to follow up as desired.

Gresswell and Hollin (1992) make a distinction between functional analyses which can be either idiographic or nomothetic. An idiographic functional analysis is the analysis of an individual case such as one person with an eating disorder. A nomothetic functional analysis is the functional analysis of a given diagnostic category such as the diagnostic label Anorexia Nervosa. In organizing this review of the literature two additional categories of functional analysis will be added. The first is the functional analysis of psychological process, such as imitation, child development or secondary reinforcement. The second is the functional analysis of complex systems, such as organizations, therapeutic environments, or prisons.

FUNCTIONAL ANALYSIS OF DIAGNOSTIC CATEGORIES

Since the early review by Owens and Ashcroft (1982) and the accompanying article by Slade (1982) on eating disorders, functional analyses of a wide range of diagnostic categories have appeared. Many examples can be found in the field of adult, child and adolescent and developmental disabilities as well as scattered articles in other fields. A summary of these reviews can be found in Table 2.1. Papers using this approach to functional analysis share a number of features in common. Typically a diagnostic category, a set of diagnostic categories or a set of apparently related behaviors or symptoms is selected. A literature review is then constructed using the notions associated with functional analysis such as the possible antecedents, behaviors and consequences that might constitute a functional analysis, and the role of learning in the development of a problem. Many such reviews use flow diagrams or charts to summarize the hypothesized development or maintenance of the problem under consideration.

In this section several illustrative papers will be discussed in detail in order to illustrate the functional analysis of a diagnostic category. Slade's (1982) functional analysis of anorexia is selected as an example of functional analysis applied to an adult psychiatric problem. Burke and Silverman's (1987) review of school refusal is selected as an example of how functional analysis can be used as a conceptual framework to review the literature and develop treatment-oriented assessment strategies (Kearney & Silverman, 1990). Finally, Layng and Andronis' (1984) functional analysis of delusional speech and hallucina-

Table 2.1   A Summary of Functional Analyses of Diagnostic Categories

Reference	Problem
Child and adolescent disorders	
Hughes and Sullivan (1988)	Social skills
Kearney and Silverman (1990)	School refusal
Burke and Silverman (1987)	School refusal
Carr and Durand (1985)	Behavior disorders
Gresham (1985)	Behavior disorders
Biglan *et al.* (1994)	Behavior disorders
Hartup (1974)	Aggression
Jones and Heskin (1988)	Delinquency
Jackson *et al.* (1987)	Recidivist arson
Mace and West (1986)	Reluctant speech
Adolescent / adult disorders	
Slade (1982)	Anorexia and Bulimia Nervosa
Loro and Orleans (1981)	Binge eating
Schlundt *et al.* (1985)	Bulimia and obesity
Ferster (1973)	Depression
McNight *et al.* (1984)	Depression
Staats and Heilby (1985)	Depression
Barnett and Gotlieb (1988)	Depression
Lewinsohn *et al.* (1985)	Depression
Dougher and Hackbert (1994)	Depression
Vandereycken and Meerman (1988)	Chronic illness / non-compliance
DeSeixas Queiroz *et al.* (1981)	Obsessive-compulsive disorders
Clark (1984)	Hallucinations
Layng and Andronis (1984)	Hallucinations and delusions
Haynes (1986)	Paranoid behavior
Upper *et al.* (1982)	Social and coping skills
Staats and Heilby (1985)	Personality disorders
Keane *et al.* (1985)	Post-traumatic stress disorder
Developmental disabilities	
Bijou (1966)	Developmental disabilities
Bijou and Dunitz-Johnson (1981)	Developmental disabilities
Carr (1977)	Self-injury
Day *et al.* (1986, 1988)	Self-injury
Iwata and Neef (1994)	Self-injury
Mace *et al.* (1987)	Stereotypy
Sturmey *et al.* (1991)	Stereotypy
Mace *et al.* (1991)	Behavior disorders
Behavioral medicine / addictive behaviors	
Ross and Schwartz (1974)	Drug abuse
Sobell *et al.* (1976)	Alcohol abuse
Norton and Nielson (1976)	Headaches
Redd and Rusch (1985)	Behavioral medicine
Redd (1980)	Cancer
Vandereycken and Meerman (1988)	Chronic illness and compliance
Wulfert and Biglan (1994)	AIDS prevention

tory behavior is used as an example of the application of functional analysis to the understanding of psychotic behavior. The reader interested in the application of functional analysis to areas of their own interest can consult Table 2.1 for possible additional references.

Anorexia Nervosa

Slade's (1982) functional analysis of anorexia is presented in Figure 2.1. Slade states that previous reviews of anorexia have emphasized antecedents rather than consequences. Here Slade uses 'antecedents' in a very broad sense, referring to predisposing factors, historical events, as well as specific triggers for anorectic behavior. The formulation of anorexia presented here is as follows. Certain necessary setting conditions exist for the development of anorectic behavior. These include initial dieting behavior and weight loss. When dieting commences this leads to feelings of success and being in control. These behaviors are positively reinforced through these feelings and negatively reinforced through avoidance of aversive situations such as weight gain and other social problems. This sets up a positive feedback loop between dieting behavior and its reinforcing consequences. Weight gain becomes punishing and weight loss becomes reinforcing.

In Figure 2.1 the principal antecedents are labelled (1) through (8). *Dissatisfaction with life/low self-esteem* include issues regarding conflicts relating to independence/dependence during adolescence. Family conflicts, commonly observed in families with anorexic members, may exacerbate these problems. Other factors that predispose towards anorectic behavior include poor relations with the opposite sex and scholastic failure in high-achieving individuals. *Perfectionist tendencies* are seen as a second group of antecedents. These may be related to the need for high achievement and control. The *need for complete control* in some aspect of life is seen as a further antecedent which may predispose the person to develop complete control over bodily appearance and eating behavior. *Specific psychosocial stimuli* refers to specific triggers such as a critical comment concerning appearance which then precipitates initial dieting in individuals who are already weight sensitive.

Figure 2.1 Slade's (1982) Functional Analysis of Anorexia. Reproduced by permission of the British Psychological Society from Slade, P. (1982). Toward a functional analysis of Anorexia Nervosa and Bulimia Nervosa. *British Journal of Clinical Psychology*, **21**, 170

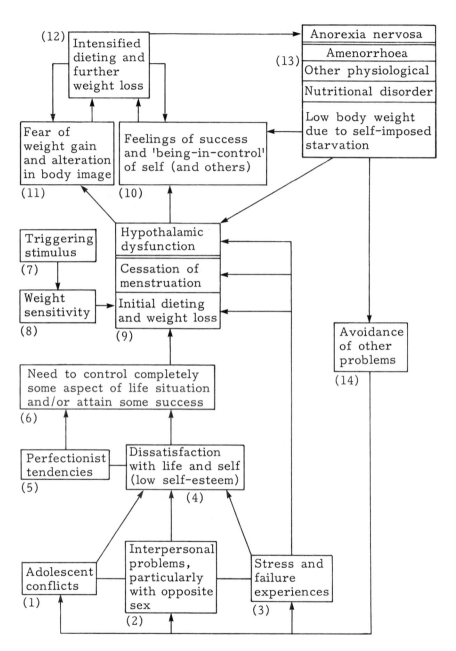

Diagrammatic formulation of anorexia nervosa

Behavior (9) refers to two major components. These are dieting and weight loss. In normally menstruating females this includes amenorrhea which may be related either to weight loss, to change in nutritional status, or to stress experiences.

Consequences are labelled (10) through (14) in Figure 2.1. They include both positive and negative reinforcers. Positive reinforcers can include feelings of success, control and increased self-esteem in the context of perceived failure in other areas of life. Negative reinforcers can include avoidance of several negative consequences such as fear of weight gain and fear of an unpleasant body image. The preoccupation with food and eating is seen as an example of avoidance of thinking about unpleasant things such as adolescent conflicts, interpersonal problems and failure experiences.

Slade's functional analysis of Anorexia Nervosa primarily emphasizes the development of anorexia. Although variables which relate to the current environment are indeed discussed, emphasis is placed upon the development of the problem.

This functional analysis was developed with implications for treatment in mind. Several feedback loops are presented which can maintain anorectic behavior. Such feedback loops could be used to identify points of intervention. Other implications for treatment of this model include developing alternate sources of reinforcement for the individual other than those related to eating behavior. Simply targeting weight gain may be insufficient if the factors maintaining anorectic behavior are not addressed. This model also implies that the development of a wide range of alternate behaviors such as alternative interests and sources of successes would be important. In this way the sources of reinforcement to the person would be broadened away from eating behaviors. A third area of intervention implied by this model is the resolution of antecedent factors such as independence/dependence issues which predisposed the person to the eating disorder.

School Refusal

A pair of articles have presented a functional analysis of school refusal (Burke & Silverman, 1987; Kearney & Silverman, 1990). Burke and Silverman (1987) review the predictors of differential treatment response in school refusal, focusing primarily on structural-diagnostic predictors. They note that school refusal has been classified in several ways, usually into two types. These have been variously called Type

I/neurotic/sudden onset/acute and Type II/characterological/gradual/ chronic. The former has usually been perceived to be mild and more responsive to treatment. The latter has usually been perceived as more severe and less responsive to treatment. A second typology of school refusal has included a three-way classification: separation anxiety, school phobia and depressed withdrawal. DSM-IV (American Psychiatric Association, 1994) does not explicitly include a category of school refusal although *Separation Anxiety Disorder*, and *Overanxious Disorder of Childhood* all might be appropriate diagnoses for school refusal. A third commonly cited empirical classification of childhood disorders is that of overcontrolled-internalizing disorders versus undercontrolled-externalizing disorders. School refusal may be related to several narrow-band disorders classified within overcontrolled-internalizing disorders such as overdependent, anxious, schizoid/anxious, or immature disorders.

The principal criticism made of all these classification systems is that none are explicitly related to treatment design. There is no strong empirical evidence that any of these classification systems are helpful in assisting the clinician in selecting or designing more effective treatment programs. Burke and Silverman do note that the three-way typology of separation anxiety, school phobia and depressed withdrawal might be closest to this.

In a subsequent article Kearney and Silverman (1990) develop a methodology for assessing the functions of school refusal by borrowing directly from Durand and Crimmins' (1988) functional analysis of self-injury. They classified the potential function of school refusal as one of four functions: (a) avoidance of specific fears or general over-anxiousness at school, (b) escape from aversive social situations at school, (c) attention-getting or separation anxiety, and (d) tangible reinforcers such as access to TV or friends. They use this behavioral diagnosis to indicate the treatment appropriate for the function of school refusal in each case.

This functional classification of school refusal makes an interesting contrast to the previous structural classifications. First, it is explicitly related to treatment selection and design rather than structural features of school refusal, such as the duration of the problem or precise psychiatric diagnosis. Second, it borrows a conceptual framework from a clinical situation-functional analysis of self-injury—which relates to a set of problems which are diagnostically and topographically unrelated to school refusal. This is a nice illustration of the functional approach to behavior where the form or topography of the problem is underplayed whereas the functional significance of the problem is highlighted.

Delusional Speech and Hallucinatory Behavior

The final example of functional analysis of a diagnostic category comes from Layng and Andronis' (1984) analysis of delusional speech and hallucinatory behavior. They begin their analysis of delusional speech and hallucinatory behavior assuming that such behaviors are operants like any other behavior, and do not assign them any special status. They note that once a behavior is seen as abnormal then people search for special causes for such behavior when it is unnecessary. They argue that it can be hard to tell what appears to be pathological or what normal behavior. A person who repeatedly seeks out violent encounters where injury and brain damage are likely may well be seen as pathological. Of course when professional boxers exhibit such behavior it is seen as a rational choice because the contingencies operating are clear. They argue that what makes this behavior bizarre is not the topography of the behavior. Rather, it is whether or not the environmental stimuli controlling the behavior are apparent and the context in which the behavior occurs that determines whether the behavior is seen as bizarre.

Layng and Andronis argue that by taking the 'ir' out of irrational the hallucinatory behavior and delusional speech can be seen as an adaptation to environments where the alternative behaviors are ineffective. Thus, psychiatric symptoms are here conceived of as successful operants when other operants have failed.

They present a case of a new in-patient tossing paper plates in the air with stars drawn on them. After one of the authors had given some assistance in this activity they asked her why she was doing this. The reason was to check the levels of electricity in the air which were bothering her and had caused power surges at home making the lights go bright. When asked if the electricity ever bothered her she replied firmly 'No, never!', however, the electricity was made worse when she had 'emotional stress'. She reported that her emotional stress had recently been made worse by serious financial and housing difficulties. She had tried to figure out what to do. The lights in her apartment started to become bright due to power surges. She then went out and threw a brick at the telephone wire figuring out that she would probably be taken to a hospital. The interviewer told her that the social worker on the unit was particularly skilled at helping people with financial and housing problems. For the first time she sat back and looked relaxed. There then followed a long conversation about the relative merits of the admission procedures of different kinds of hospitals. During this time there were no electricity surges for over an hour. This case study illustrates the situation specificity of a behavior that would often be seen as 'organic' or 'biological' rather than 'environmental'. It was clear that for this woman hospital admissions, legitimized by reporting psychiatric symptoms, gained her access to reliable help and solutions to her problems not available to her in the outside world. This paper is a nice illustration of an analysis, from first principles, of an apparently 'organic' problem using the principles of functional analysis. The behaviors are defined. They are assumed to be functional or adaptive. Environmental events are delineated which might relate to the frequency of the problem and alternative, adaptive behaviors are identified which might be used to serve the same purposes as the maladaptive behaviors. Other examples of a functional analysis approach to psychotic behavior can be found in Table 2.1.

Comment

The three papers reviewed in this section illustrate a range of approaches to conducting a functional analysis of a diagnostic category. Slade's (1982) approach presents a single functional analysis of one diagnostic category. This paper attempted to describe the development of a disorder within the terms of functional analysis. Individual differences are only alluded to within the diagnostic category. For example, Slade also presents a functional analysis of a second kind of eating disorder. Nevertheless, the impression is that of a functional analysis of a diagnostic category, rather than of an individual person's behavior. In Burke and Silverman (1989) and Kearney and Silverman (1990) individual differences related to the functions of school refusal are explicitly sought in order to place each individual within one of the four types of functions which are used to determine treatment choice. In Layng and Andronis (1984) the general principles of functional analysis are applied to a single case within a diagnostic category.

A functional analysis of a given diagnostic category clearly has some heuristic value to the clinician. It can highlight some of the common forms of the target behaviors about which to inquire. For example, it can highlight some of the common functions of the particular problem under consideration, outline assessment strategies, and indicate the interventions that are indicated and contra-indicated by the functions of the behavior (Iwata, Pace, Dorsey *et al.*, 1994). Thus, after reading Slade's review of eating disorders a clinician would be able to ask about the kinds of triggers that might precipitate eating disorders, the more common forms of the behavior, and the common reinforcers maintaining the problem.

Although the notion of functional analyses of a diagnostic category can have some practical value to the clinician there are certain inconsistencies with this approach. First, it implicitly subscribes to the psychological reality of diagnostic categories. Reviews of the reliability of even research diagnostic criteria reveal that the reliability of diagnosis is more modest than commonly believed (Zwick, 1983) and when applied to specific clinical populations their utility may be severely limited (Sturmey, 1993). Second, and more importantly, the functional analysis of a diagnostic category may subscribe to a structural approach through implying a mapping from diagnosis to treatment. As can be seen from the papers on school refusal, functional analysis can borrow freely across the boundaries of diagnostic categories. A third criticism has been made by Gresswell and Hollin (1992), namely that a single functional analysis can appear to be static. It can fail to capture the changing functions of behavior as they develop over time (see below).

FUNCTIONAL ANALYSIS OF INDIVIDUAL CASES

It would not be possible to review all the published functional analyses of individual cases. There are several hundred such cases published (Haynes & O'Brien, 1990; Scotti, McMorrow & Trawitz, 1993). The interested reader can consult West and Spinks (1988) for a compendium of analyses of single cases in a wide range of clients and settings. An extensive biography of the use of behavior-analytic methods with persons with severe psychiatric disorders is to be found in Scotti, Evans, Meyer and Walker (1991). Rather than attempting to provide a comprehensive review of several hundred papers this section will review five examples of functional analyses of single cases. These cases were selected to illustrate the range of styles used in the functional analysis of single cases. The case presentation used by Wolpe (1989) will be used as an example of the skillful kind of functional analysis which corresponds closely to regular clinical practice. The case study by Sturmey (1995a) will be used to illustrate the use of functional analytic methods from first principles to a clinical problem that is rarely reported in the literature: suicidal threats and attempts in a person with developmental disabilities. The functional analysis of tics by Malatesta (1990) will be used to illustrate an example of experimental analysis and hypothesis testing using observational data on a single case. The study by Mace, Browder and Lin (1987) was selected to illustrate the experimental analysis of psychotic speech. Finally, the functional analysis of the behavior of a multiple murderer will be used to illustrate the use of functional analysis to integrate a mass of assessment information economically. This paper also illustrates a functional analysis which focuses on the development rather than the current maintenance of a problem in order to understand an apparently random and meaningless act of violence (Gresswell & Hollin, 1992).

Anxiety Disorders

Wolpe (1989) presented a case history to contrast the analytic aspect of functional analysis with superficial behavioral analysis, eclecticism, and cognitive approaches to anxiety disorders. Wolpe alleges that these latter practices represent a misguided view of behavior analysis and believes that they are common practice.

Wolpe emphasizes the importance of very careful analysis of stimulus–response relationships in anxiety disorders before treatment is designed. This is necessary in order to reveal exactly the variables controlling the problematic behaviors. Without such information it is not possible to identify precisely those stimuli that the person with an anxiety disorder needs to be desensitized to. If this is not done the clinician is in danger of falling back on a cookbook approach to behavioral treatment, for example, placing the persons in a standard exposure program or anxiety management group, which may fail to address the route of the phobia.

Wolpe describes a 27-year-old, attractive woman, 'Jane', presenting with lack of confidence and lack of self-esteem. She had previously been treated two years ago with cognitive therapy and exposure therapy which were both unsuccessful over a four-month period.

Initial interviews and psychometric tests led to the formulation that she was extremely sensitive to being watched, criticism, the presence of her supervisor, and shortcomings in appearance. Her fears included rejection, disapproval, and being ignored. She was unable to date, had little social life, and even walking in the street was difficult. These problems began when she was 18 years old. At that time she had received an unexpected negative evaluation from a teacher.

Careful questioning led to the conclusion that what she found difficult during interactions with others was not other people's scrutiny, attitudes, demeanor, or what they said. What she found disturbing was what she *imagined* other people had thought about her. Thus, Wolpe's formulation hypothesized that distress was a clinically conditioned response to these thoughts, rather than meeting people or any actual real life situations in which these occurrences actually took place.

Desensitization based around desensitization to *imagining* other people's thoughts was therefore implemented. This illustrates the crucial role that private events can have in a functional analysis.

The previous two years of 'cognitive-behavioral' therapy had been cookbook treatment based on an erroneous functional analysis or on no functional analysis at all. These interventions had included many standard behavior therapy treatments that are commonly viewed as effective treatments for phobias such as exposure, relaxation and cognitive restructuring. However, none of these treatments had addressed the woman's reactions to her imagining what other people thought about her, and, thus, did not address the actual antecedent that precipitated fear and panic.

Treatment consisted of constructing a two by two hierarchy of critical others and critical thoughts they may have. Initially she was trained in relaxation. Jane imagined a low fear item such as the doorman saying 'Jane is a very nice person but she doesn't dress in good taste'. An admiration hierarchy was treated similarly.

This case study illustrates a key aspect of functional analysis: a model or hypothesis is developed which analytically describes the problem. The treatment is then based on this hypothesis.

Suicidal Threats and Behavior in a Person with Developmental Disabilities

At times a functional assessment has to be made on incomplete data, quickly, and from first principles. Sturmey (1995a) reported using functional assessment to develop an effective and safe form of psychiatric surveillance for a man with moderate developmental disabilities. Eduardo had repeatedly made suicidal threats and shown suicidal behavior over at least a six-month period. In line with local policy whenever he made a suicidal threat he would be interviewed by a physician or psychiatrist and asked to make a no-harm agreement. If this was not forthcoming he was then admitted to a Multiple Disabilities Unit (MDU) in the nearest psychiatric hospital for up to 30 days.

At an emergency meeting one Friday it transpired that Eduardo had been readmitted that day, had already made suicidal verbalizations and attempts, and arrangements were being made to return him to the MDU as the meeting proceeded. Interviews with medical staff, staff at the MDU, and in his regular residential facility revealed that (a) suicidal threats were only made in his home, not at the MDU, (b) suicidal threats and behavior had become more frequent over the last year, (c) Eduardo was a very socially-oriented person who showed numerous behavioral excesses which included many forms of inappropriate social behavior, and (d) Eduardo did not like participating in any of his programming in his regular home.

It therefore appeared that in some way the existing management strategy was reinforcing suicidal threats and behavior, either by contingent social attention from the special treatment he received either prior to going to the MDU or at the MDU, or that he was being negatively reinforced by removal of programmatic demands in the home. A method of psychiatric surveillance was therefore developed that would remove social attention for suicidal threats and behavior, keep Eduardo safe from harming himself, and would allow medical staff to meet their professional standards of using no-harm agreements with persons who were suicidal. Therefore if Eduardo made a suicidal threat or attempt a staff member would ask him one time for a no-harm agreement. If this was not immediately forthcoming he was escorted to the infirmary for a period of 24-hour social isolation. A staff member was always present in the room, but was generally given clerical work to do and instructed not to interact with Eduardo. All possible sources of reinforcement such as the TV, radio, pictures on the wall, had been removed. At the end of a 24-hour period Eduardo was asked to give a no-harm agreement or remain in social isolation for another 24 hours.

Over the next six months there were no further admissions to the MDU. Thus, the disruption to his programming had been successfully addressed. The procedure had not been used frequently, and procedural problems had been dealt with promptly. At six month follow-up this restrictive procedure was successfully eliminated from his program and Eduardo remained safe.

Tic Disorder

Malatesta (1990) presented a formulation of a nine-year-old boy, Mark, with multiple problems. The major problem was an eye tic, but additional significant problems included academic difficulties, despite an IQ well above average, depression, distractibility, low risk taking, fear, and anxiety in novel situations, poor peer relations, and a poor father–son relationship. The initial interview suggested that a key element in this problem was a hyper-vigilance for criticism. The person who most elicited this problem was the boy's father who was severely critical of the boy's behavior generally and his achievement in particular.

From initial interviews and psychometric assessments Malatesta (1990) stated his formulation as follows:

All seven problems were formulated as manifestations of a hypersensitivity to criticism . . . related to the boy's relationship with an insecure,
demanding and critical father . . . hypersensitivity to his father's criticism
. . . then generalized to other evaluative situations . . .' (pp. 224–225)

On the basis of this formulation Malatesta made five predictions. These
were (a) that the tic frequency would be highest when exposed to an
evaluative model, (b) the rate of tics should be highest in the presence
of his father compared to another evaluative model, (c) the rate of tics
should be higher with the therapist than the mother, (d) the presence of
the mother should be associated with the lowest rate of tics, and (e) the
presence of the father and the mother together should produce an intermediate rate of tics.

To test these hypotheses an experimental study of the frequency of the
tics was conducted as well as frontalis EMG responses. This involved
counting the rate of tics in the presence of various combinations of
adults while Mark was working on a series of puzzles. In order to test
these hypotheses experimentally a series of systematic reversals were
conducted comparing the tic rate when the boy was alone (A), when
his father was present (B), the therapist (C), his mother (D), an
unknown custodian (E), and his mother and father (F) resulting in an
A-B-A-C-A-D-A-E-A-(BD) design.

The results are shown in Figure 2.2 on the frequency of tics. All five
hypotheses were confirmed. Similar results were found with the data
on frontalis EMG. On the basis of these confirmed hypotheses Malatesta
then developed the following treatment strategy. In order to decrease
the stimulus value of the father from an evaluative to a non-evaluative
model a series of tasks were developed for the father and son to carry
out. The tasks were designed so that the father deliberately made errors
and coped with the outcome, for example, knocking over a can of paint.
Also, a series of joint activities between the father and son were
planned which were pleasurable and non-evaluative, for example,
going to a baseball game. The father's own insecurity did not allow
that the issue of changing his own behavior be directly addressed.
Three weeks later Mark's tics had completely disappeared. These gains
were maintained at 18 months follow-up.

Bizarre Speech

Although many functional analyses are based upon client interview and
psychometric assessment, systematic observation may also be a useful
method. Mace, Browder and Lin (1987) present an example of this

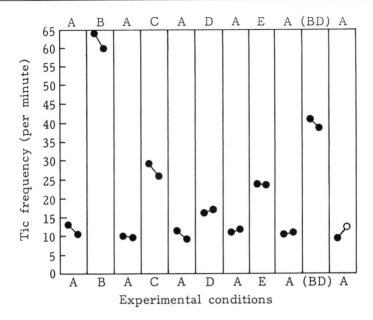

Figure 2.2   Mean Tic Frequency per Minute as a Function of the Experimental Condition

A, baseline/child working alone; B, father present; C, therapist present; D, mother present; E, custodian present; BD, father and mother both present

Reproduced by permission of Plenum Publishing Corporation from Malatesta, V. J. (1990). Behavioral case formulation: An experimental assessment study of transient tic disorder. *Journal of Psychopathy and Behavioral Assessment*, **3**, p. 226, Figure 2

method of conducting a functional analysis. The participant was a 29-year-old woman who was diagnosed with mild developmental disabilities and schizophrenia. Mace, Browder and Lin emphasize the importance of basing treatment upon an initial analysis of baseline data in order to ascertain the interactions between behavior and environment. The bizarre speech included references to things not present, inappropriate sexual comments, and maladaptive speech (e.g., 'I can't be helped'). Initially data were collected using informal observations and interviews with care staff. These data suggested two hypotheses which might account for the maintenance of bizarre speech: (a) that bizarre speech was maintained by negative reinforcement through escape/avoidance from demands to participate in activities, and (b) that bizarre speech was maintained through positively reinforcing attention from staff and peers.

Four conditions were developed in order to evaluate these two hypotheses and to develop a potential treatment. During these conditions the social environment was manipulated to simulate the kinds of naturally occurring consequences which might maintain the target behaviors according to each of the hypotheses. The *Demand* condition consisted of working at a vocational task. If, after an instruction to work, the client did not respond within 10 seconds and emitted a bizarre statement the experimenter responded to the statement and the task was discontinued for 10 seconds. Thus, in the *Demand* condition possible positive and negative reinforcers were made contingent on bizarre speech. In the *Group interaction* condition two staff were present with the client and attention was given for *both* appropriate *and* bizarre speech. In this condition the client had to compete for conversation divided between three people. During *One-to-one interaction* a single staff member asked questions similar to those asked during the *Group interaction*. Appropriate speech was responded to by speech from the staff, but bizarre speech was followed by staff glancing away and no-one spoke until at least 10 seconds elapsed without bizarre speech. Figure 2.3 shows the results from this analysis.

From this observational analysis it can be concluded that bizarre speech was strongly reinforced by escape from task demands. This information was used to develop an intervention. A *Guided compliance* procedure was used during failure to comply with demands. If the subject failed to initiate task behavior within 10 seconds of a request to do so manual guidance was used. Eye contact and attention to bizarre vocalizations were avoided during this procedure. Independent performance was praised. Thus, the treatment package used the information gained during the experimental baseline condition relating to powerful reinforcers maintaining the problem behaviors as well as the antecedents prompting it.

Multiple Murder

Gresswell and Hollin (1992) used the conventional Antecedent–Behavior–Consequence paradigm to organize case material in a segmental fashion to illustrate the development of offending behavior. This form of functional analysis emphasizes the development of a problem, which, divorced from its developmental context, appears senseless. The gradually changing functions that target behaviors and the precursors those behaviors can serve are presented in a series of seven interlocking functional analyses in chronological order.

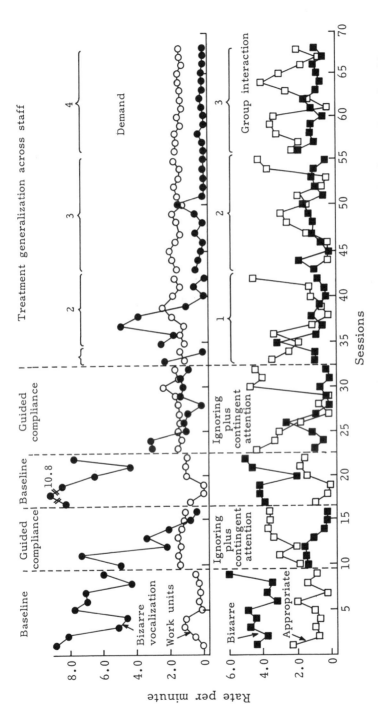

Figure 2.3 The Rate of Bizarre Vocalizations during *Demand*, *Group Interaction*, and *One-to-one* Conditions. Reproduced by permission of Pergamon Press Ltd from Mace, F. C., Browder, D. M. & Lin, Y. (1987). Analysis of demand conditions associated with stereotypy. *Journal of Behavior Therapy and Experimental Psychology*, **18**, 25–31, Figure 2

DB was a man detained under the power of the Mental Health Act without time limit following two unsuccessful attempted murders and a formulated plan to kill 20 people. The functional analysis of DB's early experiences revealed that key antecedents to the development of early problematic behavior included emotionally cold and insensitive parents, physical problems (undescended testicle and cystic acne) and rejection by peers. During early and teenage years this led to problematic behaviors such as searching through his parents' possessions and insisting that they report details of their conversations in order to get to know them. There had been three suicide attempts. Problematic covert behaviors included a feeling of being different and alienated from family and peers, fantasies of ideal parents, miracle cures for acne, and revenge fantasies of slashing other people's faces. Such fantasies gave temporary relief and feelings of power not available to him from other adaptive strategies. Other consequences also included poor relations with parents and peers, and lack of feedback from others on his behavior. He developed a further strategy of believing he was better, more sensitive and charming than others. Key learning experiences at this stage were seeing himself as very different from others in a highly negative way, and learning that revenge fantasies made him feel good.

A second functional analysis illustrates the development of problems during his early work experiences. These included the objectification of others, the use of lies to present a more normal, socially successful self, but also fear and anxiety related to dating women. This led to a further suicide attempt after an attempted and unsuccessful date.

The third and fourth functional analysis relates to DB's development of fantasies at the age of 29. At this time he was told by a plastic surgeon that his acne could not be treated (antecedent). This led him to feel angry and humiliated by the surgeon (covert behavior). The death of his mother at this time (antecedent) led him to become preoccupied with death and to fantasize about having companions when he died (covert behaviors). All of these led to still greater avoidance of others (overt behavior).

In the fourth functional analysis he moved to a public housing apartment. He became more overtly hostile at work, was more depressed and anxious, and sought help from his family doctor and a lay counselor. At this point his fantasies about the after life merged with his adolescent revenge fantasies. Revenge fantasies of massacres at work began. He began taking a knife to work.

During the next stage he began to believe that people who came to the store where he worked believed him to be sexually inadequate. He began eating lunch in the car. He also began taking a wooden doweling club to work as part of his massacre fantasy. This, again, provided temporary feelings of relief. Following an overdose he was admitted to a psychiatric hospital. After a month he was discharged and told that there was nothing anyone could do to stop him carrying out a massacre.

At this time the Hungerford massacre in which many people were murdered by one multiple killer was reported in the national media. This event acted as a key antecedent in deciding to try to beat the total number of deaths in the Hungerford massacre. He began to prowl at night in search of potential victims (overt behavior). This initially made him feel excited and confident (consequence). He also began to observe potential victims closely and open their mail. This repeats the maladaptive strategies used with his parents as a child. Eventually prowling alone came to feel pointless without action.

The final functional analysis relates directly to the offenses. Immediate antecedents included having some of his paintings rejected by an exhibition and the police making inquiry at his home relating to a local assault. Although not suspected by the police he thought that if someone else could do it so could he. He bought a crowbar and did some minor acts of vandalism. He then realized it was one year since he had told his GP about his fantasies but that nothing had changed. He gained access to an elderly female's house, attacked her with a doweling club, intended to kill her but fled when the club broke. He felt that he had done well and that his victim would never have peace. He went to bed and slept well.

At his weekly counseling session his counselor was extremely suspicious of him and would not see him in his office alone. DB went out that evening intending to slash another victim's face but found no opportunity. He returned home after several hours feeling unsatisfied. He later went back to town to find another victim. After waiting several hours outside his victim's house DB stabbed him when he got out of his car. The victim's wife called the police and DB was arrested.

Gresswell and Hollin (1992) note that this form of functional analysis is a highly economical way of summarizing material. In this case available material included 300 pages of documentation and 16 hours of interviews. These were summarized in seven tables. Second, this functional analysis makes sense of behavior which was initially without apparent meaning. Specifically, the function of the massacre fantasies appeared to be a pleasurable way of coping with extreme despair triggered by minor social events. Third, this analysis suggests strategies for change. These include training in alternative methods of coping with triggers such as social intimacy. It also identifies triggers for potential violent behavior in the future.

Comment

The functional analysis of individual cases is probably the most common form of functional analysis. The cases reviewed illustrate the wide range of assessment methods used for this task. It should be noted that these cases illustrate the full range of emphasis placed on history versus current environment in the functional analysis of individual cases. In the cases by Sturmey (1995a) and Mace, Browder and Lin little emphasis was placed upon the history of the problem. However, all were concerned with the analysis of indiosyncratic factors that would indicate correct forms of intervention and contra-indicate other forms of intervention. Assessment for the purposes of developing a treatment is a major function of this approach. The functional analysis of individual cases is treatment-oriented assessment *par excellence*.

Developing a functional analysis for an individual case is a highly complex and subtle process. It raises many issues concerning data collection, generating and testing clinical hypotheses, and developing treatments based upon these hypotheses. These issues will be discussed in greater detail in Parts II and III of this volume.

FUNCTIONAL ANALYSIS OF PROCESSES

A number of authors have used functional analysis as a method to understand and clarify psychological processes. Examples here include attempts to provide a functional analysis of normal development (Bijou & Baer, 1961, 1965) and development in persons with developmental disabilities (Bijou, 1963, 1966). Others have used functional analysis to understand other processes of behavioral change such as imitation (McCuller & Salzberg, 1982). In this section we will consider some of these papers as illustrations of this form of functional analysis.

Child Development

One of the classic functional analyses of behavior comes from a series of papers by Bijou and his colleagues on the functional analysis of the development of behavior in persons with developmental disabilities (Bijou, 1963, 1966; Bijou & Dunitz-Johnson, 1981). He states that:

a retarded individual is one who has a limited repertoire of behavior shaped by events that constitute his history . . . psychological development consists of progressive changes in interactions between the individuals, as a total functioning biological system, and the environmental events. (p. 2)

Development of a person who shows average behavior is seen as being the result of interactions between an intact biological system and an environment which facilitates average development. For the person who shows developmental disabilities the opportunities to learn have been curtailed through a damaged biological system and an environment which fails to foster normal behavior. Relevant limitations in a biological system, which may impair development, include limitations in the ability to respond to relevant environmental events. Physical or behavioral features of the individual which may elicit abnormal environments such as excessive or inadequate care, lack of opportunity to engage with the environment, or which elicit abusive or inappropriately punitive care practices may cause adaptive behaviors not to develop. Bijou goes on to suggest that environmental factors which can cause developmental delayed behavior can include infrequent or sparse reinforcement, withholding reinforcement inappropriately, reduced opportunities to learn due to social or economic factors, excessive and inappropriate aversive stimulation, and reinforcement of inappropriate behavior.

Bijou does address organic factors and internal states as part of an account of the development of behavior associated with developmental disabilities. However, they are not elevated to causal status. Rather, they are an integral part of an inextricable link between environmental and organismic factors. Bijou's functional analysis of behavior associated with developmental disabilities has been highly influential both in understanding the process of development, and in forming a theoretical basis for intervention.

Consider the following case example:

Kerry was a 21-year-old man with Down's syndrome who was non-verbal. He was admitted on an emergency basis to a large residential facility for emergency respite because of severe self-injurious behavior (SIB), self-restraint, and related medical problems.

A developmental history revealed that Kerry had several life-threatening medical problems. He had a congenital heart defect. His parents had been told when he was young that he would probably not survive. They therefore treated him as a sick child. At the age of 12 he had hyperthyroidism. This was associated with his heart beating very fast. This genuinely placed his life in danger. He subsequently had his thyroid gland partly removed and took thyroxin. Recently he had had several ear infections associated with SIB which had been very difficult to treat because of lack of cooperation. This had led to the possibility of additional hearing impairment.

His parents reported that he had always been reluctant to participate at school. At his most recent school placements teachers had just left him alone. They felt that teachers did not know how to teach him as they did not have experience of working with this kind of problem. They were reluctant to teach him because he would become disruptive or self-injure if approached. He was also in a large classroom with a variety of other adolescents, some with very demanding behavior, who took up most of the teacher's time.

Although a program was successfully implemented to address his SIB during the day implementation problems persisted at home. His parents both ran their own businesses, had years of sleep deprivation, had three young adult children in school with associated financial stress, and had a poor relationship. Presumably they had 21 years of punishment for placing demands on Kerry and were reluctant to press him too much at home. For example, they often sent him to his day program with two large pillows which he used for self-restraint, even though they had been asked not to do so.

In this case study the person's developmental history can account for both the lack of development of skills that should have occurred in this person, and the development of SIB. Kerry had reduced opportunity to learn because of medical problems, being treated as a sick child, and unskilled teachers and parents with no support on how to teach a person with avoidant behavior in teaching situations. These factors led to the lack of appropriate social and communicative behaviors that could serve the same function as the SIB. Further the SIB was low effort, easy to perform, and immediately effective in arousing parents and staff to action.

Imitation

McCuller and Salzberg (1982) provide an interesting example of the application of functional analysis to the process of imitation. As in Bijou's work on child development, functional analysis is used to clarify the nature of the phenomenon being considered, the behavioral processes necessary for imitation to occur, and factors which can promote or inhibit the development and maintenance of imitative behavior.

McCuller and Salzberg note that simply observing that two or more people behave similarly does not necessarily constitute imitation. For behavior to be considered imitation *three* conditions must be met. These are (a) the behavior of the imitator must happen after the model, (b) the imitator must perceive the behavior of the model, and (c) the behavior of the model must control the behavior of the imitator. Thus, a functional analysis of imitation would see imitation as a discriminated operant in which an antecedent, the behavior of the model, is a discriminative stimulus for the response, imitation, which is reinforced. The functional analysis of imitation is somewhat more complex than this. Since imitation only occurs at certain times or places, the three-term contingency just described must be under further superordinate control. Thus, imitation can be described as being under conditional discriminative control.

This analysis was used by McCuller and Saltzberg to point out crucial features necessary for training imitative behavior. First, the conditions of the three term contingencies (model–imitation–reinforcement) must be met. There must be clear evidence that the behavior of the subject is under control of the model. However, it must also be shown that the behavior is under control of superordinate stimuli to clearly constitute imitation. This analysis is also used to distinguish the mechanisms by which individuals can fail to learn to imitate. First, an individual could fail to learn the simple three-term contingency. Second, an individual could fail to show conditionally discriminated responding. That is, the subject may not understand under what circumstances it is required to imitate.

FUNCTIONAL ANALYSIS OF SYSTEMS

Many authors have noted the complexity of attempting to understand freely occurring behavior in the natural environment. In naturally occurring behavior there may be multiple participants. Apparently simple Antecedent–Behavior–Consequence relationships may be modified by a complex range of establishing operations and changes in organismic state, and available resources may modify the behaviors observed. In the natural environment organisms do not come with the controlled learning history of the experimental white rat. Rather, they have a complex learning history which may be unknown and unremembered, yet it forms the basis of their current behavior. The behavior observed may not be in steady state. Rather it may gradually change as the environment selects out new response classes, splits and merges old ones. Finally, the relevant environmental stimuli, both discrete antecedents as well as setting events and more subtle aspects of stimulus control, may be extremely difficult to discern.

Given the complexity of freely occurring behavior many authors have used the metaphor of ecology or system to capture the complexity of the situation (Martens & Witt, 1988; Wahler, 1975). It is probably no accident that studies which have used functional analysis as a framework to analyze systems have usually focused on social situations, larger groups of people, such as classrooms or token economies, or entire organizations. One study by Street and Butler (1987) was selected to illustrate the application of functional analysis to a dyadic social situation. Functional analysis of other, larger social systems has now become common. This approach is illustrated by four studies: one relatively simple observational study of a juvenile correctional facility (Carbone & Lynch, 1983), two complex studies of the behavioral ecology of classrooms by Leve and Burdick (1977) and by Greenwood, Delguardi *et al.* (1985), and Martens and Witt's (1988) discussion of the implications of a systems approach for behavioral consultation.

Doctor–Patient Interaction

Street and Butler (1987) were concerned with the purpose implied by different kinds of behaviors shown by the doctor and the patient. The kind of functions observed included: informative exchange, affiliation, dominance and task completion. Hence the functions they studied were not defined in simple topographical terms, but were quite abstract. For example, they state that 'a physician who holds the floor for periods averaging 30 seconds and who maintains high levels of eye contact with a patient may appear affiliative and responsive to a patient exhibiting similar behaviors but may be viewed as domineering and intimidating by a patient who talks for brief periods and who avoids eye contact' (p. 235).

The participants in the study were a group of 38 patients and 10 young physicians. Appointments were recorded on camera and varied from 16 to 32 minutes in length. They found that physicians were communicatively dominant as shown by speaking for longer periods of time and using more social touch which was not reciprocated by the patients. Patients avoided using long pauses in order to prevent taking their turn or creating a negative impression.

This style of functional analysis attempts to interpret the communicative functions served by the different kinds of behaviors shown during interactions. There are conceptually two very similar areas within clinical psychology, namely the interpretation of behavior disorders as communicative acts (Carr & Durand, 1985; Iwata, Vollmer & Zarcone, 1990) and the literature on the functional significance of bizarre behavior in persons with autism (Coggins & Frederickson, 1988; Goren, Romanczk & Harris, 1977; McEvoy, Loveland & Landry, 1988; Prizant & Duchan, 1981; Wetherby & Pritting, 1984). In all of these three different areas communicative intent is inferred from the behavior of the participants observed.

A Correctional Facility

Carbone and Lynch (1983) present an observational study of the behavior of 11 staff and 25 teenagers and young adults awaiting court proceedings in a secure setting. They present data on individual staff and residents showing characteristic profiles of the staff's use of appropriate interaction, of residents and warnings, of inmates' time spent in activities, and of appropriate and inappropriate conversation. This study is a simple descriptive study showing the time spent by staff and inmates in different kinds of activities and how they relate to environmental variables such as day of the week or time of day. The level of analysis does not proceed onto exploring either the immediate contingencies that operate or the more complex and subtle temporal relationship between the environment and behavior.

Classrooms

Leve and Burdick (1977) carried out an empirical study of social reinforcement in a classroom setting. In this study they emphasize the importance of the interdependency of contingencies between participants in a classroom setting. In many studies reinforcement contingencies are seen as a one-way process in which teachers reinforce pupils. In this study the children received immediate secondary reinforcement by way of a light going on in the classroom when the teacher smiled or emitted a positive statement. The children had been told that the illumination of the light meant that they would get candy at the end of the experiment for each teacher target behavior.

The data showed systematic increase in these teacher behaviors during a reversal design for one of the two teachers studied. Thus, although the data are not robust they do illustrate some interesting aspects of a systemic approach to modifying classroom behaviors. First, it appears

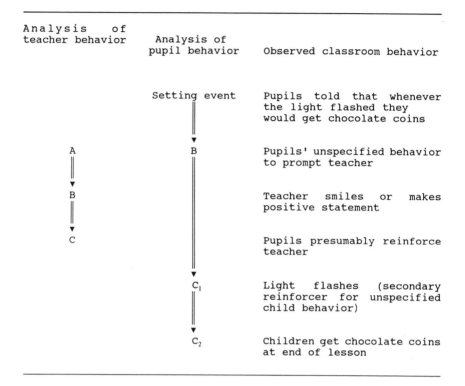

Figure 2.4 Chains of Behavior Implied by Leve and Burdick's (1977) Analysis of Child–Teacher Interactions

that the behaviors of participants can be modified indirectly by reinforcing the partner in a dyadic interaction for the presence of the partner's behavior. Second, this experiment implies that complex chains of primary and secondary reinforcement, and immediate and delayed reinforcement are at work. The chains of behavior and reinforcement as implied by this experiment are illustrated in Figure 2.4.

Classroom Ecology

Greenwood *et al.* (1985) present an example of a more complex functional analysis with two samples of 20 children from 14 fourth grade classrooms in four elementary schools, two of which served economically depressed areas. A standardized observational system was used which coded for ecological events and student behavior. The ecological events included (a) ongoing activity, (b) task type, (c) instructional grouping, (d) teacher position, and (e) teacher behavior. Student behaviors were coded as (a) academic behaviors (e.g., writing), (b) task management (e.g., attending), and (c) competing behavior (e.g., disrupting). This coding system allowed for encoding of sequences of ecological events and student behavior. This gave rise to over 23 000 sequences of data for each of the two samples of subjects. Analysis consisted of investigating the conditional probabilities of environment–behavior sequences. Thus, the analysis consisted of finding environmental events which significantly increased or decreased the probability of a student behavior compared to the overall probability of that student behavior.

These results can be illustrated by considering academic behavior within groups. For one of the samples of subjects academic responding was inhibited by arrangements such as teacher/student discussions. Here the probability of academic responding ranged from 0.000 to 0.091. Academic responding was accelerated by arrangements such as pencil and paper tasks, reading and workbooks, when the teacher was silent at her desk or at the side of the pupil being taught. Here the probabilities of academic responding ranged from 0.621 to 0.741. This study went on to show that children with lower IQs and lower socio-economic status generally underperformed compared to other children in terms of lower rates of academic responding. However, they were also more likely to be taught using individual arrangements which inhibited academic responding.

Greenwood et al. (1985) note that these data are of course correlational and do not necessarily imply causation. However, it is interesting to note here the parallel between this empirical functional analysis and Bijou's (1963, 1966) conceptual functional analysis of development. Here variables such as low IQ or low socio-economic class may solicit environments which inhibit the development of adaptive behaviors.

Behavioral Consultation

An interesting use of functional analysis comes from Martens and Witt (1988). They reviewed the implications of an ecological perspective on functional analysis in the classroom for behavioral consultation. They begin by noting the potential complexities of behavioral relationships which may occur in the classroom. These include many examples beyond the simple, temporally proximate three-term contingency relationship including the inter-relationships amongst multiple responses, environmental influences on behavior which are temporally distant, the relationship between currently available consequences, and the cumulative effect of previously available consequences and the relationship of current behavior management strategies to potential treatment strategies.

They note that teachers often prefer the refer–test–place model of professional relationship to the refer–consult–intervene model. In the latter there may be substantial costs to the teacher. These include recommendations which may be ineffective or which may produce unexpected negative side-effects, and treatment recommendations, which, though effective, may not fit in with daily routines or could involve excessive response cost to the teacher.

Martens and Witt (1985) note that behavioral consultation can broadly take two forms. If there are few or no effective rules or contingencies operating in the classroom then consultation typically consists of staff training and support to establish those forms of acceptable contingencies. If rules exist, but are inappropriate or inconsistently applied, then consultation involves developing appropriate or consistent rules and contingencies. They note that redistributing current teacher behaviors and resources probably constitutes a cheaper, more acceptable form of intervention than teaching new or complex classroom skills to teachers.

One of the implications of functional analysis for behavioral consultation is that behavioral consultation must broaden its attention span beyond the immediately referred problems to the broader context in which it occurs. Thus, a functional analytic perspective would imply three things. First, attention should be given to temporally distant events and behavior. This would include attempting to identify behavioral chains, stressful events which might increase the general likelihood of a problem behavior, and the relative costs and benefits of showing and not showing the target behavior. Second, attention needs to be focused on a broad range of potential outcomes of any intervention rather than simply changes in the single target behavior of the referred person over a short period of time. Third, the relative benefit or reinforcing effect of a consequence, and hence the likelihood of the behavior being displayed, depends upon the overall density of reinforcement available to the person. Thus, in a reinforcement-poor environment the relative efficacy of a single consequence may be relatively high. In a reinforcement-rich environment the same program may be ineffective as there may be a wide range of alternative sources of reinforcement. Thus, programs of intervention could focus on manipulating the general availability of reinforcement as well as, or instead of, simply changing the reinforcement available for the target behavior.

SUMMARY

In this chapter we have selectively reviewed the literature on functional analysis. This review has yielded a very diverse picture of what constitutes a functional analysis, the range of situations to which it has been applied, and the different styles of functional analysis. Functional analysis can be applied to a wide range of situations. Thus, it may encompass situations where change is desired or may be used to explain behavior or behavioral processes.

In Parts II and III of this volume the application of functional analysis in clinical practice is reviewed. This includes assessment methods such as clinical interviews, observational, and psychometric methods of gathering information and data for a functional analysis. In Part II the process of using these assessment methods for conducting a functional analysis is reviewed.

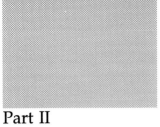

Part II

ASSESSMENT METHODS

Chapter 3

ASSESSMENT METHODS I:
BEHAVIORAL ASSESSMENT

In the early days of behavioral assessment the process was presented as a simple one. It was often perceived as a process characterized as involving little or no inference. Typically data were collected on a single topography. It was usually implicit that this target behavior was self-evidently the correct target behavior for change. Data were rarely collected on multiple topographies. If there were multiple topographies it was assumed to be acceptable to group them together under a molar behavior category such as 'aggression' without any further explanation. Data were typically collected by apparently objective methods. Observation or mechanical devices were the preferred methods of data collection. Many data collection methods were seen as a direct extension of the operant laboratory. Thus, the rate of the target behavior was often used as the preferred metric of the behavior. Methods such as self-report, rating scales, and other verbal methods of assessment were rarely used. They were rejected because they were seen as subjective, biased, and often unreliable. Their association with other treatment paradigms, such as psychotherapy, psychoanalysis, counselling, and personality explanations of behavior tainted them further.

In early behavior assessments data collection might be done in a single setting such as a classroom or an experimental laboratory. Natural settings were used alongside analog or laboratory settings. It was unusual to see studies taking place in many different settings from researchers working within the framework of functional analysis. However, studies from ecological and environmental psychologists did emphasize analyzing behavior in different settings (Proshansky, Ittleson & Rivlin, 1975). This approach was one influence that stimulated interest in observing behavior in multiple settings.

This disenchantment with the process of assessment led to its being de-emphasized in the 1960s and 1970s. Since that time things have changed substantially. The field of behavioral assessment has flourished and has become a major sub-field within applied behavior analysis. There are at least two major journals devoted exclusively to this field: *Behavioral Assessment* and *Journal of Psychopathology and Behavioral Assessment*. Numerous general textbooks have been published. Some of these have now gone through several editions (Bellack & Hersen, 1988; Cimenero, Calhoun, & Adams, 1977). Further texts have also been published addressing specific populations such as children and adolescents (Mash & Terdal, 1976) and adults (Ollendick & Hersen, 1984).

BEHAVIORAL AND TRADITIONAL ASSESSMENT CONTRASTED

Current views on behavioral assessment have greatly changed (Barrios & Hartman, 1986). Barrios (1988) notes that behavioral assessment has become more complex and subtle over time. Behavior analysis now uses and integrates many different assessment methods. It is not uncommon to see behavioral assessments that integrate interviews with the client and third parties, psychometric assessments and mini-experiments. For example, Stevenson and Fantuzzo (1984) evaluated young children's self-control strategies during math lessons. They used the children's scores on their work sheets, a permanent product measure of their behavior, and direct observation of their disruptive behavior, as measures of outcome. Barrios notes that the issue of multiple responses is now routinely acknowledged. For example, Biglan, Metzler and Ary (1994) reviewed community intervention research on child and adolescent problems. In this review they note the association often found between many different forms of behavior problems in children and adolescents. These include anti-social behavior, cigarette use, precocious and risky sexual behavior, alcohol use, dangerous driving, poor school performance, and general risk taking. Thus, this review begins with the problem of multiple responses. Barrios notes that concerns relating to how to assess, group and select target behaviors are also more commonly assessed (Kratochwill, 1985). Thus, the assumption of the validity of response selection has now begun to be addressed (Barnett & Gottlieb, 1988; Kazdin, Matson & Esveldt-Dawson, 1981; Merluzzi & Biever, 1987).

In Barrios' review he notes that the assessment process is now viewed as a hypothesis testing procedure. The purpose of a behavioral assessment is to generate and evaluate hypotheses concerning the clinical problem. Information is collected which requires careful interpretation. At times this may be a highly inferential process. Although the functions of target behaviors may be readily apparent in some situations, this is not always the case (Sturmey, 1995a).

Finally, Barrios notes that assessment, including behavioral assessments, may serve many different purposes. Thus, although the current volume is primarily concerned with the use of behavioral assessment within the context of functional analysis it should also be noted that behavioral assessment has been used in order to assist in diagnosis (Hersen, 1988), and to evaluate treatment efficacy, as well as to evaluate the most appropriate form of intervention for an individual client.

Many of these issues look remarkably like the concerns that initially motivated the development of behavioral assessment as a solution to these very problems! Nevertheless, the comparison of behavioral and traditional assessments will make a useful point of departure for the present discussion.

Aims of Assessment

The aims of traditional assessment methods are characterized as being structural rather than functional. As discussed in Chapter 1 the functions of traditional assessment methods include diagnosis, classification, identification of causes and prediction of the future course of the problem (see Figure 1.1). In a structural approach to assessment it is believed that the correct classification of the behavior based upon its form will allow the clinician to make multiple inferences of etiology, treatment and prognosis. Some diagnoses of acute physical illnesses can fulfill all of these functions. Thus, in psychoanalytic therapy the purpose of assessment is to determine the developmental stage at which the client is fixated. In cognitive therapy the purpose of assessment is to uncover the cognitive schemata and perceptual biases that the client has. In modern biological psychiatry assessment is used in part to make inferences about underlying biochemical imbalances in the brain. In personality theory the aim of assessment is to infer the personality type or traits that the person 'has'. These non-observables are given special status as the underlying cause of the client's problem.

The aims of behavioral assessment are to assist in the identification of target behaviors and the environmental conditions maintaining them, and to describe the relationship between them in analytic terms. In behavioral assessment the primary function of assessment is to describe the relationship between environmental events and the problematic thoughts, feelings and behaviors. One of the aims of behavioral assessment is also to select, develop, evaluate and revise an appropriate treatment for the identified problem. If there is a treatment failure or relapse then behavioral assessment should be able to explain these failures and use that information as the basis of a revised intervention.

Concept of Personality

The concept of personality and the causes and meaning of behavior differ between functional analytic and other approaches. In traditional views the observed behavior is seen as being a function of an unobserved, and sometimes unobservable, cause. Observed behavior is seen as a sign or symptom of intra-psychic causes, personality, illness, unresolved conflict, neurotransmitter imbalance, or genetics. In this view the behavior itself is relatively unimportant. It is only important as an index of those unobservable constructs that are believed to be the cause of the clinical problem. Thus, intervention is not aimed at changing the behavior itself directly. Rather, it is believed that changing the underlying constructs will lead that behavior subsequently to change.

In behavioral assessment the observed behavior is seen as a sample from the entire behavioral repertoire of the individual observed in a specific situation. Variations in the person's behavior are seen as a function of important environmental variables which maintain behavior and their interaction with person variables such as learning history, physiological state, genetics and personality.

In traditional assessment methods the range of situations sampled is restricted. It may be limited to one setting, such as behavior in an office or whilst completing a test. Further, traditional assessment methods tend to emphasize verbal behavior such as interviews, self-reports and writing whereas behavioral assessment is more likely to include other aspects of behavior such as motor behavior.

In traditional methods of assessment, especially personality theories, differences in behavior across settings are seen as error variance in an imperfect measurement system. Differences in behavior across different settings represent the differing extent to which observed behavior taps the underlying trait or construct.

In behavioral assessment a wide range of very different situations are explicitly sampled. Variability in behavior across settings gives evidence for the environmental variables of which behavior is a function. Thus, differences in behavior across settings are explicitly sought out. Traditional assessment methods are mono-method, mono-setting, whereas behavioral methods are multi-method, multi-setting.

Instrument Construction

Instrument construction in traditional methods places little emphasis on the situation or context of behavior. A reasonable degree of trans-situational consistency is expected, therefore it is not necessary to sample behavior across settings widely. Emphasis is only placed on sampling behavior sufficiently in order to adequately assess the underlying construct.

In behavioral assessment emphasis is placed upon fully sampling the person's behavioral repertoire and the situations in which they behave. This may mean sampling all of the person's behavior broadly and sampling certain problem situations in much more detail. For example, a child's parent and teacher might keep an ABC diary of all incidents of fear responses for two weeks. The child might then be observed in a number of specific situations such as leaving his mother, going to school, and going to an unfamiliar place in much more detail. In this way the person's behavioral repertoire is sampled in a purposeful fashion in order to understand the relationship between the environmental events that may provoke or maintain the problematic behaviors.

Schedule of Assessment

In traditional assessment, assessments are made relatively infrequently. Greatest weight is placed on the initial assessment and diagnosis rather than on repeated, ongoing assessment. In personality-type assessments the person's behavior is compared to statistical norms. Many traditional assessments involve group or norm comparisons. Thus, they are nomothetic rather than idiographic. If evaluation data are collected at all it is often only pre- and post-treatment data.

The schedule of assessment in behavioral assessment is frequent. Assessment is seen as a recursive process both in repeatedly testing and revising the model of the person's behavior. It is also repeatedly used to monitor changes in the person's behavior across time and setting. Repeated evaluation is also essential to evaluate and modify treatment. Thus, the comparison made is idiographic. The assessment procedure is often tailored very carefully to the person's own unique configuration of problems. Change is typically evaluated by comparing the person's current behavior with their own behavior at other times. If assessments are being used to evaluate treatment then it is likely that as treatment proceeds then the person will be exposed to new environments that were previously not available to them. At this point it may be necessary to revise or re-evaluate the initial functional analysis completely if new behavior–environment relationships emerge.

Level of Inference

Finally, behavioral assessment methods are seen as being direct, simple, and reliable. This is especially true for some aspects of behavioral assessment such as counting a simple, discrete target behavior, in contrast to inferring an intra-psychic process. The reliability of psychiatric diagnosis and the assessment of stages of psychological development have been characterized as indirect and complex. They often have variable and poor reliability.

Behavioral assessments are seen as having good face validity. They measure the actual problem directly. Further, they have good social validity in that they address problems of major social importance as evaluated by the person, their significant others, and society.

In contrast, traditional methods of assessment, such as protective testing, are seen as indirect since their aim is to assess non-observable constructs by making inferences about them from behavior. Such a procedure has been repeatedly characterized as having poor reliability and validity. The validity of traditional assessment methods is seen as requiring extensive research and may be a long and subtle process to establish the construct validity of such procedures. They are seen as highly inferential.

Comment

The preceding sections contrasted behavioral and traditional approaches to assessment. Such contrasts were typically published in the 1970s when the field of behavioral assessment was relatively new and attempting to define itself clearly by contrasting itself with traditional assessment methods, and by distancing itself from some of the limitations that had been recognized in some of the traditional assessment methods. Some 25 years later such contrasts continue to make important points of value although they do now seem somewhat simplistic. In Chapter 9 issues related to reliability and validity related to functional analysis will be reviewed in greater detail. Suffice it to say that the issues of reliability and validity of behavioral assessment have come back in more complex guises than was anticipated in the past.

CHARACTERISTICS OF CONTEMPORARY BEHAVIORAL ASSESSMENT

Contemporary behavioral assessment is not characterized by any specific method of assessment or by any set of procedural rules. Rather, two key features of behavioral assessment should be emphasized. First, behavioral assessment is a hypothesis-generating and -testing procedure. Second, it is a treatment-oriented form of assessment. Let us look at these two features in more detail.

Hypothesis Generation

A central dogma of functional analysis is that treatments should be designed on the basis of the functions of the target behaviors. Unless interventions are based upon the functions of the target behaviors they will not be fully effective. Without an understanding of the environmental variables which maintain the behavior and the functions which the behavior serves for the individual it will not be possible to design an effective and comprehensive treatment.

The role of assessment in functional analysis is to develop and evaluate alternative hypotheses relating to the functions of the target behavior. These hypotheses will determine what information is relevant for the process of assessment as well as what information is irrelevant. Indeed much information collected by a traditional, standardized intake will be irrelevant for many hypotheses.

A clinical hypothesis can be used to make multiple predictions about a client's behavior. These predictions can be used to evaluate, confirm and modify a hypothesis. Consider the following example from the first few moments of an initial assessment interview.

A 24-year-old, highly educated married woman with one young child is referred because of moderate depression. The referral letter states that there is no identifiable cause of the onset, which was insidious. Early during the initial interview it is apparent that although the woman's speech is slow and hesitant her social behavior is fairly appropriate, suggesting that her depression is not caused by poor social skills. When asked about her outstanding performance in national exams, which was distinctly superior to the interviewer's performance, she stated dismissively that this was only due to her good rote-memory and not to her intelligence or any personal effort.

From this initial information the hypothesis could be used to guide the assessment. Her depression is maintained by inappropriate self-talk. On the basis of this initial very undifferentiated hypothesis the following predictions could be made: (a) She will not credit herself for her achievements. She will ascribe them either to chance, or to other people, or will minimize their significance. (b) There will be inadequate opportunity in her environment for non-depressed kinds of behavior and sources of reinforcement. (c) She will be relatively confident or willing to tackle novel or unfamiliar social situations. She will do so competently, but will perceive her performance as indifferent or poor.

Some of these predictions might be incorrect. Indeed such a formulation might not appear to be very individualized at this stage. However, this initial clinical hypothesis, made in the first few minutes of the first assessment interview, can be used to guide the kind of information collected during the remaining part of the assessment. Thus, further assessment during the initial interview could explore these particular issues. Role play or *in vivo* situations could be used to assess both her skills and her self-evaluation in novel social situations. Other illustrations of this form of hypothesis testing can be found in the work of Shapiro (1966, 1970) and more recently by Turkat and colleagues (Turkat, 1988; Turkat & Maisto, 1985).

Assessment for Treatment Design

The second key feature of behavioral assessment is using the hypotheses derived during assessment to design an intervention. At first sight this might seem like an innovative idea. However, it should be recognized that much treatment, including much behavioral treatment, is not necessarily driven by assessment. Haynes, Nelson and Jarrett (1987) refer to this function of behavioral assessment as the treatment utility of assessment.

Simply placing a client with an anxiety disorder in an anxiety management group or always using exposure therapy for phobias, because the literature suggests exposure to be the most effective treatment, are both examples of poor behavior analysis (Wolpe, 1989). Indeed, this approach is, in essence, an example of a diagnostic or medical model strategy to treatment design. Namely, despite all the assessment information that may have been collected, all the clients who fall within a broad diagnostic band of anxiety disorders are placed in an anxiety management group, irrespective of the functions of their target behaviors.

This diagnostic strategy to selection of behavioral treatments gives rise to several potential problems. It requires that the diagnosis can be made reliably, a notion frequently questioned even for research diagnostic criteria (Zwick, 1983) and DSM criteria (Quay, 1986; Sturmey, 1994). Further, it requires that there is a simple mapping from diagnosis to treatment, again a notion which, even in organic psychiatry, has been questioned. Finally, it also raises the potential problems associated with implicitly labelling clients.

The keystone strategy

In her review of the relationship between assessment and treatment strategies Nelson (1988) contrasts the diagnostic strategy with two other behavioral strategies: functional analysis and the keystone target behavior strategy. By the functional analysis strategy Nelson refers to collecting information on antecedents, behaviors, and consequences and developing a hypothesis about the target behavior. The effectiveness of the treatment is then used to retrospectively validate the initial hypothesis. In developing the keystone target behavior strategy Nelson notes that many clients present with multiple target behaviors which are sometimes confusing in their number and diversity. Nelson describes the keystone target behavior as follows: 'the Keystone target behavior strategy, is to identify a target behavior that produces a therapeutic response generalization . . . alteration of the Keystone target behavior also produces desirable change in other target behaviors' (p. 162). Thus, one of the key differences between the functional analysis and keystone target behavior strategies is that in the functional analysis strategy the focus is on identifying the *stimuli* related to the target behaviors, whereas in the keystone target behavior strategy the focus is on the *behavior* which, when altered, will produce the greatest change in other behaviors. There are many examples of where targeting one behavior may influence a related target behavior. However, it is often difficult in advance to predict these changes, let alone use them strategically in treatment design. At this point we do not yet have a good technology related to the keystone target behavior strategy to assist clinicians in their work although, clearly, these ideas may be helpful.

Consider the following case example in which the client was referred initially as a simple phobia.

A young woman was referred by her family doctor for treatment of a simple wasp phobia. Early on during the initial assessment interview the woman also reported numerous child management problems and assertiveness difficulties with her mother-in-law.

This case presents the clinician with a picture of multiple topographies. It may not be immediately clear which target to select, what the relationship might be between the target behaviors, or which of the various behaviors might be a keystone target behavior.

Implications for Treatment Evaluation

Functional analysis has several implications for the issue of treatment effectiveness. From this perspective the effectiveness of treatments traditionally labelled 'behavioral' or 'non-behavioral' will depend crucially upon the match between the function of the target behavior and the treatment. Functional analysis would predict that so-called 'behavioral' treatments would not be effective in many circumstances.

For example, flooding is a procedure which typically involves taking a person with a phobia into a high fear situation for long periods of time until they habituate to the stimuli they fear. In many cases the application of this treatment principle to a problem such as agoraphobia may take the form of taking the person into a crowded shopping mall or for a standard walk in public for $1\frac{1}{2}$ to 3 hours until their fear reduces. From a functional analytic perspective the effectiveness of such a procedure will critically depend upon whether or not the person was exposed and habituated to the stimuli that they fear. Persons with agoraphobia may fear crowded situations, somatic catastrophes and the physiological aspects of high anxiety, social disapproval, social incompetence or other fears. If the particular form of exposure fails to address the relevant fear such a treatment will not be effective. Wolpe's repeated criticisms of the practice of behavior therapy make this point eloquently (Wolpe, 1989).

Another example of this principle is the use of Time Out. Time Out is short for 'Time Out from positive reinforcement'. The correct application of Time Out requires that the behavior's reinforcer is precisely identified. If a long-stay psychiatric client repeatedly shows non-compliant behaviors then the effectiveness of a procedure, such as placing them in a Time Out room, will depend critically upon the reinforcers for the behavior being correctly identified. If escape from the demands of work, heat, noise or aversive interactions with supervisors maintains the behavior, then such a procedure would negatively reinforce the behavior by consistently removing an aversive stimulus. Thus, the frequency of the behavior would increase. If it was the case that it was maintained by staff attention, such as arguments and redirection, then the treatment should be effective if, and only if, the procedure consistently removes these consequences.

Another implication of this posture is that many so-called 'non-behavioral' procedures may be effective or even indicated if these procedures address the functions of the target behavior. For example, Dougher and Hackbert (1994) consider the treatment implications of their functional analysis of depression. They note that anti-depressants can be construed as Establishing Operations that potentiate the reinforcing value of stimuli, thereby potentiating the contingencies for non-depressed behavior. Social skills training may be effective if the depressed behaviors are a function of lack of social skills, or of social anxiety if, through the social skills training, the person is habituated to stimuli that evoke social anxiety. Similarly, a functional analysis of depression might indicate that many verbal therapies such as counselling or psychotherapy might be effective treatments in a number of ways. For example, talking is a behavior and increasing the rate of talking during therapy might be expected to be reinforcing in itself. Clients who have a history of abuse or trauma may benefit from talking about them since talking about these experiences might constitute extinction of emotional responses to these verbal stimuli. Through talking about these traumatic events they may learn more appropriate self-talk. For example, the person may learn that there was no relationship between their own behavior and the incident and therefore self-blame is inappropriate. Finally, many aspects of service design and procedures may inadvertently maintain maladaptive behavior. Procedures such as how to manage so-called emergencies, procedures for dealing with suicidal behaviors, and admission procedures may all under circumstances inadvertently be counter-habilitative (Sturmey, 1995b). These procedures are rarely considered as treatment procedures but at times functional analysis can contribute to the resolution of iatrogenic procedures.

Mary was a 40-year-old client who had a history of repeated admissions to suicidal attempts of a bizarre nature. Recently she had begun trying to kill herself by jamming one or two knives down her throat. These incidents had begun to occur with greater frequency. Review of the procedure to handle these incidents revealed that she was rushed to the emergency room, had the knives removed under general anaesthetic and recovered in hospital for the next 24 hours. After these incidents were reviewed it was apparent that there was probably considerable positive reinforcement made contingent on the attempted suicide. The procedure for handling these incidents was modified so that the knives were removed under local anaesthetic after which she returned to her regular program. After the implementation of this procedure the frequency of these bizarre incidents decreased rapidly.

TYPOLOGIES OF FUNCTION

Many papers on functional analysis have espoused a completely idiographic approach to assessment. They emphasize the total uniqueness of each case. Clinicians are urged to carry out a unique analysis for each case on every occasion. Such a requirement places the clinician under a heavy burden. Every time they see a new client they start from scratch. On every occasion they should begin from first principles with no short cuts available as to the analysis of every case. Not only does this place a heavy burden on the clinician in terms of resources, but it also does so with respect to clinical decision making. It is well known that clinicians are often poor at complex decision making and combining information from many different sources, such as that related to diagnosis and treatment selection. They tend to have biases in their selection of diagnoses, treatments, and in seeking out confirmatory information rather than testing hypotheses (Garb, 1988; Rock et al., 1987, 1988). The call for a highly idiosyncratic approach to functional analysis may place a considerable information processing load on the clinician.

Perhaps as an implicit reaction to this problem a somewhat different approach to determining the functions of target behaviors can be discerned in other work. Although not explicitly described as such, this approach simplifies the decision making process by identifying some of the more common functions that a behavior may have. Guidelines are then given to the clinician on how to recognize these common functions. In this way the assessment process is simplified in a number of ways. First, the number of potential functions that the target behavior can have is reduced. Second, the information that is necessary for the clinician to discriminate between the options is specified. This can act as a structure as to the information that needs to be collected, and the kind of information that is irrelevant to the task at hand. Finally, it can guide the clinician as to the treatment options that are appropriate for each of the functions of the target behavior. It should also specify those treatments that are contra-indicated. This approach is sometimes referred to as *Behavioral diagnostics*.

An early example of this approach comes from the work of Kanfer and Grimm (1977). They suggest that clinical problems can be classified into five classes of problems. For each class of clinical problem sub-types are identified, yielding a total of 20 problem types. A treatment strategy is suggested for each sub-type. Table 3.1 contains some examples of this scheme. The five classes of problems are (a) behavioral deficits, (b) behavioral excesses, (c) inappropriate environmental stimulus control, (d) inappropriate self-generated stimulus control, and, (e) problematic reinforcement contingencies. In this schema no reference is made to the topography of the problem. The implication is that this schema could be used for many different forms of clinical problems. Any given topography might fit anywhere in this scheme. Any treatment strategy might be appropriate for a wide range of different forms of problem depending upon their function.

A second example comes from Carr's (1977) review of the motivations for self-injurious behavior. Carr suggested that there were three main motivations for self-injury. First, positive reinforcement, such as tangibles, materials, or social interaction, might occur contingent upon the behavior. Second, negative reinforcement, such as the removal of aversive academic or social demands, pain or discomfort, might occur contingent upon the behavior. Third, internal stimulation from the behavior might be positively reinforcing. This analysis suggests that the functions of self-injury can be classified into three sub-types. Each sub-type can be recognized by a characteristic pattern of environmental events. These are the reliable presentation of stimuli contingent on the behavior, reliable removal of stimuli contingent upon the behavior, and high rates of behavior in the absence of external stimulus respectively. As with Kanfer and Grimm's (1977) typology, each class of function can be associated with certain treatment strategies.

Iwata *et al.* (1994) reported on a series of 152 cases of treatment of self-injury over a ten-year period. All these treatments were conducted within the framework of Carr's typology of the functions of self-injury. Data indicated very clearly that almost all cases could be assigned to one of these three functions. Intervention was the only effective treatment which matched the three functions of the target behavior. Further,

Table 3.1   Some Examples of Kanfer and Grimm's (1977) Typology of Clinical Problems and their Potential Treatments

Type	Sub-type	Description	Treatment
Behavior deficit	Information	Person does not know details of correct performance or social standards for behavior (e.g., sexual problem)	Provide information
Behavior excesses	Excessive self-monitoring	Client attends too frequently, too long or too intensely to own behavior (e.g., somatic- or evaluation-based fears)	Thought stopping; provide incompatible responses; satiation
Problems in environmental stimulus control	Restrictive environment	Lack of opportunity for desired behavior; no reinforcement or punishment provided (e.g., college student living at home with dating problems)	Modifying current environment or seeking new environment
Inappopriate self-generated stimulus control	Discrimination internal stimuli	Internal states are incorrectly labelled (e.g., sexual arousal as anxiety)	Train client in better discrimination of more correct labelling of own behavior
Inappropriate contingency arrangements	Non-contingent reinforcement	Temporal arrangement of behavior and reinforcement is incorrect (e.g., low motivation, blandness, low affect)	Rearrange contingencies; use of short-term goals; self-management

treatments were only effective when they matched the functions of the target behavior (Iwata *et al.*, 1994, Figure 6).

The use of typologies of functions of target behaviors has been extended in a number of ways. Some authors have extended the number of types of functions by detailing more categories of potential functions (e.g., Donnellan, Mirenda, Mesaros & Fassbender, 1984; Iwata, Vollmar & Zarcone, 1990). Others have taken the work done on one topography, such as self-injury, and extended it to other problems, such as school refusal (Kearney & Silverman, 1990).

Although typologies of function have a number of potential advantages over a completely idiographic approach to functional analysis there may also be limitations. Clinicians must be able to apply a taxonomy reliably. This includes both classifying the function of the behavior correctly, and also translating the behavioral diagnosis into an intervention reliably. These issues have not yet been extensively addressed. Taxonomies such as Kanfer and Grimm's (1977) 20-category scheme might require that clinicians receive extensive training to use it reliably. Even apparently simple psychometric tools used for functional analysis may have limited reliability or their psychometric properties might be unknown (see Chapter 6). The mapping of treatment from category of function may still require considerable analytic and clinical skill. Although this approach simplifies the process of translating a functional analysis into a treatment it does not eliminate choice and decision making from that process.

MULTI-MODAL ASSESSMENT

The Primacy of Direct Observation

Early work emphasized direct observation as the *sine qua non* of behavioral assessment. Other assessment modes were rejected or de-emphasized because of their association with other theoretical orientations, because of their perceived lack of objectivity, and because of the difficulties of applying them to many populations with severe disabilities. Many early behavioral articles in the late 1960s and 1970s focused on discrete, brief target behaviors such as aggression, self-injury, and other behavior disorders and were the basis for developing observational methodology.

The application of functional analysis has expanded over the years. Part of this expansion has included the use of consumer satisfaction measures and social validity data to validate the changes measured in observational studies. Over time functional analysis has been applied to a broader range of problems. These have included problems such as depression, anxiety, hallucinations and delusions, in which private events are a central part of the presenting problem. This has forced those using the framework of functional analysis as the basis of their work to incorporate a wide range of methodologies into their work. This interest in private events has in turn been fed back into more traditional areas of functional analysis. For example, the application of relaxation training to a person with developmental disabilities involves the measurement and control of non-observable internal states such as feelings of tension and interventions involving cognitive strategies such as counting to oneself while calming down. Despite the widespread use of multi-modal behavioral assessment direct observation remains an important tool for functional analysis.

Current Practices

Behavioral assessment currently uses many different forms of assessment in many combinations as the clinician or researcher sees fit. For example, a recent issue of *The Behavior Analyst* on clinical behavior analysis (Dougher, 1994) looked very much like any mainstream, non-behavioral clinical journal with respect to the methodologies used. These included traditional verbal formats to assess and treat depression (Dougher & Hackbert, 1994; Kohlenberg & Tsai, 1994; Hayes & Wilson, 1994), and reviews of archival data on crime rate, drug abuse, epidemiological data, and correlational research using questionnaires (Biglan, Metzler & Ary, 1994; Wulfert & Biglan, 1994). Thus, even some of the most radical behavioral journals are now relatively catholic on data collection methodologies.

A wide range of data collection methodologies may be used flexibly to test hypotheses or to pilot elements of future treatment strategies as the assessment process develops. Table 3.2 illustrates the range of different assessment methodologies which are commonly used. These are discussed in more detail in subsequent chapters.

An interview of some sort almost always precedes any kind of formal data collection. The last 20 years have seen the development of interview formats for functional analysis. These have included general interview formats such as semi-structured interviews (Morganstern, 1988) and hypothesis-testing interview strategies (Turkat, 1988). Many interviews for specific topographies have also been developed (Bellack & Hersen, 1988). Self-report measures, such as questionnaires to assist in identifying topographies, and self-recorded baseline data related to antecedents and consequences have been used. Other idiographic self-report measures include individualized goal hierarchies such as card sort tasks. Behavior often leaves permanent or semi-permanent environ-

Table 3.2   Some Common Assessment Methods Used in Behavioral Assessment

Method	Comments and examples
Interview	May be fully structured, semi-structured or unstructured. Could be with the client or third parties such as family member, friends or other professions. Examples include initial assessment interviews, case conferences, follow-up interviews
Direct observation	Frequency counts and time sampling of behavior. Often in public places and often used with clients where other assessment methods not possible. Can include observation of the environment as well as the client. Examples include time on task, frequency of shouting
Permanent product	Environmental traces of behavior such as trash, damage, written materials, product of work- or education-related behavior
Standardized self-report	Questionnaires related to topographies, history or functions of behavior. Many traditional psychometric instruments are examples of this. Examples include fear survey schedules, problem behavior checklists, etc.
Idiographic self-report	Measures tailored to an individual's problems. Examples include ABC charts, thought diaries, fear thermometers, individual goal hierarchies, subjective units of discomfort, goal attainment scaling
Psychophysiological measures	Biofeedback measures such as electromyogram, palmar sweat index, heart rate variability, blood flow in finger, and physiological measures of sexual arousal

mental traces. These can be, at times, more reliable, easy to collect and sometimes more meaningful than other types of measures. Finally, physiological measures have been integrated into behavioral assessment. As technology becomes cheaper and more portable this can be used in routine clinical practice more frequently.

Some Examples

In order to illustrate the use of different forms of assessment in behavioral assessment two case studies and an observational one will be presented.

An elderly woman with a long history of obsessive-compulsive disorder was referred to an out-patient clinic. An initial semi-structured behavioral interview was conducted. This yielded a picture of high frequency hand washing precipitated by intrusive thoughts of contamination or touching many everyday objects such as door handles and food. There was much passive avoidance and use of tissues to handle contaminated objects. A self-report measure was used to assess the range of obsessive-compulsive phenomena. ABC diaries were used to assess both the frequency of the target behavior as well as the environmental events related to hand washing. During a home visit mini-experiments were carried out before and after contamination, and after a ritual using subjective units of discomfort ratings (SUDs). The client was asked to rate situations before contamination, immediately after contamination, and immediately after ritual hand washing. This revealed a classic pattern of phobic avoidance where contamination led to very high levels of anxiety, which were abolished by ritual hand washing. During subsequent flooding sessions at home SUDs ratings were again used to monitor the decay of arousal during treatment. The effects of treatment were monitored using self-recorded frequency of hand washing and tissue use.

A second example comes from a referral of a woman with severe developmental disabilities living in a large residential facility. She was referred for treatment of severe self-injury and chronic self-restraint.

An initial interview with several staff members gave rise to some of the information above, as well as a picture of chronic sinus infections. Data were gathered from medical and nursing notes over the previous two years relating to the frequency of infection, previous treatments and the pattern of use of restraint. Informal direct observation showed many examples of the client apparently requesting restraints. She would repeatedly approach staff with her hands held out apparently requesting restraint. She also showed a range of adaptive behaviors which could be important for future programs. Formal observation was used to estimate the time in restraint, time spent in adaptive behaviors, and to assess the patterns of staff-client interaction.

Another example of methods used in a broader systemic functional analysis comes from Kennedy, Fisher and Pearson (1988) who conducted an observational study of a spinal rehabilitation unit. This study used ecological mapping as a framework for data collection. Specifically they were interested to evaluate the therapeutic day environment provided by nursing and therapy staff as compared with the client's evening when no therapeutic activities were scheduled. Behavior categories were developed for both client and staff behavior. Observations were scheduled across all settings in the unit from 9 a.m. through 12 midnight. Observations were repeated eight months later.

Kennedy, Fisher and Pearson found that there were few differences between the therapeutic day and evening activities. In other words, patient behavior was largely not a function of whether or not the therapeutic day was operating. For example, patients spent most of their time in solitary activities throughout the day and evening time. There was little interaction with staff other than those activities involving having things done to the patient. There was little interaction between patients, indicating a lack of peer support and social interaction. Further, during the therapeutic day patients were only in therapy rooms some 24% of the time. Staff agreed that attendance at therapeutic activities was well below that scheduled.

When the observations were repeated eight months later the situation had changed little. Despite having had the information from the first observations fed back to staff all participants' behavior was stable. This information was used to form the basis of an action plan to develop an improved program for this group of patients with spinal cord injuries.

SUMMARY

The driving force in using functional analysis in clinical work is the use of strategies to develop and test hypotheses that will be the basis of the subsequent intervention. The importance of this approach is attested to by the fact that over the last 20 years behavioral assessment has become a sub-specialty within the behavioral literature. Behavioral assessment has expanded rapidly to encompass many different assessment methodologies beyond direct observation which are used flexibly and imaginatively.

In the next three chapters we examine some of these methodologies in more detail. These are interviewing, observation, and psychometric measures.

Chapter 4

ASSESSMENT METHODS II: INTERVIEWING

Clinical interviewing is an integral part of any functional analysis. Although it might be possible to carry out a functional analysis without an interview of some kind it would certainly be unusual to do so. What constitutes an interview might vary considerably. A brief telephone call, an idle conversation that turns into a more formal referral, formal hourly appointments scheduled over several weeks, meetings with groups of people such as families, or team meetings can all constitute interview situations in which a functional analysis might be conducted. Any of these might be situations in which a therapist might carry out a functional analysis through interview methods.

An attempt to determine the functions of a target behavior may take place exclusively through an interview. However, an interview of some kind almost always precedes other forms of functional analysis. Thus, naturalistic observation, experimental methods of assessment, and psychometric methods of conducting a functional analysis may depend upon an initial interview. An assessment interview, sometimes along with other methods, may be used to identify the target behaviors to be assessed by other methods, to help decide what other assessment methods might be appropriate, and to generate hypotheses to be tested more rigorously by other methods.

It is worth noting that many papers which use these other assessment methods usually briefly mention somewhere that interviews were conducted. However, such papers rarely describe the interview process, the methods of interviewing used, and how the information from the interview was integrated into the other methods of assessment. Thus, the importance of interview methods has been underemphasized, especially in the experimental literature.

In this chapter we will review four related topics. In the first section techniques often used in interviews to conduct a functional analysis are reviewed. In the subsequent two sections two styles of interviews are discussed: unstructured and semi-structured behavioral interviewing. In the final section we will review methods of training therapists in interviewing skills.

INTERVIEWING TECHNIQUES

A number of specific interview techniques may be used when conducting a functional analysis. It is important that the clinician and researcher alike are thoroughly familiar with these techniques and competent and fluent in their use. Many of these techniques are not specific to interviewing for this purpose. Interviewing techniques have been freely borrowed from other schools of psychology, including Rogerian techniques (Morganstern, 1988). Behavioral interviewing differs from other forms of interviewing, not in its techniques, but in its aims and format.

Rapport

Early on during the interview adequate rapport must be established with the interviewee. It must be clear to the interviewee that their concerns are taken seriously and are treated in a professional manner. The interviewer's concern for the interviewee's distress must be apparent to the interviewee.

The stereotype of the mechanical behaviorist who shows no expression of concern for their clients has not been confirmed by research findings. Several studies have shown that behavior therapists are perceived by their clients as experienced, skillful, and confident. They are often rated as more empathic, emotionally congruent and supportive than therapists of other schools (Morganstern, 1988, p. 98). Obviously, there are individual differences between behavior therapists, and some may appear cold, mechanistic and indifferent.

The importance of establishing good rapport is shown by studies that have found that treatment failure, drop-out and non-compliance rates may also be related to therapist characteristics in behavior therapy (Foa & Emmelkamp, 1983). Thus, establishing good rapport during an interview may be important in facilitating a client's giving full information concerning their problems. Clients may be reluctant to disclose embarrassing incidents, thoughts, personal weaknesses or mistakes if sufficient trust and empathy has not been established between the client and therapist. At times without this disclosure it may not be possible to conduct a complete functional analysis since the information available to the therapist will be incomplete.

After several assessment interviews with a young obsessive-compulsive client a fairly typical pattern of contamination fears and washing rituals that decreased anxiety was established. However, it was never clear exactly what the contaminant was that the client feared so intensely. One clue came from the disclosure that the problem had gotten much worse after two casual dates which, it was hinted at, turned into casual sexual encounters. Nevertheless, it was unclear what the contaminant was.

Subsequently, *in vivo* exposure treatment was conducted. There was limited success in this. One possible reason is that the therapist could not be sure that the client was actually habituated to the relevant feared stimuli.

The importance of establishing good rapport may be especially important when working through third parties such as staff, parents, or other family members. In these situations the third parties may be tired, anxious, guilty, or emotionally distanced from the problem. There may be disagreements between staff or family members, fears of blame, or even motivation to blame one another in some circumstances. In these situations it is especially important that the therapist is seen as credible, concerned, competent and fair. It is not uncommon in these situations for third parties to be engaged in strategies which might be ineffective, or be directly counter-productive. In these situations the competence of other professionals, or the competence of parents may be seen as being at stake. It is especially important that good rapport between the therapist and client is established under these difficult circumstances.

After extensive interviews with staff over several weeks the psychologist had been getting nowhere in trying to establish the functions of the newly emerging aggression in a person with moderate developmental disabilities. The aggression had started in the last two months, and typically occurred in the evening. Interviews with numerous staff members conducted over several weeks had revealed that the aggression was not directed at any particular person or type of person. It was not related to any activity, day, demands, or any other environmental variable that was assessed.

After the team meeting was over a staff member approached the psychologist to say that he never had that problem. He did something, but wanted to know if he would get into trouble if he told the psychologist what it was that he did. The staff member was informed that it really depended on what it was that he did. The staff member said that when this client got out of bed he gave him a glass of water. The client would then get back in bed. Aggression was never observed.

A review of the records revealed that some two months earlier the client had been placed on a psychotropic medication. One of its side effects was dry mouth.

Rapport alone is insufficient to conduct a functional analysis. Indeed, at times, high levels of warmth and empathy might be inappropriate, counter-productive, offensive, or culturally inappropriate to certain clients. As well as establishing empathy a number of specific interviewing techniques may be used during an interview. These are discussed below (see Table 4.1).

Open-ended and Closed Questions

A distinction is often made between open-ended and closed questions. Open-ended questions are questions that invite a wide range of material rather than a one- or two-word answer. Examples of open-ended questions are: 'How did this problem begin?', 'Tell me more about that', and 'What are your goals for therapy?' Open-ended questions are used to elicit a broad range of material from the interviewee. The material might be relatively unstructured and may not directly address the issues that the interviewer is interested in.

Closed questions invite brief answers that clarify a specific point, or provide an answer to a particular query. Examples of closed questions include: 'Which is easiest for you, walking into a store or walking into a parking lot?', 'I'm not sure about what you said earlier—did it begin before or after the auto accident?', and 'So which is the bigger problem for you and your husband, when Bobby steals or when he stays out all night?'

Often a series of open-ended questions might prompt a wealth of material. A series of open-ended questions can be clarified by a number of closed questions. Interviews often fall into naturally occurring paragraphs beginning with several or many open-ended questions which are then followed by specific closed questions.

Table 4.1   Examples of Specific Interview Techniques which may be Used during Interviews to Conduct a Functional Analysis

Interviewer behavior	Function	Examples
Open-ended question	Elicits a broad range of material; interviewee should tell you a lot	'Tell me about your main problem' 'What kinds of personal strengths do you have?' 'What makes it worse?'
Closed question	Elicits narrow range of material addressing a predetermined issue; interviewee response short	'Which is worse: stores or driving?' 'Do you argue about your child?' 'Did you have your first panic then?'
Reflection	For confirmation, shows interviewer is listening, may invite more material	'So you sweat, tremble and get butterflies?' 'So the worst problem is head banging?'
	For empathy	'I can see that upsets you.' 'I can see you feel bad about that.'
	For clarification	'. . . is that right?' 'Are you saying that . . .?' '. . . is that what you're telling me?'
Verbal setting operation statement	Indicates structure of interview, especially transition points	'You've told me about your main problem in a lot of detail, but are there any other things that worry you?' 'I've got a picture of how it started. Tell me now about what *you* want out of therapy.'
Paraphrasing	To check information, clarify and summarize	'So the problem started 18 months ago and . . . Is that right?' 'The main problem is wondering, but you also are worried about her attention and her incontinence. Have I got that right?'
	To give client a new perspective on their situation	'So with certain people you do relax, but at work and when people might criticize your performance you get uptight. Is that right?'

Consider the following example:

PS: So what kind of things make you angry? (*Open-ended question*)

K: Little stuff—stupid things really.

PS: What kind of things?—give me some recent examples . . . (*Open-ended question*)

K: When the boss asks me to do things and I think he's just picking on me, when my wife starts making demands on me . . .

PS: What else? (*Another open-ended question*)

K: When I'm tired and the kids are getting on my nerves that gets me real mad too . . . and they're only kids and they don't know they're driving me crazy . . .

PS: So which of these is the main problem for you personally? (*Closed question to clarify the client's priorities*)

K: I worry about work the most because if I hit the boss I'll lose my job.

In this example three open-ended questions are used to gather information on the situations that provoke anger. A single closed question is used to clarify the client's priority.

One of the most common errors in interviewing by untrained or novice interviewers is the excessive use of closed questions or using closed questions too early. Rather than getting the broad sweep of the problem the interviewer can get caught up in details and miss whole areas of a problem. This can lead to getting side-tracked on issues that are of lesser importance while ignoring important issues that have not been discussed. Excessive use of closed questions can also lead to the interview being very stilted as the interviewee answers a series of questions with brief 'yes' or 'no' staccato answers.

Minimal Verbals

Interviewers often grunt, say 'uh huh', 'yeh', 'go on', 'Mmm' and so on. These are known as minimal verbals and can be used in a very purposeful way. They can let the interviewee know that the interviewer is actively listening to them. They can also reinforce appropriate answers and encourage talking in people who are reluctant to talk.

Reflections

Reflections are repetitions or close repetitions of what the interviewee just said. They can be useful in prompting more material from the interviewee and, again, can let them know that the interviewer is listening. They can also be used to prompt confirmation from the interviewee that the interviewer has understood the material accurately.

Paraphrasing and Confirmation

A paraphrase is a summary of a larger portion of the interview which is followed by an invitation from the interviewer for the interviewee to confirm that the interviewer has an accurate picture of what is going on. Here is an example:

K: . . . then the kids scream and fight and that gets me mad too . . .

PS: . . . when the kids fight and scream and fight? (*Reflection inviting more material*)

K: . . . they drive me crazy some nights . . .

PS: So let's see if I've got it right . . . The main thing that gets you mad is the boss picking on you, but your wife making demands on you, and the kids fighting gets you mad too . . . Is that right? (*Para-phrase and invitation to confirm*)

K: Yeh, I guess those are the main things . . . but there are lots of little things too that get me mad . . .

Verbal Setting Operation

In order to guide the interviewee and direct their attention from one topic to another statements may be used to indicate where the interview is going. These are called verbal setting operation statements (Miltenberger & Veltum, 1988). Examples of verbal setting operations include: 'We've been talking about how the problem began, but, tell me, how is the problem affecting you right now?', 'Let's look at how the problem is affecting your family—you said that was bothering you a lot', and 'You've told me a lot about your problems, but I would like to hear about some of the good things in your life . . . what's going on right now that is good?'

Examples in the Literature

More extensive examples of the use of these techniques within the context of a full interview may be found in some of the published anno-tated interviews summarized in Table 4.2. Although these interviews

Table 4.2 Papers Containing Annotated Behavioral Interviews, Their Presenting Problems, and Type of Client

Author	Problem	Client
Brady (1986)	Psychogenic nausea and vomiting	Young adult
Chioda (1987)	Bulimia	Young adult
Levine (1987)	Anxiety disorder/phobia	Young adult
Morganstern (1988)	Various anxiety/depression	Adult
Sturmey (1991)	Behavior disorder	Child with developmental disabilities
Wolpe (1980)	Anxiety disorder	Young adult
Wolpe (1980)	Sexual disorder	Young adult
Wolpe (1980)	Anxiety disorder	Adult

have been somewhat narrow in their focus on acute anxiety and depressive disorders in young adults, the general principles that are to be found in these annotated interviews may be applied to a wide range of problems. These annotated interviews may be especially helpful for trainee therapists and for use during teaching interview skills.

Typical Pattern of Techniques

The use of the above techniques often falls into a natural rhythm to develop an understanding of a problem. This is illustrated in Figure 4.1. Typically a verbal setting operation sets the scene for the topic to be discussed. Open questions are then used to gather a broad range of information on the topic. A series of closed questions are then used to clarify issues that are still unclear. A paraphrase is then used to summarize the topic and clarification is then sought from the client. If the topic is exhausted then another verbal setting operation statement guides the interviewer and client on to another topic.

UNSTRUCTURED BEHAVIORAL INTERVIEWING

Several authors have emphasized that behavioral interviewing is a skilled, complex and subtle process that is driven by hypotheses which guide the clinician as to which areas to explore and how to interpret information gathered (Turkat, 1988; Wolpe, 1980, 1989; Wolpe & Turkat, 1985). This unstructured form of interviewing follows no predetermined structure.

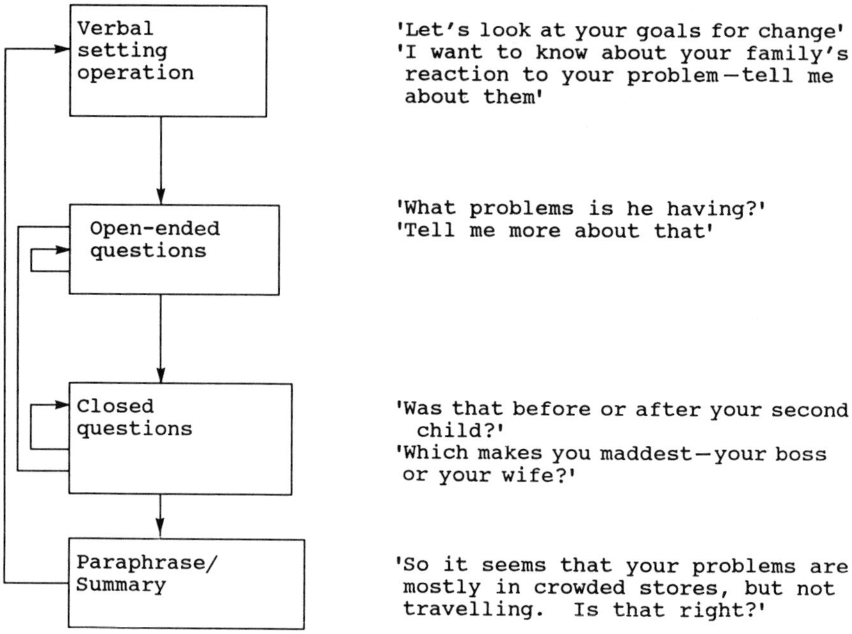

```
┌─────────────┐        'Let's look at your goals for change'
│ Verbal      │        'I want to know about your family's
│ setting     │         reaction to your problem—tell me
│ operation   │         about them'
└─────────────┘

┌─────────────┐        'What problems is he having?'
│ Open-ended  │        'Tell me more about that'
│ questions   │
└─────────────┘

┌─────────────┐        'Was that before or after your second
│ Closed      │         child?'
│ questions   │        'Which makes you maddest—your boss
└─────────────┘         or your wife?'

┌─────────────┐        'So it seems that your problems are
│ Paraphrase/ │         mostly in crowded stores, but not
│ Summary     │         travelling.  Is that right?'
└─────────────┘
```

Figure 4.1 A Common Pattern of the Use of Interview Techniques

This perspective on behavioral interviewing emphasizes the development of hypotheses very early on—perhaps prior to or during the first few moments of the interview. From this perspective it is not possible to carry out an interview without a hypothesis, since without it there is nothing to guide the interview or interpret the information gathered.

Hypothesis formulation may be possible even before the interview begins. Consider the referral letter in Figure 4.2. At first sight this letter is innocuous. Yet, there is sufficient information available to make the following speculative formulation.

A 37-year-old woman presents with a reactive depression. The A, B and C frequencies and duration are currently unknown. The move from Canada might be (a) a non-contingent, punitive event, (b) a loss of powerful reinforcers maintaining her appropriate, non-depressed behavior. Alternatively the move home might (c) have been to an environment which failed to support

Dear [Psychologist],

I would like to refer this lady, aged 37, who presents with a moderate depression. She moved back to this country two years ago from Canada when her husband obtained a job as a managing director.

Over the last year she has been presented several anti-depressant medications with some limited response to Tofranil.

I wondered if you would be willing to see her.

Sincerely,

[Physician]

Figure 4.2 An Example of a Referral Letter Which Can Be Used to Generate Hypotheses Prior to an Interview

non-depressed behaviors (e.g., failure to establish a job or other role for herself), or (d) might include excessive punishment.

Of course, this formulation may be completely erroneous. Some of these hypotheses could be eliminated very early on during the assessment. However, even if it is incorrect it can still be used to guide the initial part of the interview.

When no such evidence exists, questioning which is random or simply aimed at collecting information is unlikely to produce meaningful information. Turkat (1989) states that:

Time and again I have observed initial interviews that produce much information but provide little understanding of the patient's psychopathology . . . I have found it especially disturbing to watch a beginning student being trained by a technology-oriented behavior therapist. The student having spent four or five sessions collecting information, runs out of questions for the patient, and then asks the supervisor 'Now, what should I do?' The reply is to begin implementing ('pet') techniques matched to a patient's complaints. (p. 349)

Many of the annotated case transcripts listed in Table 4.2 can illustrate this unstructured, hypothesis-testing approach to behavioral interviewing. Here we will consider an exemplary account by Turkat (1988) which illustrates many of these features. Turkat presents the case of an insulin-dependent, freshman student having problems in injecting himself. When trying to inject himself he became angry and this interfered with the administration of his insulin. Here are the first four questions and answers of the first interview.

Dr: What's going on with you?

Pt: Trying to go to school I guess.

Dr: Are you doing that okay, or having a rough time of it?

Pt: It's pretty rough. I'm only taking 13 hours, everyone else is taking 15 or 16.

Dr: Why only 13?

Pt: Just to see if I can take it or not.

Dr: Notice any difficulties in taking what you have now?

Pt: At times, like when they force me to have lack of sleep.

(p. 350)

Turkat (1988) develops the following analysis based upon these questions, the referral information and the client's behavior. First, anger reactions to injection are unusual; anxiety reactions to injections are the common form of presentation of such a problem. Anger is usually about violation of rules or values. Therefore, some aspect of self-injection breaks an important rule or value for this person. Second, the client's account of the problem is replete with references to struggle, effort, and defiance of other people's rules. Third, during the interview the client's behavior is tough, combative and rigid. Turkat makes the following initial formulation:

Charles is angry about insulin injections because they make him appear weak. (p. 350).

From this initial hypothesis Turkat makes the following predictions. First, he will express little emotional behavior other than anger. Second, he will have few close friends since close friends are not compatible with being tough. Third, he will feel uncomfortable in any situation where he might appear weak or dependent. Fourth, he will have social difficulties since he may oversimplify social relationships into a weak–strong dichotomy. Fifth, he will come from an emotionally constricted family. Sixth, treatment should be aimed at modifying *fear of appearing weak* not fear of injections.

Turkat's paper goes on to illustrate how this initial hypothesis and set of predictions are used to structure the interview. A series of questions are asked to address each of the specific predictions made from the initial hypothesis. For example, certain parts of the interview explore other situations where Charles might feel weak or dependent. Other parts explore the kind of social relations he has and if they are consistent with these predictions. This paper contains numerous examples of masterly interviewing and interpretation of clinical material within a behavioral framework.

Comment

Hypothesis-driven interviewing is both intriguing and perplexing. On the one hand, it is an example of the best kind of clinical skill. It is flexible, tailored to the individual person and their problem, and it explicitly searches out the idiosyncratic functions of the person's problem. It is likely to yield interventions that are highly idiographic—in the case presented by Turkat the identification of modifying fear of appearing weak for what could easily be mistaken for a very mundane injection phobia is a very unusual treatment for this problem.

Despite these advantages hypothesis-driven interviewing suffers from a number of important limitations. The major problem is that of specifying a protocol to describe what constitutes unstructured behavioral interviewing. Without a clear definition of what constitutes an unstructured behavioral interview it is difficult for interviewers to learn this form of interviewing. It would be hard to specify what it is that an interviewer has to do to conduct a hypothesis-driven interview. Because of this problem it might be hard to agree on whether an interviewer was conducting a hypothesis-driven interview accurately or not. Thus, one of the limitations appears to be that it is hard to specify the independent variable.

A related concern is that of the information processing demands placed on the interviewer. It would be very easy for an interviewer to miss an important clue as to the functions of the behavior, but nevertheless continue on unaware of the omission. A more serious concern is that it would be easy to fall into the trap of confirmatory bias that has been widely reported in diagnostic interviewing (Rock, Bransford, Maisto & Morey, 1987). That is, an interviewer may have a hypothesis that is incorrect, and rather than test predictions that would disconfirm the clinical hypothesis he may tend to seek information to confirm the hypothesis. Of course, it is fairly easy in retrospect to make sense of clinical material. Thus, hypothesis-driven clinical interviewing may be fairly difficult to carry out well for novice or untrained interviewers, or for other interviewers without feedback on their performance.

SEMI-STRUCTURED BEHAVIORAL INTERVIEWS

A second approach to behavioral interviewing is known as semi-structured behavioral interviewing (Morganstern, 1988). In this approach to determining the functions of behavior a loose, flexible structure can be used to guide the interview. The main five sections to the interview are: (a) open the interview, (b) ascertain the current problem(s), (c) take a history of the problem, (d) assess the person's assets and goals for change, and (e) close the interview. An overview of the elements of a semi-structured behavioral interview can be found in Table 4.3.

The structure described in Table 4.3 can be used flexibly. It can be modified to fit within the flow of the information from the client. For example a client may initially present their problem by discussing its history. Rather than focusing on the details of the presenting problem the interview can follow the client's current interests and concerns at that moment. The interviewer can come back to the presenting problem section later on. In a similar way the elements of a semi-structured interview might be spread across several separate interviews if the problem is complex or if the interviewee is reluctant to disclose all relevant information in the first session. In this way the clinician has considerable discretion as to how the elements of a semi-structured interview are conducted.

For further information the reader is referred to the review by Morganstern (1988). For greater detail on the specific interview skills, how to discriminate them, and how to learn them the reader is referred to Miltenberger and Fuqua (1985) and Miltenberger and Veltum (1988).

Table 4.3   The Common Elements in a Semi-structured Behavioral Interview

Section	Purpose/topic
Open interview	Introduce participants; explain purpose of interview; explain ground rules; establish initial rapport
Ascertain current problem(s)	Elicit target behaviors, group into potential response classes, establish priority amongst problems; establish antecedents, consequences, frequency and duration; identify current strategies and their effectiveness
History	Identify onset (clear/traumatic vs insidious), development (gradually worsening, variable, periods of remission), reasons for seeking treatment (self-referral, other-referral, recent traumatic problem); previous treatments
Assets & goals for change	Elicit strengths such as personal characteristics, interests, hobbies, achievements and resources; elicit goals for change related to the problem and more general life goals
Close interview	Summarize interview; explain how treatment might go; how often appointments are; the expectations of therapist and client; who will be informed, how; confidentiality

Opening the Interview

Opening an interview is typically very brief. However, this section may provide the client with initial reassurance, provide key ground rules for the interview, and provide the foundation for establishing rapport. When coming to an assessment interview some people may expect to be on a couch, discuss their toilet training, talk about ink blots, or be 'psyched out'. They may be concerned that they or their significant others are in danger of being admitted to a psychiatric hospital. Some people might expect a ten-minute appointment similar to their appointments with physicians. Some may be unaware of how they got referred to the psychologist if the referral came from another professional.

Morganstern (1988) recommends that a brief summary addressing these matters be made at the beginning of the interview. For example, a statement such as the following might be sufficient to relax a client and allow them to begin talking about their problems.

'My name is   I am a psychologist here. I've had a letter from your family physician, Dr   She says that you've been having some difficulties recently. During an initial interview I often talk to someone for about 45 minutes or so to get a picture of their problems. Perhaps you can tell me in your own words what the problem is.

In the case study we reviewed earlier from Turkat (1988) he has a standard statement that he uses to try and loosen the client up.

Let me explain a little bit about what I'm trying to do. What I'm trying to do now is get an idea of what's going on with you. And, if there are any problems you are having, try to see what they are, and perhaps, why they developed, and then see if there is something we can do about it. Okay? And, if so, I'll tell you what I think. I'll tell you if there is something we can do, and if there is no problem, I'll tell you that. So, I'm just trying to get an idea of whether or not you need to do something about it. And if you do, what the options might be and how one might do that. I'm not here just to say that you're crazy or mentally ill or anything like that, because you're obviously not. (p. 352)

Such a statement, if appropriate to the person and problem, may help them relax and be more forthcoming in subsequent parts of the interview.

Assessing Target Behavior

There are two common aspects to assessing the target behavior. These are (a) establishing what the target behavior or behaviors are, and (b) establishing the relationship between the target behavior(s) and environmental variables. Many clients present with multiple forms of problems at the same time.

In an initial interview a 25-year-old woman reported that she had completely lost confidence in her ability to do anything. She was fearful in many social situations. She would get teary and run out of some situations. She reported that she was now lonely, isolated and depressed. She reported a lot of anxiety and tension in many social situations, especially when she was being evaluated by others.

In a case such as this there are numerous options for selecting target behaviors. These include anxiety, social and assertive skills, and attributions of competence. Further, the clinician has to determine the relationship between these diverse problems. Are they all one aspect of a single, broad problem, are they several independent, unrelated problems, or are they two or more problems with complex inter-relationships? One of the functions of assessing the presenting problem(s) is to determine the relationship between multiple presenting problems. Some of these issues are discussed in more detail in Chapters 7 and 8.

ABCs

The second aspect of assessing the target behavior(s) is to determine the relationship between the target behavior(s) and environmental events. A number of simple mnemonics have been used when assessing a target behavior, the most common of which has been the ABC three-term contingency. Examples of a three-term contingency would be as follows:

- Antecedent—see the door to a store as you are about to enter and see another person coming right at you;
- Behavior—turns head away from other person, hesitates to enter, tension on the abdomen increases rapidly, thinks 'Oh my God' and worries that she will catch the other person's eye;
- Consequence—temporarily avoids interaction with a stranger for a few seconds, then she catches the stranger's eye and her panic intensifies greatly.

Another example would be:

- Antecedent—the client drives past his old school;
- Behavior—the client recalls the years of punitive experiences and failure at school and has an overwhelming feeling of helplessness and disgust at his failures generally;
- Consequence—drives home in a depressed mood, cannot eat, or do anything for the next two hours.

Three-system model

Another mnemonic when inquiring about a target behavior has been the use of the three-system approach to fear. Here, information is gathered related to behavior, physiology and cognitions for each target behavior. For example, a fearful incident might involve: (a) attempting to approach a contaminated door knob and then getting a tissue to use at the last moment (*behavior*); (b) the person may feel progressively more panicky, sweat more, begin to have palpitations and her heart races more and more (*physiology*); and (c) the person may believe that the door knob is really contaminated, and after opening the door with the tissue repeatedly tell herself that everybody is safe now (*cognition*). The three-systems approach to fear can be readily extended to other problems. Thus, a client with depression might not go to work, might complete few tasks and cry excessively (*behavior*); might feel tense, have tingling feelings and feel depersonalized (*physiology*); and might feel worthless, stupid and have difficulty concentrating and remembering what to do (*cognition*). As part of a semi-structured interview a clinician might assess any of these three aspects of any target behavior as a component of assessing the functions of the target behavior(s).

Comment

Many clients will present a well-rehearsed story of their principal problems that has been repeated to many other people in the past. This presentation might be inaccurate in various ways. For example, the person making the referral may use diagnostic labels incorrectly. For example, of three clients referred for treatment for obsessive-compulsive disorder only one truly met this diagnosis. One had an embarrassing somatic fear related to social anxiety that she ruminated on a great deal. The second had a general anxiety disorder with some fears relating to germs. Thus, the initial referral information was quite inaccurate. Similarly, the way in which clients describe themselves might be inaccurate. Levine (1987) presents a case study of a 'height phobic'. Further analysis revealed that the person did indeed get fearful when alone in her apartment and looking down at the ground from high up. However, the fears were actually social fears rather than fears of heights.

Another problem in ascertaining a person's presenting problem is that the well-rehearsed story may be incomplete and too narrow. Often, after hearing about the principal problem from the client, going on to ask 'Are there any other problems in your life right now?' can often reveal a list of financial, medical, life events and other personal problems. A series of open-ended questions (see above) can often be helpful in clarifying the complete list of presenting problems.

Current Coping Strategies

As well as identifying the current problem's topography it is often helpful to get a picture of current coping strategies used to deal with these problems. These strategies may be counter-productive and directly contribute to the maintenance of the problem. Many coping strategies have short-term benefits and long-term costs. For example, giving a child who tantrums what they are asking for when the parent is exhausted provides temporary relief from an aversive situation for the parent. However, this strategy may maintain the behavior through intermittent reinforcement, and cause the child to learn to discriminate with exquisite accuracy when the parents are especially tired and vulnerable to the effects of tantrums. Similarly, when one parent gets mad and sends the child to bed as a supposed punishment, but ten minutes later the other parent goes up to comfort the child who is still crying, a mixed schedule of punishment and reinforcement is operating. This can significantly weaken the effectiveness of the strategies for management of the child's behavior.

Such coping strategies may inadvertently maintain the problem. Therefore these strategies should be identified in order to modify them. Furthermore, such modification may form the basis for future intervention strategies. Recall that Martens and Witt (1988), in the context of classroom consultancy, recommend modifying current strategies for dealing with a problem as a low-key, acceptable strategy for developing interventions. In the examples above, a simple answer would be to teach the parents to reschedule the strategies that they are currently using. They should have a shared strategy for managing the child's behavior, especially for times when they are very tired, and ensure that both parents are potent sources of reinforcement for appropriate child behavior.

History

The history part of the interviews can vary from the brief and fairly irrelevant to being long, complex and a decisive factor in designing the treatment program. The onset of a problem may be clear, such as one relating to a traumatic, potential conditioning event, or a dramatic life change that clearly signals changes in the schedules or availability of reinforcement and punishment. Alternatively the onset might have no clear beginning point and gradually escalate in a manner that is not readily described. There may be periods of remission or periods of significant worsening of the problem. These events can be useful in identifying possible functions of the problem.

Consider the following case history.

A 48-year-old lady presented with a 20-year history of agoraphobia with panics. She always considered herself an anxious, sensitive person. Although some previous problems existed, she dated the onset of the problem to after the birth of her second child. She had tolerated the problem for many years. It had fluctuated from time to time. She recalled no obvious pattern during the initial interview. The problem became dramatically worse approximately 6 months ago when her husband left her to live with a much younger and very attractive woman. Her adult children had left home several years previously and were now married. The dramatic increase in the problem had led to numerous family conferences, daughters moving temporarily back home and, indeed, her husband returning from time to time because of his wife's apparently severe, life-threatening illness.

Such a history gives rise to numerous hypotheses concerning the functions of these symptoms. Here is a woman in mid-life who has lost contact with her family and no longer has socially meaningful roles such as mother or wife available to her. She has been unable to maintain contact through appropriate and assertive social behavior. She has failed to find a set of roles for herself outside of family life. Interviews with her husband revealed a domineering, punitive individual. In his presence she literally cowered, pulled away, and repeatedly sought reassurance from him rather than expressing her own opinion. (The literature on reinforcement assessment in persons with developmental disabilities uses approach and avoidance to evaluate stimuli as reinforcers and punishers. One may therefore speculate that many of her appropriate social behaviors had been severely punished or extinguished in the past.) These symptoms were the most effective behaviors in her repertoire in gaining the social contact she needed from the only source available as few opportunities existed to support appropriate social behaviors outside the family.

Assets and Goals for Change

Evaluating a person's assets and goals for change is an important part of a semi-structured behavioral interval. It can be used to identify alternative and incompatible behaviors which might replace the target behaviors or which might be adaptive behaviors which might serve the same functions (Goldiamond, 1974).

Many clients may be surprised or somewhat embarrassed at being asked about past achievements, goals or positive personal qualities. For clients who have difficulty in reporting any current assets information relating to former interests may provide useful starting points.

An evaluation of personal strengths and assets may also identify important sources of reinforcement which are currently underutilized or unavailable. These strengths can be incorporated into treatment programs, and in the maintenance and generalization phases of intervention in a wide range of imaginative ways. The following case example illustrates some of these points.

A 48-year-old, unemployed man presented with a severe and debilitating phobia of dogs. At times he drank excessively. His wife had a long psychiatric history. His assets and goals for change included the following. He described himself as a strong family man and was very committed to do the right thing for his wife and other family members, even if it involved personal sacrifice. He had been unable to visit his relatives for over five years because of the dog phobia. In the past he had visited them frequently and had good relationships with other family members. He wished that these relationships could be reinstated now. He also had never learned to swim throughout his life. One of his goals was to do so.

His dog problem was treated rapidly in three, 2-hour sessions of flooding. However, during follow-up he was encouraged to visit his relatives and to sign up for swimming classes. On several occasions this led him to encounter dogs while travelling. These were a genuine problem in his inner city neighborhood. He also had several successful encounters with dogs at his relatives' homes. This gave him an opportunity to practice non-avoidant strategies of dealing with this problem and to re-establish motivations for travelling.

Use of assets and goals for change in therapy may be a key strategy in motivating a client to participate in therapy. It may also be a key component to maintaining change after initial intervention. For example, in people with disorders where avoidance is a key component, simply reducing anxiety or elevating mood may be ineffective strategies unless the client has a reason for regularly going out, to enjoy the outside world, and access the available contingencies of reinforcement. Examples here of common strategies include a client's getting a job, getting a better job, and establishing regular leisure activities and patterns of social behavior. In persons with chronic disabilities, such as long-term psychiatric illnesses, developmental or physical disabilities, establishing a daily pattern of life, a network of services and social support to maintain alternative behaviors, is often a useful strategy to prevent relapse.

Closing the Interview

Closing the interview may be a useful occasion to summarize the interview, to answer any remaining questions the client has, and to give information about how subsequent meetings might proceed. Some clients may still have lingering questions at the end of the first appointment which need to be solicited and answered. These might be fairly mundane matters. Some clients may simply want to know how often and when they can be seen. Others may expect more momentous pronouncements such as whether they are mad, whether it is 'just in their mind', whether they are faking, will go insane, or can be helped at all.

It may often be useful at the close of the interview to reiterate reformulations of problems at this point (Morganstern, 1988). This can be helpful to ensure that they concur with a new view on their problem. The close of the interview can also be a good time to review and clarify any tasks that must be done before the next appointment.

LEARNING BEHAVIORAL INTERVIEW SKILLS

Learning behavioral interviewing skills is a key component of any clinician's training, but this is often neglected, badly taught, or left to chance. In conducting the literature review on interviewing skills no study could be found in which the skills of psychologists were observed working with actual clients. Turkat's (1988) comments quoted earlier reflect these concerns.

The Hypothesis Testing Game

To address this issue Rickland and Titley (1988) developed a hypothesis-testing game to train some hypothesis-generating skills. The game, which can be part of a regular practicum class, consists of dividing the class into teams and allotting each team alternating 3-minute segments of interview time with a role play client. A total of 24 minutes of interview time is allotted to the class. During each 3-minute segment the interviewing team is encouraged to gather information relevant to the functions of the problem. They should use the micro-counselling skills discussed earlier, collect relevant information, generate and test clinical hypotheses and maintain rapport with the client. Students are encouraged to critique the strategies and hypotheses they are pursuing.

At the end of a 3-minute segment the team select their two best hypotheses on the basis of the evidence they have gathered. This is presented to the class as the best line to pursue in the rest of the interview. Up to 10 points are awarded on the basis of the quality of the hypotheses selected, the evidence presented for them and not missing viable hypotheses. During any 3-minute segment the second team make challenges if a lead has been bypassed or when there is a problem with the interviewer's skills. One point is awarded for any challenge. An additional 5 points are awarded for an accurate challenge and 6 points are awarded to the challenged team if the challenge is inappropriate.

Rickland and Titley (1988) found very high levels of satisfaction with the game. They reported that students benefited from both direct and vicarious feedback, and through evaluating hypotheses with other group members. Although this approach does not deal with teaching many of the specific skills during an *in vivo* situation with an actual client it may be a useful exercise early on during training interview skills.

Analog Studies

A number of studies have evaluated various methods of training semi-structured interview skills in analog settings. Brown, Kratochwill and Bergan (1982) trained interviewees in nine different scripts covering problems such as hyperactivity, enuresis and stealing. The subject interviewers were graduate students enrolled in an introductory behavioral class. During the baseline interviews they were instructed to identify the client's problem. Up to one hour was permitted. The intervention consisted of six components. These were: (a) a written outline of the interview with examples was provided; (b) a similar form was provided without examples to be used during an interview; (c) a video-tape model interview was shown; (d) the experimenter prompted the student during showing of the videotape to write examples of interviewer behavior on the form; (e) questions were answered related to the videotape; and, (f) after completion of a training interview students were given feedback on their interview skills, descriptive praise for correct performances, and corrective feedback specifying areas where student behavior needed to be changed.

The student's behavior was scored on skills such as introducing the discussion, obtaining a description of the problem, and obtaining a description of a strength. A measure of consumer satisfaction was also used to evaluate training. A follow-up interview was also held two months later.

Results showed that untrained graduates had low, variable, and often no knowledge of the skills trained. Using a multiple-baseline design across students they were able to show that large improvements in student skills occurred due to the training. Further, these gains were largely maintained after training.

Miltenberger has extended this and other earlier work to compare teaching these skills either by training manuals or by individual instruction (Miltenberger & Fuqua, 1985). In the manual condition students had to read the manual and were prompted to read it prior to each interview. In the manual ten skills were described with both positive and negative examples which the reader was prompted to critique in writing. Prior to assessment the students' manuals were checked that all the spaces had been written in. However, at no point did the students in the manual condition receive feedback or supplemental training. Students receiving one-to-one training received training broadly similar to that described earlier in Brown, Kratochwill and Bergan (1982). Miltenberger and Fuqua (1982) found that both methods were highly effective in training interview skills and both received good social validation ratings. However, the manual condition was invariably more economic to use. These findings were replicated by Miltenberger and Veltum (1988).

DISCUSSION

Future Research

Interviewing is a ubiquitous part of functional analysis. Despite its central position it is often underreported, neglected, or not reported in the research literature. In part this is because the emphasis from radical behaviorists has always been on experimental manipulation of behavior as part of the assessment process, and, allied to that, a strong preference for observational data (Baer, Wolf & Risley, 1968). Despite this very strong leaning towards this methodology it should be acknowledged that most clinicians rarely observe the behavior of their clients in the natural environment, and are most unlikely ever to conduct an experimental analysis of their behavior as Baer, Wolf and Risley (1968) require that they do. Thus, most clinicians are heavily dependent on interview data to assess the functions of the presenting problem.

If this is the case then clinical interviewing should receive far greater attention than it has hitherto been given. Research has emphasized the initial assessment interview. However, interview skills are used in other contexts also. Little attention has been paid to dealing with failures to respond, dealing with relapses, and making reformulations as new information arises or an initial hypothesis is rejected. Skills necessary for dealing with difficult, evasive or angry clients have also not been explicitly addressed. It is important to recognize that some clients are strongly motivated to report a distorted picture. Although this can be most obvious in cases where legal issues are at stake and financial compensation for injury may depend on the degree of disability incurred, this problem may arise in other situations also. We all tend to report ourselves in a somewhat positive manner. It is unlikely that every client will freely disclose their own mistakes and errors that may have contributed to their current problem at their first interview. In such situations it may not be possible to adequately assess the functions of the target behavior as full information is not available to the clinician. A third topic that future research could address is interviewing more than one person at a time. This situation presents the interviewer with additional problems such as having to monitor a group of people who may be spread out across a room, resolving conflicts among group members, allowing all people to talk, and regulating the flow of the interview with several people. Finally, the key issues of translating the information gained from an interview into a formulation and translating the formulation into an effective treatment package have not been addressed. One could imagine situations in which a therapist scored high on covering all the topics required using the skills trained, but was no closer to a formulation or treatment because they missed clues, failed to combine all the information appropriately, or made errors in translating a correct formulation into a treatment.

Learning Interview Skills

This literature on behavioral interviewing has been useful in providing models for therapists to work from in the form of annotated scripts, and in providing models for how interview skills should be trained. The implications for therapists wishing to learn or maintain their interviewing skills are clear. We would all be well advised to get our own behavior audio- or videotaped from time to time and scored up against criteria used in these studies. Peer review may be especially helpful on the general atmosphere of the interview and idiosyncrasies which might interfere with the interview. Many studies have shown that people's reports and recollections of their own behavior are often generous, and direct feedback on one's own performance is often a salutary experience necessary to learning and maintaining skills that we can all benefit from.

Chapter 5

ASSESSMENT METHODS III: OBSERVING BEHAVIOR

REASONS FOR OBSERVING BEHAVIOR

Psychology often espouses an interest in behavior. Yet, paradoxically, psychology has focused attention mainly on indirect assessment of behavior. Self-report measures of behavior, experimental studies, and questionnaires filled out by other people are all commonly used. Direct observation has received rather limited attention. This has restricted the kind of data that are available to us as well as the range of settings that have been studied. Tinbergen (1963) put it like this:

> psychology [has tended] to concentrate on a few phenomena observed in a handful of species which were kept in impoverished environments, to formulate theories claimed to be general, and to proceed deductively by testing those theories experimentally. It has been said that, in its haste to step into the twentieth century and to become a respectable science, psychology skipped the preliminary stage that other natural sciences had gone through, and so was losing touch with the natural phenomena. (p. 410)

This quotation brings us to the first main justification for observational methods in clinical practice—trying to develop a natural history of a clinical phenomenon. There are few studies which can tell us how many hours a client with agoraphobia spends out of the house—perhaps some of them spend rather longer out of the house than we think. If we do not have a good natural history of the phenomenon we wish to explain or change then our theories and treatments are based on a weak foundation.

An allied justification for carrying out direct observation related to clinical phenomena is that of trying to find out more clearly what average behavior is like. Using our own impressions of everyday behavior we might be liable to unrecognized biases and value judgements. Thus, when we come to negotiate goals with clients we might inadvertently set goals based on our own values or narrow set of experiences rather than typical behavior for the general public. For example, we do not have any good studies of how often typical members of the general public go out of the house against which to compare the behavior of people with agoraphobia.

A third reason for observational studies of the natural environment is to confirm findings made in analog settings such as laboratories or clinics. We know that people's behavior often varies dramatically from one setting to another. Thus, the possibility that behavior in laboratory or clinical settings is not representative of other settings cannot be ruled out. Therefore, naturalistic studies are needed.

Fourth, many clinical populations with whom we work are often not amenable to traditional methods of assessment. They may not have the responses in their repertoire to respond to tests or interviews. They may not be able to understand the testing procedure. They may be unable to attend for sufficient time to complete a traditional psycho-metric assessment. Thus, many groups of people, such as some older clients with dementia, some people with severe and profound develop-mental disabilities, some people with long-term psychiatric disorders, or some very young clients, may not be testable by traditional methods. Direct observation as a method of assessment has proven particularly helpful here.

Fifth, many people have become dissatisfied with the accuracy of some traditional methods of collecting data. The effects of various kinds of rater set on self-report measures, for example, faking good or faking bad. The poor reliability of reports from third parties such as care staff and relatives under some circumstances has led some clinicians and researchers to be very disenchanted with these indirect measures of behavior (Weiss & Frohman, 1985).

Finally, direct observation has been used as an effective method for studying environments as well as people. Concern over the environ-ments in which clients are found can arise from two sources. First, humanitarian concerns over the quality of some environments, such as long-stay settings or abusive or neglectful families, have often been voiced. The absence of personal possessions, materials with which to interact, staff–client interaction, and even basic cleanliness have been repeatedly raised as sources of concern in some settings. Second, the environment has also been observed in order to learn what role it might play in eliciting and maintaining client behavior. Most research here has looked at the key role of social behavior from peers, relatives and care staff. This has now become one of the major clinical applications of direct observational methods as it often has direct implications for intervention.

Comment

Despite the importance of direct observation its application to clinical problems is still relatively limited. Most research relates to work within the framework of applied behavior analysis or ethology. Observational methods have mostly been used with persons in institutional or other long-stay settings although a trend to apply these methods to a wider range of clinical populations is discernible.

In the following sections we shall discuss the properties of behavior and the implications for its measurement. Next, various practical problems relating to direct observation will be discussed. These include selecting and defining behavior, the use of time-sampling methods, continuous recording and automated devices to aid direct observation and inter-observer agreement. Finally, some applications of direct observation to identify functional relationships and to design and evaluate interventions will be discussed. The interested reader should consult Sackett's (1978) monograph for more detail on observational methods.

PROPERTIES OF BEHAVIOR

Often clinicians or researchers talk rather nebulously about the 'amount of', 'the proportion of' or 'the percentage of' a behavior that has been observed. However, this is often done in a way that does not acknowledge that behavior has clear, identifiable parameters which can be measured or estimated.

Duration

Behavior occupies time. Thus, one parameter of behavior is duration. This may be expressed in absolute units such as seconds, hours, or days. Alternatively it may be expressed as a proportion of the total observation period. For example, someone might spend 17 minutes talking over an 8-hour observation period. Thus, he spends 3.5% of his time talking.

Frequency and Rate

If behavior can be identified as occurring for discrete episodes, acts, or bouts then its frequency and rate can be measured. If frequency is divided by time then the rate of the behavior can be measured. For example, if a parent talks to a child on seven occasions in 30 minutes then the frequency of the behavior is 7 and the rate of the behavior is 0.23 interactions per minute. In operant psychology it is not uncommon to see behavior plotted as the cumulative response rate. This approach has been used much less frequently in clinical studies although it would be fairly easy to do so.

The Relationship Between Frequency and Duration

Duration and frequency are often confused but must be clearly distinguished. Duration and frequency may be independent of one another. In Figure 5.1 it can be seen that frequency and duration may vary completely independently from each other. Although operant research has focused on rate or cumulative response rate as the best measure of behavior in much clinical work, duration and proportion of time may be much more important. For example, there would be little point in reducing the frequency of rumination episodes alone without reducing the total duration of such a behavior.

Altmann (1974) introduced a useful distinction of frequency-meaningful and duration-meaningful behaviors. Frequency-meaningful behaviors are typically behaviors with very short duration which may occur relatively often. Examples include a child hits another child, a person screams or throws something. Duration-meaningful behaviors are typically behaviors which occupy more extended periods of time. Examples include the proportion of time a client with chronic pain remains in bed, the proportion of the day a client with obsessive-compulsive disorder spends washing or the proportion of a day a client with severe brain injury sits and watches television. This distinction of frequency- and duration-meaningful behaviors is useful to bear in mind when deciding how to record a behavior.

Intensity

The intensity of behavior is more difficult to define than frequency and duration. However, it has something to do with the amount of energy

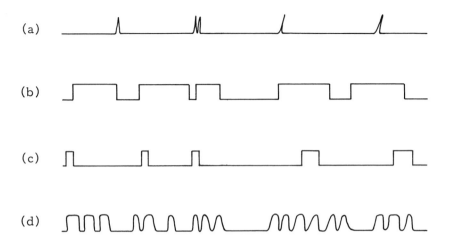

Figure 5.1   The Relationship of Frequency and Duration of Behaviors

Example (a) is a frequency-meaningful behavior, whereas example (b) is an example of a duration-meaningful behavior. Note that although in examples (b) and (c) the behavior occurs at the same rate the duration of (b) is much greater than (c). Similarly the behavior in examples (b) and (d) occupies the same duration but the behavior in (d) occurs three times more frequently. Thus, frequency and duration may be independent of each other

associated with a behavior. An example where the intensity of a behavior is the relevant dimension for measurement is voice volume (Fleece, Gross, O'Brien *et al.*, 1981). Other examples of intensity would be examples such as whether or not peers had been injured by an aggressive behavior.

Sequencing of Behavior

Behavior typically occurs in relatively ordered or predictable sequences rather than in random strings. This is sometimes referred to as *autocorrelation*. Examples here include so-called biological rhythms in behavior such as circadian and circannual patterns in behavior. Behavior may also vary systematically according to predictable changes in the environment, such as changes associated with the day of the week or regular patterns of activity associated with mealtimes which occurred at approximately 4 to 5 hourly intervals. Some behaviors, such as panic attacks and compulsive rituals, may occur together in closely packed bouts followed by longer inter-bout intervals. Thus, these behaviors are highly sequenced. A good predictor of current behavior is that behavior which occurred a few seconds ago. Other examples of sequenced behaviors include consummatory behaviors. Here, the behavior appears to be driven towards some final, consummatory act such as feeding, mating or nest-building. At any one time the organism only shows a small sample of the possible behaviors depending whereabouts in the chain of behavior it is. Clinical examples here might include behaviors which lead up to a para-suicidal gesture, or a relapse in a client with schizophrenia. The notion of a response chain has been used clinically (see Chapter 8).

Permanent Products

Behavior often produces environmental traces of damage. These permanent products can be used as an indirect measure of behavior. Permanent product measures can be quite useful and easy to measure. For example, the number of items of work a client has made in a workshop is quicker to measure at the end of the day compared to spending 8 hours observing time spent working.

Permanent product measures can be of more functional significance than some observational measures. For example, some interventions to assess the efficacy of toilet training programs have used the total weight of soiled linen as an outcome measure. Common examples of permanent product measures are those associated with the number of items made in a workshop or the number of lines written in a book by a child with hyperactivity.

Consider the following example.

A young male medical registrar was referred because of extreme difficulties in completing any kind of written work. After an initial assessment interview he was asked to bring with him the content of his trash can from the previous day to the next appointment. He appeared the next week with two black trash bags of screwed up paper, each with two or three words written on it, from his previous day's efforts.

Here is a still more florid example of permanent products of psychopathology.

A client was referred for treatment of a severe obsessive-compulsive neurosis of at least 15 years history. The letter stated he had hoarded everything over the last 15 years and had thrown nothing away. Upon arrival at the house the clinical psychologist struggled from room to room brushing past ceiling-high piles of newspaper, magazines, empty cartons, milk bottles and a carefully arranged line of decaying dead vermin on the kitchen sink.

SELECTING AND DEFINING BEHAVIORS

Selecting and defining behavior categories are two related issues which pose a number of important conceptual and practical problems. The selection of a suitable category of behavior to record is dependent upon a number of important judgements on the part of the observer. Categories of behavior which need to be decreased are most commonly selected. However, it is also useful to have at least one other category of behavior used to monitor increases in desired behavior. In this way one can be more confident that only the target behaviors are being selectively reduced rather than a general suppression of all behaviors. Also, from a constructional point of view it is important to demonstrate that an intervention increased desirable or functional behaviors. It is not adequate to merely remove the undesirable behavior.

Trying to identify a desirable behavior to increase may not always be easy. For example, some undesirable behaviors serve important functions for some individuals. They may not have any alternative, more acceptable response that is both effective and easy to perform and that serves the same function. Also the person may be in an environment which does not support alternative, acceptable behaviors. Consider this example.

Sally, a 28-year-old, non-ambulant woman with profound developmental disabilities, was referred for help relating to her throwing tables. Two days of informal direct observation led to the following formulation. Sally did have some limited speech, typically one or two phrase utterances (e.g. 'Ah dolly', 'Gimme'). She appeared to use these appropriately in context. A typical sequence of disruptive behavior would probably begin by Sally saying 'Nurse' in a rather quiet voice. This was gradually repeated, getting louder and louder. Then she would begin slapping and banging a table and begin to try to throw it. Finally, a nurse would come over to see why she was so upset and ask her what she wanted.

In this case it would appear that the social environment did not support desirable behavior, which was extinguished. Rather, in a noisy and often chaotic environment only loud shouting and banging was an effective method of communicating with care staff.

Multiple Topographies

Quite often clients might present with several topographically dissimilar behaviors which may or may not all serve the same function. If they do all serve the same function it might be quite legitimate to combine them into some superordinate category. For example, one might legitimately group screaming and throwing things together under 'disruptive behavior' if both behaviors served the same function for the client. The decision as to whether or not to combine individual topographies in this way can be a matter of careful judgement.

Similar problems can arise in attempting to define observational categories of desirable behavior. For example, an intervention could be based upon reinforcing other alternative or incompatible behaviors. Thus, a decision has to be made on whether the category of behavior to be reinforced is to consist of simply not showing the target behavior, a specified other response, a set of behaviors which are physically incompatible with the target behavior, or a specified set of other behaviors which might serve the same function as the target behavior.

Defining behavior categories presents a number of problems. First, behavior categories should be operationalized and defined topographically. Global labels such as 'Communication', 'On Task', or 'Engaged', require further careful definition. Some examples of operationalized behavior categories can be found in Table 5.1. The situation can become complicated further by different authors using the same term, e.g., 'Engaged', but using different operationalizations which differ substantially from each other both procedurally and conceptually (Sturmey & Crisp, 1994).

Molecular and Molar Behaviors

A useful distinction which is sometimes made is that between molecular and molar classes of behavior. Molecular categories of behavior are

Table 5.1 Some Examples of Operationalized Behaviors Selected to Illustrate a Range of Clinical Problems; How 'Fuzzy' Behaviors such as these Can be Operationalized

Subject/setting	Behavior category	Operationalization
Children/school	Specific academic response (Greenwood *et al.*, 1985)	Writing, reading aloud, reading silently, asking questions, answering questions, academic talk, academic game play
Doctor & patient/ general practice	Illustrative gestures (Street & Butler, 1987)	Hand and arm gestures used to convey meaning or which were indicative of interest and expressiveness
Dually diagnosed adult/state hospital	Bizarre vocalization	One or more of: (a) referred to stimuli not present or not being discussed; (b) inappropriate sexual content; (c) maladaptive
	Appropriate vocalization (Mace, Webb, Sharkey *et al.*, 1988)	Any question, phrase or statement of fact or opinion that was relevant to the conversation
Excessive drinkers/ various	Inappropriate limited drinking	Before work day, at an AA meeting, interactions where prohibited, to relax recurrent stress, to cope with loneliness, etc.
	Appropriate heavier drinking (Sobell, Sobell & Sheahan, 1976)	Ritual drinking in some cultures, beer parties, drinking to drunkenness with preparations to minimize risk—such as not driving.

usually narrow and defined by topography. For example, 'speaks' or 'hits' would probably be considered examples of molecular behavior categories. Molar categories of behavior are usually broader and are more likely to have connotations of the function or purpose of the behavior. 'Communication' and 'Aggression' would be examples of molar behavior categories.

The combination of molecular behavior categories into superordinate molar behavior categories lies at the heart of the problems outlined above. Combining molecular categories into molar categories should be done on the basis of some explicit rationale rather than on the basis of intuition. For example, if a definition of 'Engagement' was made on the basis of behaviors which promote learning in school children the definition might look substantially different from a definition of 'Engagement' made on the basis of behaviors which were likely to reduce disruption (Sturmey & Crisp, 1994).

RECORDING METHODS

Continuous Recording

Continuous *in vivo* observational data collection is most often used for observing a relatively simple situation such as counting the frequency of a discrete, low or moderate frequency behavior which is readily observable. Observers tire quickly. Multiple behavior categories or complex sampling schedules can be difficult to record and using continuous recording *in vivo* is unusual.

Many studies have used technology to assist in data collection. This might consist of simple devices such as golf counters and stop-watches. Recently the advances in microcomputer technology have enabled data collection using lap top computers (Repp, Harman, Felce *et al.*, 1989) or bar codes and optical scanners (Tarnowski, Rasnake, Linscheid & Mulick, 1989). Data may also be collected on video or audiotape which allows repeated observation of the behavior. These methods have also allowed more complex analyses of sequential data than have hitherto been readily feasible. Practitioners should be aware that this technology does involve some cost. Maintenance, debugging computer programs and hardware failures may all cause significant problems from time to time.

Time-sampling Methods

Continuous recording may be difficult, especially for long periods of time and for many behavior categories. Thus, a number of methods which do not require continuous observation have been developed. These are collectively known as time-sampling. All time-sampling methods share two features in common. First, time is divided into a

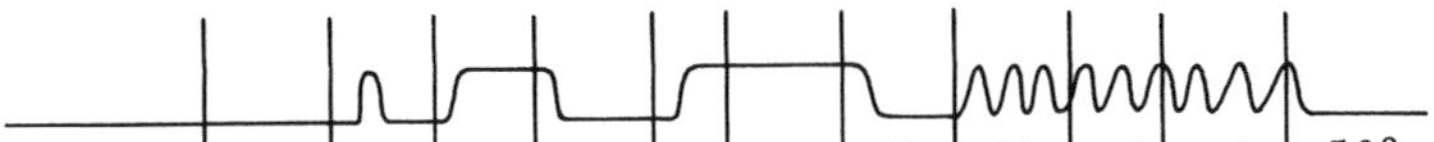

MTS	X	X	✓	X	✓	✓	X	X	✓	✓	50%
PIR	X	✓	✓	✓	✓	✓	✓	✓	✓	✓	90%
O & R	X	R	✓	R	✓	R	✓	R	✓	R	80%
WIR	X	X	X	X	X	✓	X	X	X	X	10%

Figure 5.2 Four Different Time-sampling Methods and their Relationship to Frequency and Duration of the Target Behavior

number of regular intervals. These might be quite close together for short periods of observation, perhaps 10 to 60 seconds apart over a 15- to 30-minute observation. Alternatively, they might be quite far apart for longer periods of time, perhaps every 30 or 60 minutes over an entire 16-hour day. Second, a rule is used to score the interval. It is this scoring rule which defines the difference between different time-sampling methods.

The four main methods are: (a) Momentary Time-Sampling (MTS), which is also known as instantaneous time-sampling; (b) Partial-Interval Recording (PIR), which is also known as zero-one recording or Hansen frequencies; (c) Whole Interval Sampling (WIS); and (d) Observe and Record (O&R). In MTS an interval is scored if the behavior is occurring at the precise moment that the observation is made. It is like a camera shot of the behavior. In PIR an interval is scored if the behavior has occurred at any time during the interval. The O&R is a variant of PIR in which alternate intervals are used for recording and observations. Finally, in WIS an interval is scored only if the behavior occurred throughout the entire interval. For all four time-sampling methods the results are then expressed as a proportion of the intervals scored. The four time-sampling methods are illustrated in Figure 5.2.

The major controversy with time-sampling methods is the relationship between the scores and the frequency and duration of behavior. There have been numerous evaluations of these time-sampling methods (e.g., Goodall & Murphy, 1980). Briefly, this literature can be summarized as follows. None of the four methods bears any simple relationship to the frequency or rate of behavior. Only MTS accurately estimates the proportion of time spent in a behavior. Even so, there is error variance associated with it. Thus, if the number of observations is small or the actual duration of the behavior is very low MTS may be quite inaccurate, although it will not be biased. WIS consistently, and often grossly, underestimates the proportion of time spent in behavior. This is because the behavior has to occur throughout the interval for the interval to be scored. When the behavior occurs even for a substantial proportion of the interval, the interval is not scored. PIR tends to systematically overestimate the proportion of time spent in behavior and at times grossly so. This is because any occurrence of the behavior causes an interval to be scored. O&R is essentially a variant of PIR, and, thus, the same comments apply.

One recent refinement has been the work of Harrop and colleagues on the sensitivity of time-sampling methods to change. They demonstrated that although MTS was more accurate than PIR in estimating duration, that MTS was less sensitive to change than PIR (Harrop & Daniels, 1986, 1993). Therefore, they recommend the use of PIR over MTS in situations where the investigators are interested in detecting change, but do not need to know the actual proportion of time spent in behavior.

When time-sampling is to be used it is therefore necessary to combine MTS, for behaviors which are duration-meaningful, and simple frequency counts for frequency meaningful behavior. It should be noted that in order to carry out a frequency account of a behavior there must be a clear rule for the beginning and end of an occurrence of a behavior. This is relatively simple for very brief behaviors such as a tic, 'hits' or 'shouts'. However, for behaviors which are more extensive in time it is not always readily apparent how to score a single act, episode or bout of a behavior. For example, it may require some pilot work to develop rules to define the beginning and end of a bout of social interaction in order for the frequency or rate of social interaction to be observed.

PROCEDURAL ASPECTS OF OBSERVATIONS

When carrying out direct observation a number of important procedural aspects require clarification. These relate to the use of pilot observations, the design of recording forms, the scheduling of observations, observer reactivity and the use of videotape.

Pilot Observations

Pilot observations are an essential step in any use of direct observation. They can take the form of simple running, narrative notes of the behavior used to derive draft behavior categories. Piloting out initial definitions of behavior categories, initial reliability studies (see below) to assess the robustness of the definitions of behavior categories, clarifying disagreements, and assessment of how comfortable different schedules of observations are for the observers, are all important preliminary stages in observational studies. It is unwise to carry out any observational data collection without a pilot phase and some initial reliability data. If the observations are carried out using other workers' definitions of behaviors, then piloting is still commonly needed to clarify confusing situations.

Designing Recording Forms

The design of recording forms often needs careful attention. A good recording form can help an observer to record, allow rapid recording of observations, and be readily understood when completed. Having sufficient space to make some narrative notes on the setting conditions, any salient events, hypotheses or any other relevant details which might be forgotten is often helpful. The use of spaces between columns, double lines or thick lines to help guide recordings is often helpful. Figure 5.3 illustrates an original and a modified version of a recording form to illustrate these points.

Observation Schedules

It is rare for observations to be made throughout the day. Breaks should be scheduled to allow observers to rest, especially if observations are made frequently, are complex, or are for long periods of time. If observations are made throughout a day then breaks should be scheduled in a pseudo-random format. For example, a break could be scheduled for any one 10-minute block in each half an hour period. In this way the results will remain representative of the whole day. Alternatively, if more than one observer is available a rolling schedule assigning observers to observation periods is possible which could also schedule in periods for inter-observer agreement.

Reactivity

Reactivity is a problem often cited with direct observation. It is difficult to be certain when people are completely habituated to being observed.

(a)

Time	Engaged	Disengaged	Hits	Shouts	Swears
—					
9.10	✓				
9.11					
9.12					
9.13					
9.14	✓			✓	
9.15					
9.16	✓				

(b)

NAME: <u>Mrs Smith</u>   DATE: <u>9.1.76</u>
PLACE: <u>Alveston Ward Day Room</u>   PAGE <u>1</u>
TIME: <u>9 a.m.–11 a.m.</u>   ONGOING ACTIVITY: <u>Few residents
sat in day room. Staff attending to end of breakfast in
dining room. 4 residents present. TV on.</u>

Time	E(ngaged)/ D(isengaged)	Disruptive?			Comments
		Hits	Shouts	Swears	
9.10	E	X	X	X	Sat on own, reading
9.11	D	X	X	X	—
9.12	Missed observation	X	X	X	—
9.13	D	X	X	X	—
9.14	D	X	✓	X	Other resident tried to take book. Staff involved also.
9.15	D	X	X	X	—
9.16	E	X	X	X	Reading

At times it may not always be possible to achieve this. A number of precautions can help minimize these problems. First, people often habituate most rapidly early on. So, a period of pilot observation may help to minimize observer reactivity. Discarding some of the early data may be advisable. Second, it often helps to minimize eye contact with observers although it may take some time for people who know the observer to get used to this. Third, it helps if observers are discrete and inconspicuous in their appearance and behavior. Finally, if people do approach the observer it may be useful to have some stock reply such as 'I'm sorry, I'm busy now'.

Videotaped Observations

Videotaped observations are now commonly used. Whilst this offers some advantages over *in vivo* observation it also raises a number of other problems. Videotapes of behavior allow the possibility to repeatedly observe a sequence of behavior and to analyze it in finer detail than is possible with *in vivo* observations. However, it should be noted that the quality of both picture and sound is not always as good as is desirable. Consequently, some detail may be lost. Also, the angle of the lens is not as wide as with *in vivo* observation. Consequently, observing groups of people can be difficult. Data loss can also occur when people stand in front of the camera. Finally, observer reactivity may be greater on some occasions with videotape than with observers present due to the novelty of the situation.

INTER-OBSERVER AGREEMENT

Assessing agreement between two observers is important in order to assess that the observations are public and that they do not simply reflect the whim of one observer. Inter-observer agreement is also important to establish that the definitions of the behavior categories are clearly operationalized and can be interpreted similarly by two observers. Carrying out inter-observer agreement checks raises two main sets

---

Figure 5.3   Two Versions of the Same Recording Form

In (a) there is no space for description of the person, or running comments. Spaces are left, which are ambiguous. In (b) extra lines are added to simplify scoring. All spaces have something written in them. Missed observations are clearly distinguished from the behavior being absent

of problems—those relating to procedural aspects of inter-observer agreement and those relating to how to calculate inter-observer agreement.

Procedural Aspects

In a typical inter-observer agreement trial two observers will train together until adequate agreement is reached. Subsequently, observers will work independently except for occasional checks on inter-observer agreement. Taplin and Reid (1973) assessed the adequacy of this procedure by comparing overt checks with checks which continued when the observers were unaware of being observed. They revealed a number of artifacts. Inter-observer agreement dropped immediately after training ceased. When overt checks were carried out agreement jumped up immediately, but fell back after the check ended. Also there was a trend across sessions for agreement to gradually drift and get worse. This study illustrates how reactive inter-observer agreement checks can be.

Several solutions exist. If two observers work together observing several people together the order in which they observe people can be randomized. In this way from time to time they will observe the same person simultaneously and carry out an inter-observer agreement in a less reactive fashion. Although some inadvertent communication between observers might occur, this procedure should reduce reactivity. An alternative procedure, which is more robust, involves using videotape. In this procedure a primary observer scores up all the tapes and a second observer scores up a random sample of the tapes. The primary observer is kept blind to which tapes are being scored (Sturmey, Newton & Crisp, 1991). A review of procedural aspects of inter-observer agreement checks can be found in Kazdin (1977).

Statistical Aspects

The most common method used to assess the degree of inter-observer agreement is to express agreement as an overall percentage of intervals where both observers have agreed divided by the total number of observations made. Conventionally, overall percentage agreement should exceed at least 70% although inter-observer agreement above 90% is very often reported. Although overall percentage agreement seems a simple solution it is highly affected by chance levels of agreement. For example, if two observers both score a behavior as occurring during 90% of intervals they will agree *by chance alone* 81% of the time.

A wide range of solutions have been proposed. Only two will be discussed here (see Hartmann, Roper & Bradford, 1979, for a review). Firstly, it is useful to cast the data into a two-by-two matrix and simply look at it (Harrop, Faulkes & Daniels, 1989). An example is to be found in Figure 5.4(a). In this example 100 observations were made by two observers. On 64 occasions they agreed that the behavior occurred and on 17 occasions they agreed that the behavior did not occur. Thus, overall percentage agreement is 81%. Simple observation of the matrix shows that both observers were scoring occurrences on about the same number of occasions. If two observers differ in their leniency in scoring the behavior then the matrix is asymmetrical as in example 5.4(b).

One solution to the problem of chance levels of agreement inflating overall percentage agreement is to calculate agreement separately for intervals in which occurrences occur and for intervals in which non-occurrences occur. Only if both occurrence and non-occurrence agreements are high is inter-observer agreement deemed adequate. Examples of these calculations are found in Figure 5.4(a). Here it can be seen that the percentage of non-occurrence agreements is unacceptable in this example. A second solution is to calculate Cohen's *Kappa* (κ). This is the observed level of agreement corrected for chance levels of agreement (Cohen, 1960). It involves directly calculating levels of chance agreements for both occurrence and non-occurrence. Again Figure 5.4(a) contains a worked example. Conventionally *Kappa* should exceed 0.6, that is 60% better than chance levels of agreement. In the worked example in Figure 5.4(a) the value of K is only 0.441. Thus, the observers only agree some 44% better than chance. This confirms the results of the alternative method of calculating inter-observer agreement which also indicated that the observations were not acceptable.

Inter-observer agreement should be presented separately for each behavior category. In this way individual behaviors which are not acceptable can be identified.

IDENTIFYING FUNCTIONAL RELATIONSHIPS

The use of observation to establish a functional analysis can take a number of different forms. Prior to any observations taking place it is likely that a clinician will have already developed some hypotheses about the behavior to be observed. These might come from interviews, case notes, referral letters, reading the literature, or the clinician's previous experience. The simplest form of observation consists of unstructured observations without data collection. In the hands of a

(a)

Observer 1

Observer 2		✓	X	Total
	✓	64	9	73
	X	10	17	27
	Total	74	26	100

Overall percentage agreement $= \dfrac{(64 + 27) \times 100\%}{100}$

$= 81\%$

Occurrence agreement $= \dfrac{64}{(64 + 10 + 9)} \times 100\%$

$= 58\%$

Non-occurrence agreement $= \dfrac{27}{(27 + 10 + 9)} \times 100\%$

$= 43\%$

Kappa (the proportions of observed agreements corrected for chance agreement)

$$\kappa = \frac{P_o - P_c}{1 - P_c}$$

$$P_c = \left[\frac{73}{100} \times \frac{74}{100}\right] + \left[\frac{26}{100} \times \frac{27}{100}\right]$$

$P_c = 0.660$

$P_o = 0.810$

$$\kappa = \frac{(0.810 - 0.660)}{(1 - 0.660)}$$

$\kappa = 0.441$

(b)

Observer 1

Observer 2		✓	X	Total
	✓	57	26	83
	X	4	13	17
	Total	61	49	100

skilled clinician this may be an economical method of clarifying target behaviors and generating hypotheses. Many studies of naturally occurring behavior which systematically collect data can show significant variations in the target behavior and hence can give clues concerning stimulus control of the behavior. Many systematic observational studies have often included data on environmental events, such as the setting, group size, behavior of peers or staff which can be relevant variables in a functional analysis. Some observational studies have not confined themselves to passive observation. Rather they have systematically manipulated environmental variables such as staff interaction and use of materials to test a hypothesis. In this section we review and illustrate a range of observational studies which have been used to develop a functional analysis.

Informal Observation

One of the simplest forms of functional analysis using observation is informal observation without data collection. As with other forms of functional analysis the key strategy is the development and evaluation of hypotheses. The following example will illustrate this approach.

During an early assessment walk with a patient with severe agoraphobia several observations were made when walking around a crowded shopping area: (a) she frequently kept her head down, apparently avoiding eye contact with strangers; (b) she would walk in a fairly relaxed manner in open spaces between stores away from people, but would hesitate and attempt to find other routes past crowded parts of shops; (c) she would walk around stores that were not too crowded but would get into minor, embarrassing situations when steering the trolley around the supermarket during which she would blush; (d) she was observed to take an anxiolytic medication in the middle of the session which she said she always carried out with her because it made her feel safe. None of the details had been apparent during her assessment interview. Subsequent interviewing using this information showed that social avoidance, especially avoidance of appearing stupid, was a major motivator of avoidance. She reluctantly admitted to abusing tranquilizers as being one of her problems, which she had not previously admitted.

Figure 5.4 Methods of Presenting and Calculating Inter-observer Agreement

Example (a) is a symmetric matrix, but (b) shows an asymmetric matrix indicating different criteria for scoring behaviors

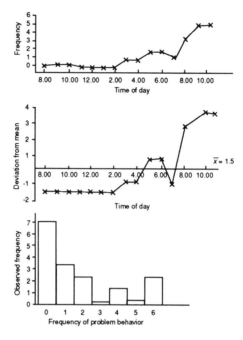

Figure 5.5 Variations in the Frequency of a Target Behavior across Times of Day which are Suggestive of Stimulus Control

The upper panel shows a plot of the frequency. The middle panel plots deviations from the mean. The lower panel plots the frequency distribution and shows a possible bimodal distribution

Systematic Observation

Simple observation of the behavior

Observations on the frequency or occurrence of a behavior can give some useful clues as to potential stimuli which might inhibit or facilitate the occurrence of the target behavior. It is important that the data on frequency counts are combined with relevant information from the environment such as the people present, and ongoing activities. Figure 5.5 shows an example of the variation across time of day which can occur in a target behavior. Simply plotting at the frequency (upper panel) gives some indication of this variability. Sometimes plotting the deviation from the mean (middle panel) can make this clearer. From this graph it appears that the behavior is more frequent after 4 p.m., and is especially low from 8 a.m. through 3 p.m. A histogram of the frequency of the target behavior (lower panel) suggests a bimodal distribution. These data suggest that there may be stimuli which inhibit and stimulate this behavior that are closely correlated with time of day. Further information concerning this person's schedule might help identify what these might be.

Hypothesis-driven observation of behavior and environment

Repp, Felce and Barton (1988) developed an observational methodology to observe behavior in the naturally occurring environment and to use this information to develop hypotheses concerning stereotypic and self-injurious behavior. The subjects were three children aged 6 and 7 with severe developmental disabilities who were observed in special education classes. During baselines data were collected for each of three hypotheses. For the *positive reinforcement hypothesis* consequences of the maladaptive behavior were noted including teacher proximity, verbal attention, touching from staff, and so on. For the *negative reinforcement hypothesis* events which were removed after the behavior were noted. These were overwhelmingly removal of task demands. For the *self-stimulation hypothesis* observers coded whether the child was engaged in activities, was held, being addressed, walking during the 10 seconds prior to the onset of the behavior. Thus, during each baseline a hypothesis concerning the motivation for the behavior was developed.

This study is important as it also offers validation data for this assessment method. For example, data for subject one showed that head banging was usually preceded by task demands and consequated with removal of these demands, thus suggesting a negative reinforcement hypothesis. Figure 5.6 shows this baseline and subsequent comparisons of two treatments, one based on the negative reinforcement hypothesis and one based on the positive reinforcement hypothesis. The first treatment consisted of extinction, that is task demands were never removed as a consequence of the behavior. The second treatment also consisted of extinction, but was consistent with the positive reinforcement hypothesis. Thus, this treatment consisted of removing staff approach, eye contact, touch and verbalization as a consequence of the behavior. As is seen in Figure 5.6 only the treatment based on the hypothesis supported by the baseline functional analysis was effective.

Taylor and Romanczyk (1994) reported a study that is conceptually similar to that reported by Repp, Felce and Barton (1988). The subjects were 15 children aged 3 to 11 years, with a variety of developmental and emotional disabilities. They were observed in small group or individual teaching settings. The distribution of attention was an index of

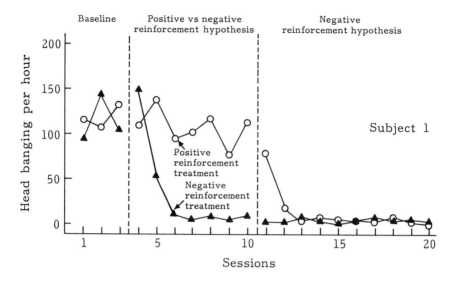

Figure 5.6   The Rate of Head Banging in a Student with Severe Developmental Disabilities during Baseline

This figure shows alternatives of treatments based upon the positive and negative reinforcement hypotheses and full implementation of the treatment based on the negative reinforcement hypothesis.
Source: Repp, A. C., Felce, D. and Barton, L. E. (1988). Basing the treatment of stereotypic and self-injurious behaviors on hypotheses of their causes. *Journal of Applied Behavior Analysis*, **21**, 281–289, p. 285

whether the children's behavior disorders were maintained by attention or escape avoidance. Taylor and Romanczyk hypothesized that children who received the greatest amount of attention had behaviors maintained by attention, whereas children with the lowest rates of attention had behavior problems maintained by escape avoidance.

In the first part of the study Taylor and Romancyk identified those children who had very high or very low rates of attention during their teaching situations. In the second part of their study they experimentally investigated the hypotheses derived from the naturalistic observations by conducting brief experimental functional analyses. In these experimental analyses they compared the behavior of the children in low and high attention conditions and while working on easy and difficult tasks. In 14 out of 15 students the experimental analyses confirmed the hypotheses generated from the naturalistic observations.

ABC charts

Another approach to using observational data to develop a functional analysis has been to use ABC charts. ABC charts consist of noting each occurrence of the behavior operationally, the antecedent and consequence of the behavior. These observations are frequently supplemented by other information such as time, place and any additional comments that might be relevant.

ABC charts are useful in that they supply more information than a simple frequency count as shown in Figure 5.7. ABC charts specify the antecedents, consequences, time and setting. They also can provide additional information. Comments from the observer can also provide useful information about the care giver, if they are doing the observation. An example of an ABC chart is shown in Figure 5.7. ABC charts can be used as a general method of functional analysis and are not just restricted to observational data. They can be used for self-report data, transcribing and summarizing notes (Gresswell & Hollin, 1992), to structure information from an interview, and as a tool in staff training. ABC charts can be a highly effective method of assessment. However, ABC charts are very dependent upon the ability of the observer to be able to report behavior sensitively and accurately. The observer must

Date time	What happened before?	What did you do?	What happened
2 July 1984/ 5.30 pm	Walking home	Ate: 4 Wispa bars, 2 Marathons	V, went home feeling
2 July 1984/ 6:15 pm	Preparing tea	Ate: 4 sandwiches 1 chocolate cake (family size) 1 pizza 2 bars (4 oz) of chocolate	
2 July 1984/ 12:15 pm	Walking around	Ate: 4 barm cakes 2 Wispas	V
2 July 1984/ 5:30 pm	Walking home	Ate: 2 Wispa bars	Felt tense

Figure 5.7   An Example of an ABC Chart for a Bulimic Patient

Note the rewording of antecedent, behavior and consequence. Letter 'V' indicates an incident of vomiting

also be able to discriminate antecedents and consequences accurately. This may require substantial training efforts for some observers. In some situations the ongoing behavioral processes may be exceedingly subtle, such as low frequency, intermittent reinforcement. In these situations it may be difficult to interpret the data when they are available.

Scatterplot

One variant of these methods is the scatterplot (Touchette, McDonald & Langer, 1985). A scatterplot is a matrix of time of day by day of the month on which occurrences of the behavior are noted. See Figure 5.8 for an example. Touchette, McDonald and Langer use open circles for low frequency of the behavior and a filled circle for high frequency of the behavior. This can assist in analyzing the pattern of behavior across time.

Scatterplots are extremely useful in identifying stimulus control. Periods when the behavior is least and most likely to happen are often very apparent. The utility of scatterplots in identifying stimulus control is dependent upon the controlling stimuli being correlated with time of day. If they are not the stimulus control will not be apparent. A further problem is that often the pattern of stimulus control may not be readily apparent from scanning several months of scatterplots. Often simple histograms of frequency by time of day, day of the week or some other graphical representation related to a specific hypothesis (e.g., graphing data pre- and post-menses), might be helpful. A final problem can be that even when some form of stimulus control is evident it may not be apparent what the controlling stimuli are. For example, knowing that a bulimic patient purges mainly in the weekday evenings and very frequently all day during the weekend does not, by itself, identify the antecedents for purging.

Detailed Behavior Report

Another method of structuring observations is the Detailed Behavior Report (DBR: Groden, 1989). This is, in effect, a rather expanded ABC chart with accompanying forms to assist in the analysis of the data arising out of many individual incidents of a problematic behavior. For each occurrence of a target behavior a detailed, descriptive record is made. This includes a careful, operationalized description of the behavior as it occurred on that occasion, its physical location, immediate and distant antecedents such as activities, social events, overt events, and organismic factors. Programmatic and other consequences

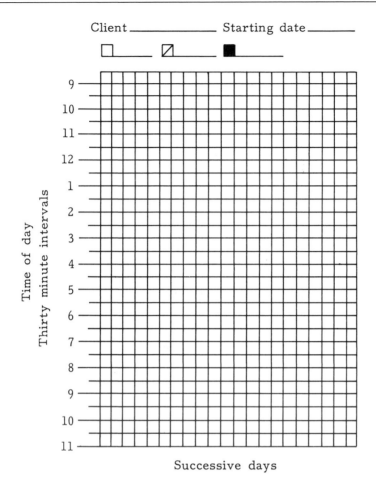

Figure 5.8 A Blank Scatterplot

Reproduced with permission from Touchette, P. E., MacDonald, R. F. and Langer, S. N. (1985). A scatterplot for identifying stimulus control of problem behavior. *Journal of Applied Behavior Analysis*, **18**, 343–351, p. 347

are also recorded for each incident. The data from all these incidents are then summarized using the DBR Checklist. On the checklist the information is summarized with regard to day of the week, time of the day, location, and antecedents.

Currently, no data are available as to the reliability and validity of the DBR procedure. It is clearly a useful tool in collecting data prospectively. It is also helpful in providing tools to analyze and summarize the data in a format directed towards deriving a functional analysis. It is also a helpful procedure in directing data collection to be highly specific. The DBR would also be very useful for low frequency, intense behaviors that can be reviewed in detail at every occurrence. A potential disadvantage to the DBR is that it may generate a lot of paperwork quickly for high frequency problems. Thus, it might generate response cost for both the client or informant and for the clinician analyzing the data.

Observations of treatment environments

Ideas and hypotheses for functional analyses can also be based upon naturalistic observation of entire environments. Numerous eco-behavioral studies exist. As one illustrative example we will consider a study of a pediatric burn unit. Tarnowski *et al.* (1989) note that intensive medical treatment environments for children may be associated with psychological problems. They may involve separation from parents, painful medical treatments, observation of other sick individuals, and reduced sensory stimulation. Previous research had suggested that children in pediatric burn units may develop behaviors such as anxiety, depression, aggression, exaggerated dependency and inability to play.

In this study they observed 40 children and their environment over a 6-month period. Most children were young (mean age 52 months) from predominantly white, intact, lower socio-economic status families. Children typically had accidental burns due to scalds or flame burns. About 40% had moderate disfigurement. The average stay was 18 days. Data were collected on the behavior of the children and their environment. Child behavior categories included observations of verbal/vocal behaviors, affective state and position. Care provider behavior categories included verbalization, number, type and proximity of staff.

Tarnowski *et al.* present both simple descriptive data and some analyses of the relationship between child behavior and environmental events which are suggestive of functional analyses. For example, the overall percentages of molar affective responses were: good—60%, fair—0.2%, poor—11.4%, and very poor—27.8%. However, when analyzed by setting marked situationality was observed. For example, the proportion of positive affective responses was 82.5% in the playroom, but 44.4% in the patients' rooms. Similarly the highest rates of positive affective behavior were seen in the presence of child life staff (84.2%) and the lowest in the presence of medical (53%) and nursing staff (52%). Positive affect was related to ongoing activities. Positive affect was most likely to be seen during play (41%), and least likely during medical procedures (5%). Modest, but statistically significant, correlations were found between positive affect and child activity ($r = 0.31$), the presence of other individuals ($r = 0.30$), and the presence of other children ($r = 0.28$). The presence of other people or burn severity was not related to affective state.

These data were used by Tarnowski *et al.* as the basis of speculation concerning the possible factors maintaining these behaviors. They note that, in contrast to studies of pediatric intensive care units, the children's behavior was more active and had much higher rates of positive affective behavior. Previous studies of pediatric intensive care units had involved the concepts of learned helplessness to explain the behavior of the children. The learned helplessness hypothesis used in other studies revealed that the children showed little active behavior because of non-contingent aversive events. Tarnowski *et al.* contrast this with the profile of active behavior found in their study. They suggested that in the burn unit the highly aversive medical procedures were very predictable because they occurred only in certain rooms, at certain times, and with certain staff present. They also note that these children could also control and delay the timing of these procedures in this setting.

Experimental Observation

Any kind of naturalistic observation is subject to the possibility that the naturally occurring sequences of behavior may be confounded with other variables. These other variables rather than those measured may be responsible for the observed changes in behavior. Further, in naturally occurring sequences of behavior the functions of the behavior may not be apparent. For example, in the case of a long established escape avoidance behavior the client and significant others may both be so shaped up by each other's behavior that the avoided situation is rarely presented or is presented in a very mild form and rapidly removed.

For these reasons experimental observational methods have been developed. These include experimental, single subject designs such as analog baselines (Iwata *et al.*, 1982, 1994), variants on this procedure, and the creative use of single subject designs. Many of these studies have been used with behavior disorders in persons with developmental disabilities and with children. This general approach could readily be expanded to other populations, settings and behaviors.

Analog baselines

Based upon Carr's (1977) analysis of the motivations for self-injurious behavior Iwata *et al.* (1982) developed four analog conditions. In *Social Disapproval* the experimenter asks the subject to engage in an easy task such as toy play. The experimenter sits opposite the subject and appears to read. No interaction occurs except that contingent upon every occurrence of the target behavior the experimenter expresses concern and disapproval and makes non-punitive physical contact with the subject. In the *Academic Demand* condition the experimenter teaches the subject a task they are likely to succeed at only some of the time. Contingent upon every occurrence of the target behavior teaching is stopped. In the *Alone* condition the subject is placed in a room with no materials or others to interact with. High rates of the target behavior associated with only one of these conditions is interpreted as evidence for the positive reinforcement, negative reinforcement and self-stimulation hypothesis respectively. The *Unstructured Play* condition is a control condition for the presence of materials, the experimenter and social interaction. These four conditions, which are typically implemented for 15 minutes, are rotated in blocks of four sessions to yield a multi-element design or as histograms using z-scores. Analog baselines can be used as the basis for a treatment based on a functional analysis (Day, Rea, Schussler *et al.*, 1988; Mace, Lalli & Lalli, 1991; Parrish, Iwata, Dorsey *et al.*, 1985).

Analog baselines have been extended both methodologically and clinically. Methodological developments include tracking the integrity of the independent variable (Sturmey, Newton & Crisp, 1991), tracking adaptive as well as maladaptive behaviors, individually tailored modifications to the analog conditions, and more rapid method of implementation for use during routine clinical practice (Northup, Wacker, Sasso *et al.*, 1991).

One potential limitation in the use of analog baselines is that they can become an ossified procedure. The driving force behind functional analysis is individually based hypothesis testing. Analog baselines may be helpful in doing this if the hypotheses tested are relevant to the subject's behavior and if this is the optimum method for doing so. One trend in the literature that illustrates this flexibility has been the trend to modify analog baselines on a case by case basis or to use the general methodology of analog baselines but to develop conditions in a much more idiographic way. For example, Day *et al.* (1988) modified the *Alone* condition to include variations of an adult being present or absent during this condition to test if the presence of a staff was a discrimination stimulus for self-injury. Northup *et al.* (1991) added a *Tangible* condition, in which a tangible item (such as toys, other materials, drinks or edibles) was presented contingent upon the target behavior. This is a condition to test an alternative form of the positive reinforcement hypothesis. More flexible and idiographic uses of this methodology include comparing activities requiring high and low rates of responses, familiar versus novel task demands, avoidance and partial demand avoidance (Mace, Lalli & Lalli, 1991) comparing descriptive language with demands, and consecutively presented requests versus requests dispersed into the context of an entertaining story (Carr, Newsom & Binkoff, 1976).

Analog baselines have thus been a major thrust forward in the literature on observational methods to develop functional analyses. Areas for further development related to analog baselines include how to translate them into effective programs of intervention and further evaluation of their validity (Oliver, 1991; Sturmey, 1995c).

SOME CONCEPTUAL ISSUES

Observational methods have been the hallmark of behavior analysis. Many authors have presented observational data as if they were the least inferential and most believable kinds of data. This assumption has now been challenged. Jacobson (1985a, b) suggests that the relationship between observational measures and the primary targets of change is not simple. He points out several potential pitfalls and misuses of observational data. For example, at times an observational scheme might code behavior categories that are easy to observe and readily coded. However, these behaviors may be unimportant or only indirectly related to the real target behavior. Clinically significant target behaviors may be selected on the basis of differences between normal and clinical groups. For example, observational codings for marital therapy might be validated on the basis of statistically significant differences between distressed and non-distressed couples. These behavior categories may then be selected as the relevant target behaviors for marital therapy. Jacobson describes these kinds of behavior categories as 'signs' or indexes of what may be going on, but not necessarily the key, or even the important, variables for change. He notes that for many couples presenting for marital therapy the use of predetermined, standard behavior codes to establish either target behavior or for use as outcome measures in therapy may be misdirected since it does not reflect the idiosyncratic nature of each couple's problems. Jacobson's main point here seems to be that simply using observational data is no guarantee of carrying out an adequate functional analysis. On some occasions, other kinds of data are to be preferred.

A second area of concern is the cost of observational data. Observational data can be quick to collect and easy to analyze. Observational data can also quickly yield tens of thousands of observations in a few days. This can involve round the clock observation by teams of observers Monday through Sunday, and vast amounts of time spent on data entry, analysis and interpretation. In these situations, where other, cheaper methods of data exist which correlate well with observational data, these data are clearly preferable.

There is a final problem that relates to the way in which observational data are used. Jacobson notes that often observational data can be used as an assessment of treatment outcome (the dependent variable) when they are truly an assessment of the implementation of therapy (independent variable). For example, consider training a couple to show more frequent positive and affectionate interactions. Here observational data on rates of positive and affectionate interactions are a check on the implementation of the treatment rather than evidence of a treatment outcome. Treatment outcome should be assessed by a second, independent measure such as marital satisfaction ratings, divorce rate, or some separate observational method.

In replying to this article Weiss and Frohman (1985) and Gottman (1985) point out that self-report data, as an alternative to observational data, may often be severely limited by biases such as faking good and other demand characteristics. They also point out the many pitfalls when subjects attempt to assign meaning to observational data. For example, what can be made of a statement such as, 'He means affection when he hits me?' Jacobson's (1985b) reply to these criticisms is that he did not intend that other methods should replace observational data, but rather that observational data should be viewed cautiously and not as a necessarily direct or meaningful measure of the problem at hand. He goes on to argue that the role of observation in functional analysis is to determine empirically for each individual a set of target behaviors rather than to impose an externally determined set of target behaviors. He also notes that private events (feelings and thoughts) are often what propel people to seek therapy. There would be little point in increasing a couple's rates of interactions if they both still felt unhappy and dissatisfied with their marriage. Thus, Jacobson (1985b) argues that self-report data may be an important component of a functional analysis which also uses observational data.

CONCLUSION

Observational data began as the primary methodology associated with functional analysis. As both this and the previous chapter have shown, observation no longer occupies the unquestioned position it previously did. As behavioral assessment has matured into a more complex field, many assumptions made early on in behavioral assessment no longer seem self-evident. Nevertheless, observational data remain a central part of many functional analyses. For some it will remain the preferred methodology.

Chapter 6

ASSESSMENT METHODS IV: PSYCHOMETRIC MEASURES

We have seen in previous chapters that a wide range of different methods are available to assess the functions of behavior. Methods such as clinical interviewing and observation are not without costs. Both interview and direct observation can be time-consuming to conduct. Direct observation can also generate massive amounts of data which are often time-consuming to collate and analyze and interpret. Similarly multiple interviews can be time-consuming to organize, conduct and interpret. These methods also require highly specialized skills and considerable amounts of specialized training. Although they can be taught, sometimes quickly, the number of professionals and third parties who possess these skills is relatively small. This limited pool of available expertise limits the application of functional analysis in routine practice using these methods.

In response to these problems a number of short questionnaires have been developed to assess the functions of behavior. Psychometric instruments may offer a solution to some of the limitations of other assessment formats discussed above. It has been suggested that they are quick and easy to complete. Further, because they produce scale scores and profiles they can be easy to interpret. For these reasons a number of psychometric measures have been developed as methods to rapidly assess the functions of behavior.

DESIRABLE PSYCHOMETRIC PROPERTIES

All psychometric instruments, including those designed to assess the functions of behavior, must have certain technical properties in order for them to be psychometrically adequate instruments. Without firm evidence of these psychometric properties such scales are seen as inadequate measures.

Reliability

Inter-rater reliability

For a measure to be objective the same results should be obtained whoever completes the measure. Two sources of extraneous variability can contribute to unreliability—the informants and the interviewers. If significantly different results are obtained from different informants, for example, classroom teachers versus parents, or different interviewers, for example, psychologists versus technicians, then it is unclear if the results of any single assessment reflect the informant, the interviewer, or the actual behavior of the person assessed.

Inter-rater reliability is typically assessed by correlating the scores from two sets of informants or two sets of interviewers with each other. Inter-rater reliability is typically assessed using Pearson's r. If the value of r is greater than 0.7 that is usually perceived as adequate, although inter-rater reliabilities of the order of 0.9 are usually seen as more acceptable.

It should be noted that r does not measure agreement between raters. Rather it measures the degree of association between the scores. Thus, high inter-rater agreement can be obtained if one rater scores are consistently more liberal than another.

Because of this problem some researchers have also calculated exact agreement, or agreement plus or minus one point on a seven-point rating scale. This is then expressed as a simple percentage (e.g., Sigafoos, Kerr & Roberts, 1994). Percentage agreements should typically exceed 70%, although percentage agreements of 90% or better are possible.

Test-retest reliability

A second source of extraneous variability is when the ratings are completed. If the functions of the behavior are fairly stable across time then the same results should be obtained at different times. The assumption that the functions of the target behavior are stable is important. If the functions of the behavior changed then the initial treatment would become inappropriate and would have to be revised accordingly. The same statistics used to assess inter-rater reliability are used to assess test-retest reliability.

Internal consistency

Psychometric instruments designed to assess the functions of behavior have one scale for each function assessed. For these scales to be good measures of several different functions the scores and the items that belong to the same scale should be more closely correlated with each other than the average inter-item correlation.

Internal consistency can be assessed in several ways. A simple statistic is the split-half reliability. This is simply the scores from the first half of the scale correlated with the scores from the second half of the test. An alternate form of this is the odd–even item correlation. As before this should exceed 0.7 although values of 0.9 or greater are both desirable and possible. A more commonly used statistic is Cronbach's alpha (α). Cronbach's α is the average of all possible split-half reliabilities for a given scale. Conventionally it should exceed 0.6.

Comment

The problem of reliability has a number of subtleties to it. One possibility is that informants actually do experience different behavior from the same person. This can be most obvious when informants and settings are confounded. An example of this would be when teachers and parents report on child behavior. The teachers report on the child's behavior in the classroom, where there are many academic demands and extended periods of work on difficult tasks are common. The parents may report on the child's behavior at home where there may be less structure and fewer academic demands, but more chores to do. Although differences in the environment that are correlated with setting are most apparent it should be remembered that people may exert stimulus control over the child's behavior. Thus, even in the same setting different adults may correctly report different child behavior because the behavior of each adult is different. Recall from Chapter 2 Malatesta's case study that analyzed the rate of tics according to the presence of each adult. In this example each adult would have given a different account of the boy's tic behavior during the same task and setting. The father would have accurately reported high rates of tics, whereas the mother would have reported low rates of tics. This would lead to poor inter-rater reliability, even though both raters would have been accurate. In fact these differences in behavior across settings and other people are a valuable source of information on the functions of the behavior. Thus, it should be no surprise that in some circumstances the same behavior could have different functions in different settings or with different people present.

Validity

Validity refers to the confidence one can have in the meaning of scores from a test. Validity is no simple matter. A test may be designed to measure a certain construct, but the evidence to support the belief that the scale actually measures that construct has to be built up gradually. The names given to tests and scales can be deceiving. Further, the notion of test validity as an absolute quality of a test is false. A test may be valid for one purpose, or be valid under certain circumstances. However, it is nonsense to declare a test to be valid in some absolute sense. Finally, it should be recognized that there are different kinds of validity that can be used to evaluate a test.

Predictive validity

Predictive validity is the extent to which a test score correlates with some important outcome or variable. For example, in classic psychometric studies one might validate IQ scores by seeing if IQ at age 6 years predicts academic grades at age 10 years. For psychometric measures of the functions of behavior the most important predictive validity they can have is to predict which kind of treatment the client will respond to and which kind of treatment is contraindicated. Thus, a key issue of psychometric measures of the functions of behavior is the ability to predict effective treatment.

Factor validity

The factor analysis is a multivariate statistical procedure that is used to group together items that are most closely correlated with each other. Thus, it is very useful in empirically developing scales from larger pools of items. For scales that are not developed empirically factor analysis can be used as a method to validate the scales after they have already been constructed. (See the study by Singh, Donatelli, Best *et al.*, 1992, discussed below for an example of this.)

Construct validity

Construct validity refers to the gradual accumulation of evidence that attests to the meaning of the scale scores. It does not refer to any single procedure or statistic. Rather, it refers to the progressive interplay of data and theory that progressively helps us both understand the meaning of the scale and develop theory further. For example, consider the validation of two scales that purport to distinguish clinical problems that are positively reinforced by attention from others and those that are negatively reinforced by the removal of aversive demands. One might predict that people with high scores on the social attention scale should receive high rates of interaction in naturally occurring situations, and those scoring high on the negative reinforcement scale should receive low rates of interaction. One might also predict that clients scoring high on the social attention would learn quickly when given social attention contingent on learning a task and would not work for a break. Similarly one would predict that clients with high scores on the negative reinforcement scale would work for a break and that the frequency of their behavior would reduce if it was consequated with attention. The gradual accumulation of such evidence constitutes the construct validity of an instrument.

Robustness

An important property that scales must have to be clinically useful is that they must be usable by many different kinds of raters and informants, in many different settings, and with many different topographies. If a scale can only be used by highly trained raters for a single topography that occurs fairly frequently then the clinical utility of the instrument is compromised.

Psychometric robustness is demonstrated when the instrument has good reliability and validity in many different settings and with minor modifications. If an instrument is known not to be robust then it may be necessary to routinely conduct reliability and validity checks every time the instrument is used in order to assess its adequacy in each particular situation.

REVIEW OF MEASURES

In this section we review several psychometric measures designed for functional analysis. In the first section generic measures which could be applied to a wide range of different problems are reviewed. In the last section three measures which are designed for use with specific clinical problems are discussed. Finally, a number of recurrent conceptual and practical issues are discussed. A review of these measures can be found in Sturmey (1994).

Generic Measures

Functional Analysis Checklist

The Functional Analysis Checklist (FAC: Van Houten, Rolider & Ikowitz, 1989) is a 15-item measure which collects information on aspects of the physical environment, such as crowding, adjunctive behaviors, transitions from one activity to another, escape from demands and positive reinforcement related to behavior problems. Van Houten and Rolider (1991) note that information should be collected on potential causes other than those directly on the FAC such as medical problems, illness and physical discomfort. Thus, the FAC casts its net fairly broadly as to the potential causes of the target behavior. The FAC seems to be relatively quick to administer and could readily be incorporated in an assessment battery.

Van Houten and Rolider (1991) are properly cautious about the use of the FAC. They state that 'questionnaires . . . can provide useful hints as to the causes of behavior. The next step is to perform a clinical assessment to confirm whether these hunches are correct' (p. 573). It appears that Van Houten and Rolider (1991) see the FAC as a hypothesis-generating procedure which would occur early during assessment. Hypotheses generated by this, and presumably other procedures, would be evaluated subsequently using other experimental procedures.

Sturmey and Bertman (1992) reported on the inter-rater and test-retest reliability of this measure. A wide range of topographies and rates of behaviors was selected by randomly sampling 30 persons with developmental disabilities living in an institutional setting. All subjects were currently on behavior therapy programs. Raters were either Qualified Mental Retardation Professionals in charge of the person's living area or the shift supervisors. Test-retest reliability was evaluated by assessing the subjects 2 weeks after the initial testing.

Inter-rater reliability was poor. Percentage agreement was relatively high for individual items. The median percentage agreement was 80% (range = 43% to 100%). This reflected the fact that items were usually not endorsed frequently. The median percentage of items endorsed was 33% (range 0% to 77%). Thus, most items did not apply to any one subject. Agreement across raters was not much better than chance.

Since this is the only evaluation of the FAC, it must be interpreted cautiously. As with other psychometric measures of functional analysis, the effects of target behavior salience, behavior frequency and rater characteristics may all be significant. Also it should be noted that raters in this study did not have extensive experience with the measure. It may be that greater reliability would be obtained if the informants and interviewers had extensive training in using this instrument.

Functional Analysis Interview Form

The *Functional Analysis Interview Form* (FAIF: O'Neill *et al.*, 1991) is part of a suite of materials developed by O'Neill, Horner, Albin *et al.* (1991) to assist clinicians in conducting a functional analysis. These materials include forms for direct naturalistic observation, and for observation using systematic manipulation of the environment. O'Neill *et al.*'s guidebook provides many worked examples, completed forms and case material which the clinician will find helpful. There are nine sections in the FAIF. These are the behaviors, potential ecological events, antecedents, functions of the behavior, efficiency of the target behavior, the person's communication skills, functional alternative behaviors, and history of the behavior and its previous treatments. Each of the nine sections has a series of open-ended questions and several short forms used to assess the target behaviors. The administration time is about 45 to 90 minutes. The FAIF and the related procedures are designed to be used by staff already experienced and trained in behavior management.

The FAIF and the related procedures are capable of producing a mass of complex information. Indeed, it is unlike some of the brief questionnaires discussed below. It is much closer to clinical practice in the breadth and complexity of the information generated. Unlike some of the other instruments discussed it does not include any simple method of summarizing the information and translating the information into a treatment program based on the functional analysis.

So far no psychometric data are available on the FAIF and the related procedures. It is a potentially lengthy procedure which requires the clinician to exercise considerable judgement in the selection, combination and interpretation of the assessment procedures available. It would be a useful basis to train up interviewers who do not have previous experience of conducting a functional analysis.

Problem-Specific Measures

Several instruments have been designed to carry out a functional analysis of a specific problem. These include the Motivation Assessment Scale (MAS) for the evaluation of self-injury (Durand & Crimmins, 1988), the Motivation Analysis Rating Scale (MARS) to assess the function of stereotypy and/or self-injury (Weiseler, Janson, Chamberlain & Thompson, 1985), and the School Refusal Assessment Scale (SRAS), an extension of the MAS to evaluate school refusal (Kearney & Silverman, 1990).

All of these share a number of common features. These include a relatively small number of questions which can be rated on Likert-type scales by third party informants such as staff or parents. The scores on these items are combined into a small number of scales corresponding to the potential functions of the behavior. The scale with the highest score is assumed to indicate the function of the behavior. Thus, these measures circumvent the problem of combining and interpreting the information available by using simple scores.

Motivation Assessment Scale

The MAS (Durand & Crimmins, 1988) is a 16-item instrument which was originally designed to assess the functions of self-injury. However, it has also been used to assess a wider range of behavior problems (Newton & Sturmey, 1991; Sigafoos, Kerr & Roberts, 1994). So far it has been used exclusively with persons with developmental disabilities. Items are rated on a 7-point scale from 'never' to 'always' and are combined into 4 scales: Attention, Escape, Tangible and Sensory consequences. It takes only five minutes to complete. It is very easy to score.

The MAS is the most extensively evaluated instrument reviewed in this section. Durand and Crimmins (1988) reported inter-rater agreements of 0.66 to 0.92 (all Ps < 0.001) for individual items and 0.80 to 0.95 for scale totals. Test-retest data were all of similar magnitude.

Validation of the MAS was provided by comparing the results of it with Iwata *et al.*'s (1982) analog baselines. The MAS and analog baselines correlated 0.99 in terms of ranking the functions of the behavior. Further, Durand, Crimmins, Caulfield and Taylor (1989) showed that the reinforcers for problem behaviors identified by the MAS could be effectively used as reinforcers for skills teaching. Thus, it appears that the MAS was highly effective in identifying the motivation for self-injury. Moreover, it could also be used as the basis for effective habilitation.

Singh *et al.* (1992) conducted a factor analysis of the MAS on two samples. The first sample was an institutional sample who showed high rates of self-injury. The second sample was a school sample with lower frequencies of self-injury. The factor analysis of the scores for the institutional sample yielded a four-factor structure which corresponded almost exactly to the four scales of the MAS. In the school sample there was only modest correspondence between the factor analysis and the MAS scales. This study would suggest that the psychometric basis of the four scales is good, at least in populations with high rates of self-injury. It may be that the relative lack of correspondence between the factor structure and the four scales in the school sample may simply reflect attenuation of the correlations between items due to lower frequencies of the behavior.

Although the initial studies appeared to indicate that the MAS was psychometrically adequate several independent studies have found clearer evidence for the lack of robustness of the MAS. Newton and Sturmey (1991) evaluated the reliability and internal consistency of the MAS with a wide variety of behavior problems including stereotypy, self-injury and aggression. Recall that for an instrument to be really useful to clinicians it should be reliable and valid in different settings and for different behaviors.

Newton and Sturmey found inter-rater reliabilities of only 0.20 to 0.70 for individual items. Also, the reliabilities for the four scales were only 0.25 to 0.49. Further, evaluation of the internal consistency of the scales, an essential requirement for scale construction, was negligible.

Subsequently, Zarcone, Rogers, Iwata et al. (1991) conducted a more liberal evaluation of the MAS. They evaluated the function of self-injury in 55 adolescents and adults with moderate through profound developmental disabilities. The frequency of the self-injury ranged from several times per hour to less than once per week. Zarcone et al. also provided some initial training on functional analysis to staff completing the MAS. Zarcone et al. found similar evidence of poor inter-rater reliability. Inter-rater reliabilities were low. Raters agreed on the function of self-injury in only 16 out of 55 subjects.

Sigafoos, Kerr and Roberts (1994) assessed 18 clients with developmental disabilities living in an institutional setting who displayed aggressive behavior. The frequency of the aggresssive behavior occurred on average from 1 to 6 times per week, and up to 10 times per day for some clients. The raters were a direct care staff and a professional staff each of whom had known the client for at least 6 months.

The average correlation between the pairs of rates was only 0.034 (range –0.667 to 0.772). On individual items and the four sub-scales all correlations were small and non-significant. Similar results were found if the results were calculated as percentage agreements. Sigafoos, Kerr and Roberts do note that there was some modest agreement on the function of the target behavior in a minority of cases. Thus, Sigafoos, Kerr and Roberts found little evidence that the MAS was robust.

Thompson and Emerson (in press) assessed the reliability of the MAS by assessing 41 topographies of challenging behaviors in 5 children with developmental disabilities. Topographies included self-injury, aggression, and stereotypy. Whether agreement was calculated as agreement on individual items or on the principal motivation for the behavior inter-rater agreement was unacceptably low. Agreement on individual items did not exceed 27%, and agreement on the function of the target behavior ranged from 10% for attention to 58% for tangible.

Similar reports of poor reliability of the MAS have been reported by Kearney (1994) and by Lawrenson (1993). It therefore seems reasonable to conclude that the MAS is not psychometrically robust.

In some studies the MAS has demonstrated good evidence of reliability and validity as well as high levels of clinical utility. Other studies have found it to be psychometrically weak or at least only able to generate reliable information in a minority of cases. What accounts for these differing findings? In their first study Durand and Crimmins (1988) used a rather restricted pool of subjects and raters. The subjects were all children who self-injured at least 15 times per hour. Their raters all had at least a 2 to 4 year degree in social sciences. Thus, the behavior was high rate, salient, and significant. The raters may have been well educated in behavioral methods. Other studies have used a wider range of behaviors, a wide range of behavior rates, and routine informants such as care staff. It may well be that this combination of factors may limit the robustness and utility of the MAS.

Motivation Analysis Rating Scale

The MARS (Weiseler *et al*, 1985) is a 6-item questionnaire. Each item is rated on a 4-point scale. There are three scales: Positive environmental consequences, Task escape-avoidance, and Self-stimulation. Weisler *et al*. used ratings of self-injurious behavior on 23 individuals completed by 58 staff. They found 73% agreement on the primary motivating consequence. When compared with a direct observational assessment of function they found 95% agreement. Thus, this study appears to indicate that the MARS is reliable and valid in identifying the functions of self-injurious behavior.

So far this has been the only report on the use of the MARS. Like the MAS, it is brief, quick to administer and easy to score and interpret. However, three potential problems exist. First, there are only two items per scale. This is psychometrically unusual. Scales as short as this would have to be carefully designed to ensure internal consistency and be sensitive enough to provide a range of scores. This has not yet been demonstrated. Second, reliability is only given for the primary motivation of stereotypy or self-injury. No reliability data are presented for items or scales totals. Third, given a reliability of 73% a validity coefficient of 95% is surprisingly high since reliability limits validity. This may in part be due to different scales of measurement or to the fact that validity data were only collected on a subset of subjects for whom raters both agreed on the primary motivation of the behavior.

School Refusal Scale

The SRS (Kearney & Silverman, 1991) is a scale directly modelled after the MAS (Durand & Crimmins, 1988). Thus, four items relate to avoidance of fear or anxiety-provoking conditions, four items relate to escape from aversive and evaluative social situations, four items relate to attention-getting consequences, and four items relate to positive, tangible reinforcement. Each item is rated on a 7-point scale from 'never' to 'always'. Child, parent, and teacher versions of the scale have been developed. The scale with the highest score is used to identify the primary motivator for school refusal. Scale scores within 0.25 of each other are considered tied.

Kearney and Silverman's report on the SRS focuses on the clinical use of the scale and deriving treatments from its scores. Thus, they do not directly present any reliability or validity data on the 7 children in the study. However, in their Table 2 (p. 351) they do present the raw scores from multiple ratings of each child by self, mother, father and teacher. A total of 25 ratings were made on the 7 children. (Not all children were rated by all 4 possible raters.) Of the 25 ratings 18 agreed with the final evaluation. This gives a reliability of 72%. In three of the seven cases all three or four raters agreed on the function of school refusal. In two cases two out of three and three out of four raters agreed on the behaviors. However, in two cases the raters were split across two or more functions.

Despite the moderate degree of reliability there was some good evidence of validity. Treatments were developed based upon the functions of school refusal as indicated by the mean SRS rating. Thus, the child who was identified as fearful/anxious was treated using imagined and *in vivo* desensitization and relaxation training. Four children, identified as avoiding aversive social situations, received cognitive behavior therapy, restructuring of negative thoughts, and social skills training using role play and feedback. The child who was identified as attention-getting/anxious relating to separation received contingency management and shaping procedures using staff attention to reduce attention at home. The response cost of remaining at home was increased by requiring that school work was completed. Reinforcement was also used for increased school attendance. Finally, the child who was motivated by positive reinforcers at home was treated by contingency contracting using the reinforcers believed to maintain school refusal.

Treatment results were good. Six of the seven children were attending school full time, both at post-treatment and at 6-month follow-up. All children evidenced modest improvements in anxiety, depression or distress. Thus, these results offer good validation of the SRS as a tool to develop a functional analysis of school refusal which can be used as the basis of subsequent treatment.

The SRS has not yet been independently evaluated. Thus, it is not possible to judge its robustness.

DISCUSSION

Evaluation

Psychometric instruments were developed as a simple, inexpensive and rapid way to develop a functional analysis which can be used as the basis of a treatment program. To what extent have these promises been fulfilled?

Several of these instruments have shown good clinical utility in prescribing treatments which are effective (Kearney & Silverman, 1990) or in identifying powerful reinforcers which can be reprogrammed to increase desirable behaviors (Durand et al., 1989). The package by O'Neill et al. (1991) appears to be a useful training tool for staff who are new or inexperienced in behavior analysis. The prepared sets of forms, guidelines for their use, and worked examples would be especially helpful. Thus, this approach has made a clear contribution to clinical work. However, a critical examination of the approach shows it to suffer from several problems.

Several measures, such as the MAS, MARS and SRS, focus almost exclusively on the motivating consequences of the behavior. Whilst a consistent motivation for a target behavior often implies stimulus control these measures do not directly assess the antecedents of the target behaviors. Indeed, the complexity of the functional analysis for some behaviors is not addressed by these instruments. Issues such as multiple functions of one problem, setting-specific functions, establishing operations are not addressed. Further, the range of consequences evaluated by these instruments is restricted. Thus, they may not be very helpful in identifying the functions of behavior when the behavior is maintained by idiosyncratic consequences.

Other instruments such as the FAIF (O'Neill *et al.*, 1991) and the FAC (Van Houten, Rolider & Ikowitz, 1989) produce a wealth of information. In the measures discussed above the results can be summarized in a few scale scores. For these measures that is not so. There is no clear, simple procedure for summarizing the data, interpreting it, and translating it into a program of intervention. In such cases there is considerable latitude for the clinician to use judgement, skill, and experience to interpret the available information. In such cases questions assessing reliability and validity are complicated procedures. The simple reliability of a single item or set of items becomes a necessary condition for the reliability of the entire process rather than sufficient in itself. Reliability of these items does not guarantee the reliability of the over-judgement of the function of the behavior or translating it into an intervention. In these cases it is clear that the behavior of the clinician, the manner in which certain data are highlighted and others de-emphasized, the decision to select certain assessment procedures rather than others, the decision as to when to stop data collection and when to collect further information, are paramount in evaluating the use of these instruments.

The only instrument which has received any extensive psychometric evaluation has been Durand & Crimmins' (1988) MAS. No other instruments have been independently evaluated. Indeed, several, such as the FAC and the FAIF, have no psychometric evaluation. The psychometric information on the MAS indicates that although it can be reliable and valid under certain circumstances, it is not highly robust. Given this there is an urgent need for the psychometric evaluation of these instruments by independent researchers and practitioners in order to evaluate their robustness.

Recurrent Issues

A number of issues have repeatedly been discussed in relation to psychometric instruments to assess the functions of clinical problems. These include how to combine the information from many items into some form of readily interpretable summary, how to translate the functional analysis into a treatment program, how informants perform when interviewed or completing such an assessment, and the status of non-experimental methods of functional analysis.

Several instruments used simple summary scales which are easy to score and interpret. This process requires little technical knowledge. It could be performed with little technical training. Other instruments produce a more complex set of narrative summaries or no clear guidelines on how to summarize the total complex of the available information. This problem is complicated still further by the fact that the taxonomy of function used has varied from author to author. Weiseler et al. (1985) use three classes of function (self-stimulation, attention and escape). Durand and Crimmins (1988) add tangibles; O'Neill et al. (1991) use a six-fold classification. Others do not use a typology at all.

A second issue is how to translate the functional analysis obtained from the questionnaire. Kearney and Silverman (1990) offer a simple solution—a one-on-one mapping of function to treatment. They imply that such a functional analysis can be used as a prescription for treatment. Durand et al. (1989) demonstrated that the MAS can be used to identify powerful reinforcers which can be reprogrammed to increase desirable behaviors and thereby extinguish problematic behavior. Others are not explicit about how to translate the assessment information into a treatment program. One important point, which is often not acknowledged, is that the functional analysis is only one consideration in designing a treatment. Other factors may also be crucial. The current management strategies of the client and significant others, the resources available to implement a program, the acceptability of an intervention strategy to the client and/or caregivers, the likelihood that the client and/or caregivers can be readily trained to carry out the procedure, and their motivation to continue the procedure are all crucial factors above and beyond the functional analysis. These other factors are also crucial in determining what treatment is actually implemented.

Another recurrent issue is the ability of informants to give accurate and meaningful answers to the items or questions found on the instruments reviewed. At first glance these items are straightforward. However, closer examination of them shows that they are often abstractly behavioral in nature. Thus, they require that informants can both discriminate and report the behavior in question in behavior-analytic terms. This is not a simple matter. For example, questions related to demand, escape-avoidance, or self-stimulation do not refer to a simple, single, observable topography or single instance of behavior. Rather, they refer to the function of the behavior which is abstracted from repeated observation in many different settings or many different forms of behavior. Thus, these questionnaires require the informant to make discriminations about behavior and the environment which are not intuitively obvious. Such observations may require extensive training (Lalli, Browder, Mace & Brown, 1993; Wilkinson, Parrish & Wilson, 1994). It is notable that several studies have used raters with a considerable degree of training in this area (Durand & Crimmins, 1988). Others have suggested that raters should already have some training in behavioral methods (O'Neill et al., 1991). Still others have provided training prior to using these questionnaires (Zarcone et al., 1991). Providing training to informants prior to using these instruments suggests that naïve, untrained informants may not be adequate informants. Future research could evaluate the efficacy of various forms of training on the reliability and validity of the information gained from trained and untrained observers.

In Chapter 1 it was noted that for several authors a functional analysis must include an experimental component (Baer, Wolf & Risley, 1968; Iwata, Vollmer & Zarcone, 1990; Skinner, 1953). Thus, for these authors any psychometric assessment of the potential functions of behaviors cannot constitute a functional analysis. This is implicitly acknowledged by several authors of these questionnaires who recommend that they are used for generating hypotheses early on during assessment. Subsequently, an experimental analysis of observed behavior should be conducted on the basis of the initial hypotheses derived from the psychometric assessment (O'Niell et al., 1991). On the other hand, the cost of an experimental analysis may often be too great for a practicing clinician. Thus, the studies that initially validated the MAS (Durand & Crimmins, 1988; Durand et al., 1989) appeared to promise that these measures might be an effective short cut around this aspect of a functional analysis.

Future Research

All of the questionnaires reviewed here have been recently developed—all were published after 1985. Although they show promise a major area of effort should be to ascertain their psychometric properties and, in particular, their robustness. To date, no studies have been carried out on the concurrent validity of these measures with each other. Although Weiseler et al. (1985) found good agreement between psychometric assessment and direct observation, at least one study has found poor agreement across different methods of functional analysis (Oliver, 1991).

A second issue has been deciding what behavior or behaviors to assess using these instruments. Many clients present with multiple topographies, some of which may have the same function. O'Neill *et al.* (1991) recommended recording as many behaviors as possible initially and scanning the data for patterns of response covariation or patterns of escalating chains of behaviors. A separate assessment can then be conducted for each response class.

A third area for future research is that of validity. Some data on these questionnaires are already available which suggest their potential validity (Durand & Crimmins, 1988; Durand *et al.*, 1989). However, this issue has received limited attention so far.

Finally, many of these instruments have been applied to only a limited range of clinical problems. It appears from the work of Kearney and Silverman (1991) that these instruments could be modified to a range of other problems (e.g., child behavior problems, chronic psychiatric symptoms, etc.). As with the measures reviewed here, extensive empirical evaluation will be necessary.

Part III

PROCESS ISSUES

Chapter 7

PROCESS ISSUES I: As, Bs, AND Cs

The preceding section reviewed several assessment methods which are important and useful in developing a functional analysis. However, using these tools is only a partial account of functional analysis. Many issues related to developing a functional analysis still remain to be addressed. Being able to accurately complete a questionnaire on the function of a behavior is insufficient to conduct and use a functional analysis. There are many other considerations to be made in the process of assessment and treatment when working within the framework of functional analysis. The preceding chapters have focused on the methods rather than the process of assessment (Mash, 1985). In this section we look at some of the issues related to the process of functional analysis.

OVERVIEW OF PROCESS ASPECTS OF FUNCTIONAL ANALYSIS

One of the most common tasks which faces the clinician is deciding which behavior or behaviors require treatment. Many clients will present multiple problems (Nelson, 1988). Many factors may directly influence the conception of the presenting problems, such as the resources available for intervention, and the prioritization of presenting problems by the client, significant others, and by the therapist. Consider this example of multiple presenting problems.

A 49-year-old woman presented at an out-patient clinic for fairly typical symptoms of Generalized Anxiety Disorder including tension, anxiety, panics, and periodic mild depression. She appeared to be quietly spoken and unassertive. After initial discussion of her presenting problem she also revealed that she had a chronic, painful medical condition of her legs and feet. This was made worse by working in the family store all day which involved prolonged periods of standing without a break. The family business caused her much worry. Her husband had previously been bankrupted in an earlier business venture. He would often write large personal checks from business accounts without informing her or recording the checks written. He would arrive home laden with large, expensive presents and household items whereupon arguments and recrimination might ensue if the presents were not gratefully received. Further, when tax returns were due she would discover additional substantial spending had occurred without her knowledge.

When she left work at 4 p.m. she would engage in two to four hours of meal preparation and washing dishes. Successive adult sons would arrive home, often unannounced, expecting meals on the table at short notice. She had little time to herself for her own interests and pursuits.

In this example one could select any of the following target behaviors or some combination of them: general anxiety, panic attacks, mood, assertiveness, increasing time in preferred activities.

When there are multiple presenting problems, as in the above example, the clinician must group them rationally into one or more functionally related categories of behaviors. A functionally related set of behaviors is known as a *response class*. Some behaviors may form relatively orderly sequences or *response chains*. If there is a relatively orderly sequence of responses then the order in which they typically occur should be described in detail. Analysis of the presenting problems may allow many, seemingly disparate, behaviors to be grouped together in useful and meaningful ways.

Target behaviors must be operationalized prior to collecting baseline data. The process of operationalizing a target behavior is a highly subtle one. Yet, the problems associated with this are rarely acknowledged. It is relatively easy to produce some kind of operational definition of a target behavior. However, the process of operationalizing a target behavior can sometimes introduce serious problems in making an adequate formulation. For example, an easy, cheap measure of a behavior may be readily available. However, it may have little validity in that it may not accurately represent the presenting problems. The process of operationalization can distort the presenting problem if it is not done carefully.

The clinician must also correctly identify establishing operations, setting events, antecedents and consequences. Again, this is not necessarily as simple as it may seem. Even getting informants to recall or record a sequence of events in time is not always easy. This task requires them not only to collect this information, but to do so within a behavioral framework. This method of working may not be intuitively obvious to the client or may even run directly counter to the way they have perceived their own behavior for many years. Such a task also requires that they are able to discriminate and report their experiences using behavioral concepts, or at least report events in such a way as the clinician can interpret the information within a behavioral framework. The importance of this problem is attested to by several papers which have trained third parties, such as parents or teachers, to discriminate, record, and report data in behavioral terms (Lalli et al., 1993; Wilkinson, Parrish & Wilson, 1994).

During the assessment process the clinician has to make decisions as to how to proceed. Throughout the initial assessment interview itself the clinician has to determine which topics to pursue in detail, and which can be left without further evaluation. At the end of the initial assessment interview the clinician has to decide whether or not the information gathered is sufficient for a functional analysis or whether further information should be collected. It is possible that in subsequent interviews the client may reveal additional information when they are more comfortable with the clinician or when they have learned from the clinician the kind of information that is important. If further information is required the clinician has to decide how it should be collected. If the assessment phase consists of several different kinds of information then the clinician has to decide how the information from different sources should be combined. When there is conflicting information from different sources the clinician has to decide which information should be given greater weight in the formulation, which information should be attended to, and which ignored.

The clinician also has to decide when the initial assessment phase should stop. There may be diminishing returns from collecting additional information. Even though additional information could be collected the clinician has to judge whether this additional information will make a significant difference to the intervention that is indicated from the current available data. In some circumstances it may be that the functional decision during the initial assessment interview is simply whether or not the client may benefit from one of the standard treatment groups that are available. For example, it may merely be necessary to decide whether to place the person in an anxiety management group, a social skills group, a depression group, or that they should be seen individually. It may not be necessary at the first interview to develop a comprehensive functional analysis of the presenting problem(s) if this can be done subsequently in a treatment group.

The clinician also has to decide how the assessment information should be summarized. Different kinds of summaries may be necessary depending on the audience for whom it is intended. A summary formulation may be a useful tool to educate the client as to the nature of their problems. It may also be a suitable opportunity to educate the referral source as to how the clinician works and views the problem referred. A concise summary of the functional analysis may also be made for the clinician to use as a framework within which the subsequent assessments and interventions are to be made.

Another set of decisions for the clinician to make is how the information gathered during assessment is to be used to develop an intervention. Insufficient attention has been given to the process by which a formulation is translated into an intervention. Several critics of poor behavioral practice have been very critical of methodological behaviorists who use treatments that are called 'behavioral', but who do not use the functional analysis as the basis for designing individual interventions (Turkat, 1988; Wolpe, 1989). An adequate formulation may be useless if the clinician is insensitive to the implications that the individual differences in the functional analyses have for designing interventions.

The busy clinician has to balance the resources necessary for this decision-making process against other factors. As services become more and more cost-conscious, assessments and treatments that are extensive and expensive will require greater and greater justification. Services which are expensive may be difficult to justify unless the problem is seen as serious by the purchaser of the services and it is perceived that the additional benefits accrued from the extra resources allocated to the enterprise are justified by additional client gains. Only if the extensive evaluation is likely to lead to substantially greater benefits for the client will a purchaser buy these services. In some services funded by private health insurance companies insurance may simply not cover the costs of functional analysis. In the subsequent sections of this chapter we go on to explore these issues in greater detail.

OPERATIONALIZING BEHAVIORS

Given the importance of operationalizing behavior it is surprising how little attention has been given to this issue. The only comprehensive review of this topic identified is that by Kazdin (1985). He notes that the problem of operationalizing a target behavior can vary in its complexity. He contrasts the relative simplicity of operationalizing self-

injury versus the relative complexity of operationalizing marital dishar-
mony. (Of course those of us who work with self-injury might take
umbrage with Kazdin over the apparent ease of operationalizing self-
injury. Although describing head-banging is indeed relatively easy that
is still no guarantee that you have described the response class to
which it may belong.)

One of the problems facing the clinician in operationalizing a target
behavior is the range of different options that exist in operationalizing
the behavior. Even an apparently simple problem such as nocturnal
enuresis can be operationalized in many different ways. This problem
could be operationalized in any of the following ways:

- number of bed wets per night;
- number of nights during which a toileting accident occurred;
- time in between wetting incidents;
- size of wet patch;
- number of dry nights;
- number of times correct, independent voiding occurs;
- weight of wet bed linen and clothes; and,
- amount of fluid child can drink prior to sleeping without voiding.

Each of these measures may be suitable in some circumstances. They
may each vary as to their validity for different purposes. During classroom exercises with postgraduate students considerable confusion can
arise even over an apparently simple problem such as this. Selecting the
number of correct voidings is often selected in order to emphasize the
positive, constructional aspects of an intervention. However, such a
choice fails to address the fact that wetting and correct toileting might
be independent. Hence, increasing correct voiding may or may not
decrease nocturnal wetting. The patch size may be a more sensitive
measure of change than simple frequency of wetting early on during an
intervention as the child begins to learn to inhibit voiding. However,
number of dry nights and time in between toileting accidents will both
directly capture the principal outcome of interest in this situation. If
these do not change then the intervention is unlikely to be considered
effective. While all of these measures are readily implementable for a
single client, in communal settings, such as residential facilities where
incontinence may be relatively common, these measures might be too
costly to implement. In such circumstances the permanent product
measure might be preferred, i.e., weight of wet linen and clothes. This
measure would probably be both cheaper and easier to carry out than
many individual assessments.

One of the key problems behind selecting a correct operationalization of a target behavior is that of validity. Because of this the clinician must be absolutely clear about the purpose of the assessment. Only when the clinician is completely clear as to the purpose of the measurement can the measure selected can be evaluated as to its validity for that purpose.

Kazdin's Validational Assessment Model

Kazdin (1985) frames the problem of operationalizing target behaviors within a *validational assessment model*. He notes that the validity of many behavioral methods of assessment has been questioned. Many analog methods such as role play, behavioral avoidance tests, and so on are only useful if they correlate well with the actual behavior itself. Thus, operationalizing problems using such analog methods may sometimes have little validity. Many behavioral assessments use multi-channel methods of assessment (e.g., physiology, behavior and cognition) in order to overcome the potential bias of using a single channel of assessment. In any case the relationship of the operationalized target behavior to the analog assessment methods is rarely demonstrated.

A further problem is that a particular operationalization may be taken to represent a much broader range or constellation of problems. For example, mood may be used as an index of eating, social and sexual functioning in a person with depression. Again the issue of validity arises because it is assumed that other behaviors co-vary with the index behavior selected to represent a wider portion of the person's behavioral repertoire.

In his validational assessment model Kazdin (1985) borrows from psychometrics the various kinds of validity that can be used to evaluate the validity of an operationalization of a target behavior as an index of the client's presenting problems. The notion of *concurrent validity* can be used if several operationalizations are believed to measure a single behavior domain or syndrome. Thus, ratings of anxiety from the client and a third party should be fairly closely correlated. Similarly, changes in the operationalized target behavior should correlate strongly with changes in the broader constellation of behaviors or syndrome it is believed to represent. Thus, if anxiety ratings reduce one might assume that independent travel would increase.

Predictive validity refers to the likelihood that the behavior will correlate well with some important future outcome. Kazdin suggests that the parallel here is that the target behaviors selected should be good predictors of maintenance and follow-up of change. Kazdin notes that the concurrent and predictive validity of a target behavior may be independent of each other. Behaviors which accurately represent the current overall problem may not predict outcome especially well. For example, in the case of childhood aggression target behaviors such as hitting might have good concurrent validity. However, long-term progress might be better predicted by measures of social skills. Thus, a measure that is valid to assess initial behavioral change in response to intervention may not predict maintenance and relapse particularly well.

It is clear that the process of operationalizing a target behavior is not a straightforward one. The clinician needs to continually check and confirm with the client and significant others that the operationalization of the problem does not inadvertently trivialize the presenting problems. The operationalization of a problem must not inadvertently distort the presenting problem by sacrificing validity on the altar of simplicity of data collection.

Frequently the process of identifying and operationalizing a target behavior is done through third parties such as parents, other family members, or staff such as teachers, residential staff or other professionals. In such situations a number of potential dangers might arise. Passively accepting the presentation of the problem according to the informant's viewpoint can, at times, lead to grossly erroneous conclusions. At times third parties may focus excessively on negative aspects of the client's behavior. They may demand eliminative strategies of change and be perplexed by being asked to focus on the client's skills and assets. In such situations one of the tasks of the clinician is to reformulate the problem for the informant. The therapist must be able to place the presenting problem in context and protect the client from potentially abusive treatment. At times this is a subtle and complex process of negotiation.

Comment

The process of operationalizing a target behavior is clearly a complex one. Hitherto it has not received sufficient attention. The process can be subtle. It can require considerable sensitivity to the client's entire behavioral repertoire, their situation, and the motivations of third parties. Operationalizing the target behavior occupies a pivotal role in functional analysis since the rest of the assessment process hinges upon it.

MULTIPLE RESPONSES

Target Behavior Selection

The early literature on behavioral treatment emphasized the treatment of a single response which apparently had self-evident validity as the target behavior of choice. Since then emphasis has been placed on multiple behaviors (Delprato & McGlynn, 1988; Kratochwill, 1985). This has variously been described as response structure, response covariation, behavioral covariation, response pattern (Delprato & McGlynn, 1988), or response–response relationships. This view has led to a wide range of different criteria used to select target behaviors (Kratochwill, 1985; Wilson & Evans, 1983). Here are some of the criteria suggested by various authors.

- Select problem most aversive to client, parents or care givers.
- Select mild problem to ensure cooperation from client or care giver.
- Select behavior which is easy to change (O'Leary, 1972).
- Select the 'keystone behavior' which produces greatest change amongst many target behaviors (Nelson, 1988).
- Teach functionally-related, incompatible behaviors (Carr & Durand, 1985; Goldiamond, 1974).
- Select target behaviors that pose a physical danger to the client and/ or others (Kratochwill, 1985).
- Select target behaviors that are likely to maintain (Kratochwill, 1985).
- Select a replacement behavior that is very valuable (Kratochwill, 1985).
- Select replacement behaviors that are important for development of other behaviors (Kratochwill, 1985).
- Select replacement behaviors that increase adaptation to the environment (Kratochwill, 1985).
- Consider the effectiveness in changing current contingencies (Kratochwill, 1985).
- Select behaviors to change that are consistent with developmental and/or local norms (Kratochwill, 1985).
- Select target behaviors that are relevant to successful performance (Kratochwill, 1985).
- Select target behaviors that have positive social validation ratings (Kratochwill, 1985).
- Select target behaviors that lead to greater ability to discriminate between successful and unsuccessful performance (Kratochwill, 1985).
- Select target behaviors whereby the client would have poor prognosis if that target behavior went untreated (Kratochwill, 1985).

As can be seen from this list the range of guidelines put forward vary from each other considerably. Indeed the different guidelines may conflict with each other. Some guidelines are relatively *ad hoc*. For example, some authors have advised choosing a mild problem to ensure cooperation from the client and significant others. Many such *ad hoc* guidelines have not been validated. For example, Wilson and Evans (1983) note that the advice to select an easy target first (O'Leary, 1972) has been shown *not* to be related to overall outcome (Eyberg & Johnson, 1974). Many of these *ad hoc* guidelines directly conflict with each other. For example, the advice to select behaviors which are easy to change *versus* behaviors which are most aversive to the client or care givers may conflict with one another in some cases.

Kratochwill (1985) distinguishes between *empirical* and *conceptual* criteria which have been used to guide selection of target behaviors. Among conceptual criteria are the likelihood of physical danger, good maintenance and the positive valence of the replacement behaviors. Among the empirical criteria are the consistency of outcomes with developmental and local norms, and the relevance of outcome to successful performance. Many of the earlier guidelines on target behavior selection were merely clinical opinion. They lacked empirical validation and did not have a conceptual framework to aid decision making. However, Kratochwill (1985) notes that as time has passed the criteria used have gradually been made more explicit.

Organization of Responses

Several conceptual tools have been proposed which can be useful in addressing the organization of individual molecular behaviors into groups. Evans (1985) developed the notion of response hierarchies as a method of organizing responses and identifying which of the various responses should be targeted to ensure maximum benefit for the client. Other methods of grouping responses together include the notions of *response class, response chain* (Frankel, 1975) and Nelson's (1988) *keystone behavior strategy*.

Response hierarchies

Evans (1985) has suggested that understanding the organization of multiple responses can be made explicit. Understanding multiple responses can be enhanced by the use of graphic models borrowed from systems theories. Within this framework the many elements in a

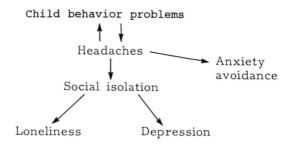

Figure 7. 1   A Diagrammatic Summary of Evans' (1985) Case Example

behavioral repertoire were conceived of as elements in a complex system. Thus, a particular problematic response may not be seen as necessarily being the primary target for change even if it is reported to be the most important target for change by the client or significant others. The problem may lie elsewhere within the system of responses. Changes in the target behavior itself may result from changes in other parts of the response system as well as direct intervention with the target behavior itself.

Evans (1985) gives a simple case example summarized in Figure 7.1. A client presented with severe tension headaches. These headaches were believed to be caused by her child's behavior problems. The headaches in turn appeared to cause her to have difficulty in using effective strategies with the child's behavior problems. Thus, a bi-directional feedback loop was set up (Owens & Ashcroft, 1982; Haynes & O'Brien, 1990). Headaches were also given as a reason for avoiding meeting males at social gatherings. Meeting males at social gatherings made her anxious. This social isolation appeared to cause her both loneliness and depression.

Evans' (1985) systems model would predict that intervention with any of the behaviors lower down in the response hierarchy would result in little or no change in other parts of the behavioral system. To maximize change and produce maximum response generalization intervention should focus on the superordinate problems. In this case intervention should focus on the feedback loop between the child behavior problems and headaches.

Evans (1985) goes on to suggest that hierarchical models of symptoms can be used to organize disparate symptoms. A second, less complex example can be found in Figure 7.2. In this example one would conclude that maximum change would result from intervention with

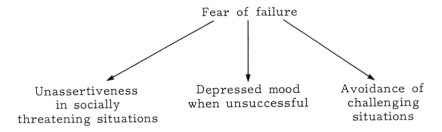

Figure 7.2   A Simple Hierarchical Model of Symptom Organization

impulse control rather than individual expressions of the superordinate problems such as bulimic behavior and shoplifting.

A hierarchical symptom model can suggest a whole range of possible relations between superordinate and subordinate behaviors. Some of these are shown in Figure 7.3. The simplest model is shown in Figure 7.3(a). Here all subordinate behaviors are related to a single superordinate behavior or process. Figure 7.2 is an example of this kind of simple hierarchy. A slightly more complex variant of this is shown in Figure 7.3(b). Here there are two or more hierarchies of behaviors which are independent of each other. In (c) the situation is more complex. Here the problem hierarchies interact with each other. Although some subordinate behaviors are a function of only a single superordinate variable some subordinate behaviors relate to more than one superordinate behavior. In the final model (d), the organization of behavior is still hierarchical, but the behaviors are part of a complex web of inter-relationships.

Evans goes on to suggest that the everyday language of informants can provide potentially useful hints of the way in which individual responses might be organized. For example, terms such as 'fearfulness' or 'a tantrum' may indicate groups of responses that are functionally equivalent.

Response classes

A *response class* refers to a group of topographically different behaviors which all have the same relationship to environmental events as each other. All responses in the same response class share common antecedents and consequences. In other words they all serve the same function for the organism, even though they may be topographically very different. For example, a child might get candy by asking for it,

(a) Simple hierarchy

(b) Multiple, independent hierarchies

(c) Overlapping, multiple hierarchies

(d) Complex, hierarchical symptom systems

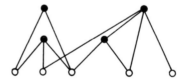

Figure 7.3 Some Examples of the Range of Complexity of Hierarchical Symptom Models

pointing to it, crying, whining, or tantruming. If these behaviors are also under the same stimulus control then the behaviors are said to be a member of the same response class. Members of a response class can be identified from any assessment method which gives information about antecedents and consequences.

Clinicians should be sensitive to the fact that very different forms of behavior can serve the same function. Equally, the same behavior may serve different functions in different settings. For example, a child's whining may solicit candy from parents whereas in the classroom it may function to delay aversive teacher interactions.

Finally, the clinician should be sensitive that the function of one topography may change over time (Lerman *et al.*, 1994). For example, a child may initially learn whining when the child was sick. In this initial environment whining may serve the function of soliciting medical attention and relief from pain more rapidly than conventional communication. Later, the child may learn that whining can serve the function of delaying or removing a number of aversive stimuli. Finally, as time proceeds adults may be shaped up not only to delaying or removing aversive stimuli, but also to delivering positive reinforcement on an intermittent schedule.

Response chains

Frankel (1975) discussed and illustrated the clinical use of the notion of a *response chain*. He defined a response chain as 'a repetitive sequence of responses, each of which acts as a discriminative stimulus for the next response member, and as a secondary reinforcer for the previous response member number' (p. 255). Response chains may occur over a relatively long period of time, perhaps several hours, or may occur fairly rapidly in a couple of minutes.

Identifying response chains can be useful in several ways. First, identification of a response chain should lead to the identification of the terminal reinforcer. Second, it can also be a useful tool to organize a sequence of very different responses which may be spread out over a long period of time. In such circumstances a simple ABC analysis of the terminal behavior may result in an incomplete functional analysis. Third, an analysis of a response chain may also allow identification of adaptive behaviors early in the chain, which may not be supported by the current environment. Thus, an analysis of a behavior sequence can be used to identify functionally equivalent, adaptive behaviors that could form the basis of a group of replacement behaviors to be reinforced in the intervention. Fourth, it is most efficient to disrupt a response chain as early on in the chain as possible. If the frequency of only the terminal response is reduced then a number of functionally equivalent responses remain in the person's repertoire. These may form the basis of relapse through relearning the maladaptive response, or learning a new terminal response to the chain that is also maladaptive.

Response chain applied to childhood non-compliance. Frankel (1975) illustrates the intervention implications of the notion of a response chain to

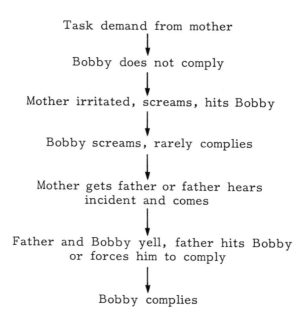

Figure 7.4   A Chain of Behaviors Described by Frankel (1985)

guide selection of a target behavior in a case study. Frankel (1975) describes a case of non-compliance analyzed as a response chain. A six-year-old boy was referred who showed non-compliance both at home and school. Figure 7.4 shows the response chain at home. This analysis suggested that after Bobby had been non-compliant, aggressive, and begun screaming he got access to his stepfather often some hours later. When requests were made by his father Bobby would comply and the aversive situation for the parents would be removed. This suggests that access to his father was a powerful reinforcer for Bobby. Recall that in a response chain each behavior acts as a secondary reinforcer for preceding members of the chain. This suggests that the mother's screaming and hitting might also be secondary reinforcers to Bobby's non-compliance. This could be because they consistently predict access to his father. Alternatively, it might be that the mother's behavior does not function as punishers because the consequences are delivered late, at low intensity, with a mixed schedule of reinforcement and punishment, or because Bobby can escape the most aversive consequences through non-compliance.

The intervention in the home used the response chain analysis in two ways. First, the father was taught to play and communicate with his stepchild. The father and the son set up a behavioral contract for the father to spend three hours per week with the child on an activity that Bobby chose. In this way the son got access to his father without resorting to non-compliance. Second, the mother was taught to respond to behavior incidents by remaining calm. If she could not remain calm then she agreed to leave the room until she could calm down. Then she would return to Bobby to gain compliance in a calm manner. Under no circumstances was she to call in the father.

A second response chain was identified for aggression and non-compliance at school. This response chain began after aggressive behavior in the playground. After an initial interaction with his regular teacher Bobby intermittently gained access to a second teacher. The intervention was a simple rearrangement of the existing contingencies. If Bobby showed any aggression, non-compliance, or approximation to any of these behaviors he was placed in time out in his own classroom. He did not get access to the second teacher. Bobby was also allowed to have access to his preferred teacher by scheduling three, one-hour homework sessions per week with the teacher. This latter procedure was gradually faded out after the first month.

At follow-up three months later Bobby's behavior was much improved both on teacher ratings of behavior problems and on the frequency of aggression which was now down to near-zero levels. One year later these gains were maintained, even when Bobby had transferred into a new classroom with a new teacher.

Response chains applied to self-induced seizures. A similar analysis of response chains by Zlutnick, Mayville and Moffat (1975) was used to treat a seizure disorder. In their initial analysis they identified chains of behaviors that preceded a seizure. The intervention was to reduce the frequency of early members of the response chains. By reducing the frequency of the early members of the response chain they were able to reduce the frequency of the terminal response—seizures—without directly intervening with the target behavior itself.

Clinical Implications of Multiple Responses

Record more than one behavior

Delprato and McGlynn (1988) provide an elegant analysis of some of the implications of working with multiple responses. The first, and most simple implication, is that the clinician must observe and record more than one behavior. For example, one might record both target behavior that is being reduced and a functionally equivalent response that is being increased to replace the maladaptive response. Alternatively, if there are several independent target behaviors one might record each of these to monitor progress.

Delprato and McGlynn make a useful distinction between narrow and broad-based assessment of multiple behaviors. Narrow-based assessment would include recording more than one behavior where all behaviors are relatively closely related. For example, recording mood and activity in a person with depression would be narrow-based assessment since both behaviors are probably very closely related. Recording mood, social activity, and anxiety would be an example of broad-based assessment of multiple responses since it is less likely that all of these three behaviors would necessarily be closely related.

Analyze response–response relationships

A second clinical implication of multiple responses is that the relationship between multiple responses should be analyzed. There are a number of complex multivariate and probabilistic methods available for this purpose. However, these are too time-consuming to conduct for routine clinical work and may require large data sets not available in typical clinical practice. A number of very simple methods of analyzing response–response relationships might be used fairly readily. One method is simply to graph behavior rates against each other. Figure 7.5 shows the relationship between SUDS ratings of anxiety and lower back pain in an adult out-patient. The data were collected during a 2-week baseline assessment in between the first and second appointments. As can be seen from Figure 7.5 these behaviors were positively correlated, but not in a simple linear fashion. Many observations of high levels of back pain were independent of anxiety. This information suggested: (a) that there might be some organic basis to the back pain, although this was often exacerbated by anxiety; and (b) that reduction of anxiety might result in some reduction of reported back pain, but not elimination of it. Similar methods such as plotting behaviors together on a simple graph of behaviors against time might often yield the same result.

Analyzing the relationship between multiple responses by scatterplots and simple graphs is feasible only when the number of behaviors is small. For example, to analyze the relationships between only 6 behaviors would require 15 graphs. Wahler (1975) used a *correlogram* to summarize multiple response–response relationships. A correlogram is

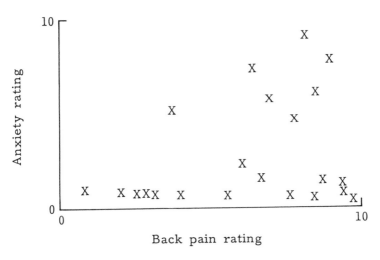

Figure 7.5 The Relationship between Ratings of Lower Back Pain and Anxiety in an Adult Out-patient

simply a plot of the correlations between multiple behaviors. Correlations which are smaller than 0.3 in absolute value are typically omitted in order to simplify the results. A correlogram can be used to identify clusters of behaviors which tend to occur together as well as groups of behaviors which are inversely related to each other. Sturmey, Newton and Crisp (1991) reported the response–response relationship in a group of three individuals with profound developmental disabilities whilst they were using an operant device. The responses recorded included turning away from the task, affective behaviors, such as smiling and vocalizing, and stereotypies, such as head weaving and foot movements. Figure 7.6 shows the relationship between these behaviors for each of these three individuals. For example, Mary tended to show positive affective behavior *and* stereotypies together. She appeared very excited when using the device. Vocalizing and turning away also co-occurred and this pair of responses was inversely related to the first two behaviors. Her vocalizing appeared to be distressed. This latter pair of behaviors tended to occur when the toy was turned off.

Select functionally equivalent replacement behaviors

A third implication that Delprato and McGlynn (1988) discuss relates to selecting target behaviors and indeed parallels Nelson's (1988) ideas on keystone target behavior strategies. Changing one behavior might lead

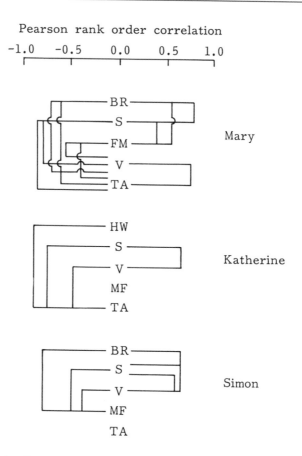

Figure 7.6 An Example of a Correlogram to Describe Response–Response Relationships

BR, body rocking; HW, head waving; S, smiling; V, vocalizing; MF, movement of feet; TA, turn away

Reproduced with permission from Sturmey, P., Newton, T. and Crisp, A. G. (1991). Validation of the Pethna toy through changes in collateral behaviours. *Journal of Mental Deficiency Research*, **35**, 459–471

to multiple changes within the ecology of the person's response repertoire. There are at least three strategies which the clinician can use to identify a keystone behavior. Correctly identifying the response classes and their functions can give strong clues as to the motivation of the behavior. This can also be used to identify functionally equivalent replacement behaviors. A good example of this comes from Carr and Durand's (1985) work on the communication hypothesis for behavior disorders. Here, it is assumed that behavior disorders and communicative behaviors can serve the same functions. Thus, they may be said to be members of the same response class. For example, behavior disorders might serve either to gain assistance on a difficult task or to gain attention. In their intervention Carr and Durand therefore taught children to say either 'Help me' or 'Am I doing good work?' as functionally equivalent responses to their maladaptive behavior. The first communicative response helped only those children whose behavior had been shown to be task-avoidant. The second phrase helped only those children whose behaviors were believed to be maintained by attention. A similar behavior-diagnostic strategy was used by McNight, Nelson, Haynes and Jarrett (1984) to determine the most effective treatment for depression. Using a comprehensive assessment battery they determined that for three subjects their depression was related to social skills deficits. Three other subjects had depression characterized by irrational cognitions. For the three last subjects their depression was related both to social skills and to maladaptive cognitions. Using an alternating treatment design they showed that depression in the first group was effectively treated only by social skills training whereas cognitive therapy was ineffective for these subjects. Similarly, for the second group depression responded only to cognitive therapy but not to social skills training. Similar results were also found in the area of interpersonal problems by Trower, Yardley, Bryant and Shaw (1978). Clients were assessed as being either deficient in social skills or being excessively anxious. Clients with social skills deficits responded more to social skills training than to systematic desensitization. The keystone behavior strategy appeared to be less important for the socially anxious clients who responded to both forms of treatment.

The third strategy that clinicians can use to identify keystone behaviors is to use Evans' (1985) hierarchical models of symptom organization. In this model it is suggested that targeting superordinate behaviors will produce the greatest cascade of behavior change. Targeting lower elements will simply pick off isolated problems without producing any generalized change within the behavioral system.

Comment

A range of strategies are now available for working with multiple responses. However, we have little technology that is both quick and easy to use which has been explicitly developed for assisting the clinician in this task. Interviews, self-recording, and direct observation can all give useful information regarding behavior sequences in many cases.

However, it is likely that this information is most likely to be accurate in the more simple situations. Notice that in Figure 7.3 the behavioral hierarchies can be highly complex. As yet we have little information available as to how to assess these more complex relationships between responses and the behavior of the clinician while attempting to unravel the relationships.

Predicting changes in other behaviors

A fourth implication that Delprato and McGlynn (1988) outline in their review of working with multiple responses is that eventually we should be able to predict changes in so-called 'side-effects' of treatment. A wide range of positive and negative side-effects of both reinforcement (Balsom & Bondy, 1983) and punishment procedures (Axelrod & Apsche, 1983) have been reported. What is clear is that there is no simple relationship between whether an intervention is reinforcement- or punishment-based and the likelihood of side-effects.

Identifying functionally equivalent adaptive behaviors

A final implication for the clinician that Delprato and McGlynn (1988) draw out is the relationship of multiple responses to Goldiamond's work on constructional tactics. Rather than merely eliminating problematic behaviors, the constructional approach emphasizes developing repertoires of adaptive behavior which can replace maladaptive behaviors and serve the same functions as those behaviors did. It can be seen from some of the preceding sections that the work by Carr and Durand amongst others is a good example of such an approach. Thus, analyses of multiple responses should include some analysis of why functionally equivalent, adaptive alternative behaviors have not developed or are not effective within the current environment. When examining the behavioral repertoire of many clients such behaviors may well be present. However, they may only be shown at a low frequency because within the current context of the person's environment they are not effective instrumental behaviors compared to alternate, more powerful and effective maladaptive behaviors.

Conclusion

Clinicians work with multiple responses every day of the week. This is nothing new. The real issue is how to assess, analyze and use multiple responses within the confines of regular clinical practice. As can be seen from this section, functional analysis has begun to provide some frameworks which can be used to conceptualize multiple responses, some tools to analyze response–response relationships, and some strategies to use to attempt to produce the greatest response generalization possible in order to provide maximum benefit to the client and provide a more efficient method of working. Future research could attend to the development of new, simple tools for analyzing response–response relationships. They should be both simple to use, robust, and effective in designing interventions.

ANALYZING ANTECEDENTS AND CONSEQUENCES

In preceding chapters we have reviewed many methods of identifying potential antecedents and consequences of a particular target behavior. Antecedents and consequences are intimately tied together. Antecedents are those stimuli which precede behavior, which alter the probability of the behaviors and which predict the likelihood of punishing or reinforcing consequences. In some circumstances identifying antecedents and consequences can be relatively easy. In more complex situations it may be a highly subtle process. As we have seen people may not be able, or may be reluctant, to report truly functional reinforcers accurately. Third parties may be rather inaccurate at reporting stimuli which function as reinforcers for others (Pace, Ivancic, Eduards *et al.*, 1985). Similarly, identifying antecedents for behavior—one's own or another's behavior—may require considerable powers of observation, discrimination, and reporting.

Self-recording is an example of a commonly used process in which a client may record their own behavior, its antecedents, and consequences in the form of an ABC diary. This procedure can illustrate some of these commonly experienced problems. Nelson (1977) suggested that self-recording consists of two stages. First, there is discriminating one's own behavior and relevant aspects of the environment too. Second, there is recording the behavior and related aspects of the environment in some form. Thus, self-recording is a discriminated operant behavior which may or may not already be in the client's repertoire. As a learned behavior it too may or may not be currently supported by the client's environment. The client may, therefore, need training in this task. For example, it is not an uncommon experience to ask a client 'When do you feel tense?' and to get the reply 'All the time'. Collection of baseline data early on can be used as a procedure to train the client to discriminate between different degrees of tension and events that are related to changes in tension. In a similar way, one of the functions of training tense clients in Jacobson relaxation exercises is to teach them to discriminate between tension and relaxation.

The process of learning to discriminate and report behavior can be particularly difficult if the relationship of environmental events and behavior is subtle or complex. This problem can arise if there are intermittent schedule contingencies that maintain the behavior, if the chains of behavior and events are spread out over a long period of time. For example, in the case report discussed by Frankel (1975) the environmental events maintaining the child's aggression and non-compliance were not apparent to the parents or teachers because the behavior was maintained by intermittent reinforcement and the relevant environmental events took place over several hours.

The process of self-recording can be reactive, i.e., it can change the behavior being recorded (Fremouw & Brown, 1980). Thus, the process of trying to ascertain the antecedents and consequences may change the behavior being analyzed.

The process of determining antecedents and consequences may be substantially effected by the kind of problem studied. For many clinical problems the state of the client may directly inhibit their reporting the data or substantially affect its accuracy. Clients involved in substance and alcohol abuse, clients with severe anxiety or depression may be unable to discriminate their behavior at relevant times or may be unable to recall it subsequently.

A second example of some of the difficulties in identifying antecedents and consequences accurately is when events happen quickly, in a complex manner, or when key events are very difficult to observe. Examples of this can include target behaviors that are covert, such as stealing, or subtle social behaviors, such as aggressive staring, or another person quietly cursing somebody else as they walk past them.

Many of our clients may not have the kind of learning history to enable them to describe and report their own behavior accurately (Skinner, 1989, Ch. 3). Indeed some of them may have had learning histories relating to their verbal behavior which directly teach inaccurate verbal behavior. At times cheating, lying, and inaccurate talk can have major pay-offs, whereas telling the truth and reporting accurately may be punished. For staff in residential settings, complaining at the right time and place to the right person and exaggerating the severity of a behavior might gain them extra staff, remove an aversive client, get the staff transferred to a more reinforcing place to work, or get the client transferred elsewhere. Many models for such behavior may be available. In a similar way the verbal repertoire of clients may be inappropriately shaped over the years so that they do not report their own behavior accurately.

Establishing Operations

Michael (1982) introduced a new distinction into behavior-analytic vocabulary: the establishing operation. Michael argues that there are two classes of stimuli that precede behaviors and that change the future probability of that behavior. The familiar one is a discriminative stimulus. He defines a discriminative stimulus as 'a stimulus change which (1) given the momentary effectiveness of some particular types of reinforcement (2) increases the frequency of a particular response (3) because that stimulus change has been correlated with an increase in the frequency with which that type of response has been followed by that type of reinforcement' (p. 149). Michael goes on to argue that there are also other stimulus changes that change the future probability of behavior, but that are not discriminative stimuli. That is, there is no prior learning history whereby the organism has learned that the stimulus predicts future reinforcement. One example of this is the effects of deprivation such as thirst or hunger. He notes that conditions of deprivation can have two distinct effects. These are (a) to enhance the reinforcing value of the stimulus that the organism has been deprived of, and (b) to increase the frequency of all behaviors that have a history of being reinforced by the stimulus that the organism is deprived of. For example, being thirsty both increases the value of water as a reinforcer and evokes behaviors that have a history of being reinforced by water, e.g., licking at a water spout. In this example licking the water spout is not under the control of a discriminative stimulus (e.g., a light indicating the availability of water), because there is no such discriminative stimulus present.

Michael goes on to give examples of various emotional states that are establishing operations. Being angry is an establishing operation because it (a) establishes the reinforcing value of signs of discomfort in others, and (b) evokes behaviors that produce these kinds of behaviors in others. Being anxious is an establishing operation because it (a) increases the reinforcing value of removing certain stimuli, and (b) increases the frequency of those behaviors that remove those fearful stimuli.

There are many implications of establishing operations for making clinical functional analyses and that can be used to account for some of the complexities of functional analysis. First, the simple ABC paradigm can be refined to account for the variability in the way in which a person may respond to an antecedent. An ABC relationship may only be true in certain situations. For example, a person may avoid social interaction only when in a depressed mood. Thus, social avoidant behaviors are reinforced by the removal of other people only when depressed mood acts as an establishing operation that increases the punishing effects of social interaction. During these times a social initiation from another person (antecedent) is followed by turning away and mumbling (behavior) and is reinforced by shortening the interaction (negative reinforcement). Further the negative mood evokes avoidant responses from the person. When the person is in an average mood social interaction has not been established as a punisher. In this situation a social initiation from another person (antecedent) is followed by extended social interaction (behavior), and is reinforced by interaction from others (positive interaction). The notion of establishing operations can be used to produce more complex and subtle formulations. In particular it can be used to describe how ABC relationships change in different environments.

ABCs AND PRIVATE EVENTS

Within behavior analysis 'private events' refers to thoughts and feelings. A full account of private events can be found in the various writings of Skinner (e.g., Skinner, 1953, 1989) as well as in other more recent sources (Dougher, 1993). There are a number of popular misconceptions about a behaviorist's perspective of thoughts and feelings, such as that behaviorists do not believe in them or that behaviorists believe that they are unimportant. Private events are an important part of behavior analysis. Skinner (1989) writes: 'Behaviorists are not supposed to have feelings, or at least admit that they have them. Of the many ways in which behaviorism has been misunderstood for so many years, that is perhaps the commonest . . . how people feel is sometimes as important as what they do' (p. 3).

The controversy is not that behaviorists ignore thoughts and feelings. Rather, that they do not give them any special status. They are not elevated to the status of causes of behavior. Like any other kind of behavior thoughts and feelings are under environmental control. Thus, part of a behavior-analytic account of private events is to describe their relationship to environmental events that control them. Thus, thoughts and feelings are seen as a kind of perceptual behavior. Thought and language is seen as behavior which is gradually taught through observation. Thus, a child falls, experiences pain, and someone says, 'That must have hurt' or, before a meal, someone says, 'You look hungry'. In this way internal states become labelled through language. Feelings are seen as a kind of perception of bodily states associated with emotions. For example, when someone says 'I am tense' they are reporting how they perceive an internal state.

Skinner (1989, Ch. 2) provides an extended discussion of the etymology of words related to thoughts and feelings. Skinner shows that language related to thoughts and feelings is derived from words originally related to actions associated with those thoughts and feelings. For example, *consider* originally meant to look and wonder at the stars and *image* originally meant a colored bust.

Thinking is seen as an efficient method of representing, and sometimes misrepresenting, the world and its contingencies. If all learning was done through trial and error or contingency shaping, then learning would be incredibly slow. Much of our everyday conversation serves to ascertain the prevailing contingencies. For example when we ask 'What kind of a mood is he in now?'or 'What is it like?' we are asking about information on the prevailing contingencies.

The main point of controversy that people have is that behaviorists do not elevate private events to causal status. Thus, from a behavioral perspective the causes of behavior can be ultimately traced to environmental events. Reaching for a glass of water is not caused by a feeling of thirst, a high motivational state, or the thought 'I need a drink'. Ultimately the causes of behavior, including thoughts and feelings, reside in environmental events and the person's learning history.

Private Events and Formulations

Since private events have no special status, there is no reason why they cannot enter into a functional analysis in the same way as observable events do. Private events can enter as antecedents, behaviors, or consequences. Examples of this can be found in Figure 7.7. The principal problem with using private events in functional analyses is in assessing their validity. Since two independent observers observed these behaviors it can be very difficult to be confident of the validity of the self-report data that have to be relied on.

Private Events and Depression

The status of private events can be illustrated by discussion of Dougher and Hackbert's (1994) functional analysis of depression and its implica-

Example	Antecedent	Behavior	Consequence
(a)	**Think about impending meeting while travelling to office.**	**Feelings of panic and** get off bus.	**Feelings of panic removed.**
(b)	Watching TV alone at night.	**Delusional voices get loud and angry.**	Call sister and get reassurance.
(c)	See news item on TV about children starving in Africa.	Turn TV off; and go to bed.	**Feel stupid and hopeless; tell self 'cannot cope'.**
(d)	**Intrusive image of dead bodies.**	**'See' the words of the Lord's Prayer roll off a scroll quickly.**	**Feeling of terror removed; intrusive image removed.**

Figure 7.7   Some Examples of Private Events (in bold) in ABC Formulation

Note private events can be (a) antecedents, (b) behaviors (c) consequences, or (d) a formulation can be wholly cognitive

tions for intervention. Depression is a good example for illustrating the behavior-analytic perspective on private events as the most commonly reported complaint in depression is how people feel and the way they think about themselves, the world, and others.

Dougher and Hackbert note that DSM (American Psychiatric Association, 1994) lists the following as features of depression: sad mood, loss of pleasure in activities, disorders of appetite, psychomotor retardation, agitation, loss of energy, feelings of worthlessness and guilt, and selective recall and attention to negative events. They also list some of the following behaviors: excessive crying and rumination, expressions of hopelessness and helplessness, dissatisfaction, anger, substance abuse, problematic social and personal relationships, and work-related problems.

Dougher and Hackbert go on to propose a number of consequences that could maintain depression. These include a low density of reinforcement, or low rate of response-contingent reinforcement, and poor social skills to solicit reinforcement. Extinction may be important in persons who have undergone a major loss of a source of reinforcement, such as a death or unemployment. Punishment may also be an important element for some people. For example, people who have a history of abuse, or punishing social relationships. Finally, distressed behavior may be reinforced negatively by the removal of aversive stimulation by others and positively by sympathy and attention.

Depressed behaviors can be under stimulus control. For example, certain social situations may be learned to be aversive and may thus be the discriminative stimuli for avoidance. Alternatively, certain people may be seen as especially understanding and thus be the discriminative stimuli for complaining, crying, and other behavioral excesses.

Respondent aspects of depression are illustrated by the affective aspects of depression such as sad feelings and anger. Emotional behaviors may be associated with insufficient reinforcement, extinction, and punishment. Emotional responding can occur in response to these processes which are unconditioned stimuli for behavioral excesses.

Establishing operations for depressed behaviors could include the presence of other people who indicate that reinforcement is available for depressed behaviors. Certain places or tasks may indicate that avoidance will be a powerful negative reinforcer.

The person's thoughts may be an important part of the maintenance of depression. When people reproach and blame themselves or (mis)label their negative affective state as evidence of psychopathology or permanent personal flaws, this can lead them to perceive that there are no contingencies of reinforcement available to them. They may believe that the only source of reinforcement available to them is the removal of their current aversive situation through suicide.

Next, there are cultural influences on the process of learning depressed behaviors. These include learning the beliefs that thoughts are the causes of behavior and that negative affect is an indication of trait-like psychopathology. Further, the media portrays the good life as one of high personal resources and free from any inter-personal strife. If people learn these beliefs through the popular media and socially, then they are likely to believe that feeling depressed is a sign of something much more serious.

Finally, there is the role that verbal processes can play. Here, Dougher and Hackbert refer to the role that stimulus equivalence can play in thinking. If depressed people learn that 'I', 'failure' and 'sick' are in the same set of equivalent stimuli then the depressed mood and other negative behaviors associated with 'failure' can be elicited by 'I'.

Dougher and Hackbert (1994) present a comprehensive behavior-analytic account of depression. In this account the role of thoughts and feelings is central, but they are not elevated to the causes of the observed behavior. Rather, thoughts and feelings enter into the functional analysis in a number of ways. Their functional analysis seeks to find the stimuli that evoke depressed thoughts and feelings and the role that verbal regulation of behavior can play in (mis)representing contingencies. Thoughts and feelings are only one part of the experience of depression, and they take their place alongside depressed behaviors. Note that the implications for treatment are very broad. These will be reviewed in the next section. In particular we will review Acceptance and Commitment Therapy (ACT) as a behavior therapy that attempts to alter the way depressed people think.

Behavior-Analytic Therapies for Depression

A functional analysis of depression has a number of implications for both traditional therapies for depression. For those persons with social skills deficits related to depression social skills training would be appropriate (McNight et al., 1984). Many traditional verbal therapies could be effective in a number of ways. Repeatedly talking about certain traumatic events might extinguish the negative emotional responses associated with them, which could not happen if the person persistently avoids thinking about them. Shaping up a gradually more active pattern of behavior might be useful for some people, especially as it brings them into contact with new contingencies that may support non-depressed behaviors.

Hayes has taken this functional analysis of depression one step further by developing ACT (Hayes, Strosahl, & Wilson, in press; Hayes & Wilson, 1994). In ACT there are three main goals. These are to treat emotional avoidance, to correct literal responses to thoughts, and to make and keep commitments to behavioral change. According to ACT depressed people actively avoid excessive depressed or anxious thoughts because they are seen as a sign of serious psychopathology— for example, evidence they are going mad. In ACT the therapist seeks to undermine the strength of the client's belief in these thoughts. The therapist points out that what have appeared to be reasonable solutions in the past have brought no relief to the problems. Literal responses to cognitive content refer to the process of learning about the world indirectly through language, rather than directly experiencing the contingencies. In many cases this is a very efficient way of learning. However, when depressed people learn from others 'Don't think about that' they learn that depressed thoughts and feelings are a sign of serious mental illness and not merely thoughts and feelings. Further, because they are effective at avoiding very high intensities of depressed or anxious thoughts and feelings there appears to be some veracity in the proposition that they would have gone mad if they had not controlled those thoughts and feelings. Keeping commitment to behavioral change refers to encouraging the client to make an explicit choice to engage in certain behaviors, to adopt behavioral change as a goal rather than only changing their feelings. More detailed examples of ACT techniques and transcripts of therapy sessions can be found in Hayes and Wilson (1994), Kohlenberg and Tsai (1994) and Dougher and Hackbert (1994).

Comment

The example of behavior-analytic therapies for depression, which are primarily verbal, nicely illustrates the role of private events in behavior analysis. They are not excluded. Rather, they can occupy a central place in the formulation and treatment of a clinical problem. The key difference between a behavior-analytic approach to understanding and treating a clinical problem is that a behavior-analytic approach does not elevate private events to be the cause of behavior. Rather, private events are behavior with no special status. They have a relationship to environmental events like other behavior. It may often be more difficult to ascertain that relationship because of the difficulty in obtaining reliable data. However, that is no reason to elevate private events to some mysterious status as special causal agents of observed behavior.

Such an approach to private events and 'cognitive' therapies means that there may be times when many interventions other than traditional behavior therapies may be highly appropriate, depending upon the functions of the target behaviors. There may also be times when many traditional behavior therapies can be misapplied and be inappropriate (Wolpe, 1989). A behavior-analytic approach to case formulation does not necessarily imply intervention using a traditional behavior therapy.

CONCLUDING COMMENT

Discussion of the methods of assessing antecedents, behaviors and consequences reviewed in earlier chapters was relatively concrete and simple. Methods can be reliable or unreliable, convenient or costly. The process of identifying antecedents, behaviors and consequences, of deciding when to use which assessment method, of using clinical judgement as to the adequacy of current information, is more flexible and imprecise. Much less attention has been given to process issues in functional analysis than to issues of assessment method. Consequently there are no fully developed procedural rules for how to conduct the process of a functional analysis. This is a key area for future research.

Chapter 8

PROCESS ISSUES II: DEVELOPING AND USING A FUNCTIONAL ANALYSIS

In this chapter we will continue to examine the process of functional analysis. Four issues will be discussed. First, we will explore the task of writing down a functional analysis. Second, we will review the process of testing functional analysis. Third, we will review the process of translating a functional analysis into a treatment program. Finally, we will review the issue of reformulating problems.

WRITING A FUNCTIONAL ANALYSIS

Writing a functional analysis is a skill which is usually ignored. No papers were located which addressed this clinical skill. Although it is not addressed in the research literature this is an important skill. Writing a functional analysis is a good discipline in making a clinician commit to an explicit formulation of the problem. A functional analysis can also be used to concisely summarize information from multiple sources of assessment which might give rise to a large amount of diverse information. Writing functional analysis may also be a requirement of certain accreditation agencies in order to show that treatment is both individually designed and based upon a functional analysis. Finally, a written functional analysis may be a useful tool for communicating with a referring agent to indicate how a clinician works and how a functional analysis can be used to design treatment.

Many written case summaries do not constitute a functional analysis. Consider the following case example.

At the time of his first admission to a state hospital at the age of 24, the patient, an unmarried and unemployed laborer, already had a long history of anti-social behavior, promiscuity and addiction to alcohol and other drugs

. . . There had been eight brief admissions to private sanatoria for alcoholics, a number or arrests for public intoxication and drunken driving, and two jail terms for assault.

The patient had been born into a wealthy and respected family in a small town. The patient's father, a successful and popular businessman, drank excessively and his death at the age of 57 was partly due to alcoholism. The mother also drank to excess. The parents exercised little control over the patient as a child, and he was cared for by nursemaids. His father taught him to pour drinks for guests of the family when he was very young and he reported that he began to drain the glasses at parties in his home before he was 6; by the time he was 12 he drank almost a pint of liquor every weekend and by 17 he was drinking up to three bottles every day. His father provided him with money to buy liquor and shielded him from punishment for drunken driving and other consequences of his drinking.

The patient was expelled from high school in his freshman year for striking a teacher. He then attended a private school until the eleventh grade, when he changed the date on his birth certificate and joined the Army paratroops. After discharge, he was unemployed for six months; he drank heavily and needed repeated care at a sanatorium. When a job was obtained for him he quit within a month. On his third arrest for drunken driving he was jailed. His father bailed him out with the warning that no more money would be forthcoming. The patient left town and worked as an unskilled laborer—he had never acquired any useful skills—but returned home when his father died. During the next few years he was jailed for intoxication, for blackening his mother's eyes when he found a male friend visiting her, and for violating probation by getting drunk. He assaulted and badly hurt a prison guard in an escape attempt and was sentenced to two additional years in prison. When released, he began to use a variety of stimulant, sedative and narcotic drugs as well as alcohol.

(Rosen, Fox & Gregory, 1972, p. 312)

A number of observations may be made on such a case summary. First, it is mainly descriptive rather than analytic. It describes a range of behavior and describes the history of the problem in rather general terms. However, it does not offer any extensive understanding of the problem in psychological terms. Second, it is history-oriented rather than being concerned with the current environmental variables which maintain the behaviors. Third, it describes the problems in rather general terms (e.g., 'anti-social behavior', 'drank heavily', 'began to use a variety of . . . drugs') rather than precise behavioral descriptions of the form, frequency, duration and intensity of behavior. Finally, the manner in which the information is presented is oriented more to diagnosis than to treatment; it is unclear from this case description how treatment should proceed based on the information presented.

As part of a teaching exercise I have asked students or workshop participants to write a functional analysis of a current case: the result is often one of perplexity. Consider the following example of an attempt at writing a functional analysis.

A 30-year-old lady was referred for fear of using stairs. She is living at home with both her elderly parents. When climbing or descending stairs she feels tense and anxious, which often will result in injury and sitting down where she is. The antecedent is almost any staircase, but particularly open-sided ones without banisters. The consequences of this are that she receives attention from strangers when in public and a reaction from her parents, usually anger.

A clear onset of this problem dates back to an incident, at age 15 years, when she fell down the stairs in her home whilst running to answer the phone. The problem appears to have worsened over the past year since the death of her fiancé.

Treatment for this process consists of systematic desensitization in vivo to her fear of staircases, and grief counselling since this lady has never been 'allowed' to express her feelings about the loss of her fiancé.

This example is clearly more behavioral in character than the previous case description but still only partly addresses the functional analysis of this presenting problem. First, there appears to be a reasonable description of at least some of the target behaviors. However, one is tempted to wonder if there are additional related problems such as the relationship between the lady and her parents and/or possible grief-related issues. Second, the manner in which the consequences are described is somewhat superficial. What is it about 'attention from strangers' that is reinforcing? There is no mention of anxiety reduction and phobic avoidance, a common element in a phobic behavior. Third, and most striking, is that the proposed treatments appear to be rather standard, cookbook proposals based on the form of the problem—systemic desensitization for the phobia, counselling for the grief. These treatment proposals are rather general and are not linked to the formulation of the case. If the avoidance of stairs was related to attention from strangers how would systemic desensitization address this? How do either of these proposed treatments address anger from the parents? How will allowing the lady to express her feelings over the loss of her fiancé address these problems, or are there other problems not described here?

In order to facilitate training clinicians to write better functional analyses a set of criteria were developed. These are summarized in Table 8.1. These criteria were developed as a teaching tool, as a method of scoring up written functional analyses, and as feedback during teaching. A limit of 250 words was set in order to ensure concision and to encourage a concise style of writing a functional analysis. At some workshops participants have written very extended case descriptions of up to 1000 words, and yet still omitted many important aspects of a functional analysis. A relatively short word limit can also be helpful in forcing clinicians to abstract key features of a case, rather than attempting to be all-inclusive. A brief demographic and psychiatric description is justified in order to give a rapid summary of the kind of problem and content of the presenting problem. An operationalized target behavior can include either overt, physiological or cognitive targets. Students are often confused about the status of cognitions in a 'strictly behavioral' approach (see Chapter 6) and often believe that it is wrong to talk about thoughts or feelings, therefore the consideration of thoughts and feelings as potential target behaviors is explicitly included. Good examples of cognition as target behavior for change include recurrent, intrusive images such as are reported by people with obsessive-compulsive disorder. Of course, the methodological and conceptual problems relating to the measurement of private events and their elevation to causal status still fully apply. A written functional analysis should also explicitly state the antecedents and consequences of the target behaviors if they are known. A clear distinction should also be made between the onset and maintenance of the target behaviors. The onset may require an entirely separate functional analysis since onset and maintenance may be entirely separate. Note that this idea was developed substantially by Gresswell and Hollin (1992). In their paper they summarize a complex history using functional analysis. They present multiple functional analyses at various points in the development of the violent behavior. Again the emphasis here is on a brief summary of the history which highlights variables associated with increases or decreases in the target behavior and key learning experiences which account for the presenting problems. The pair of criteria relate to ascertaining the secondary gains from the problem and the functions that the problems might serve. An explicit link between the formulation and the treatment might be made. This is one of the most difficult aspects of functional analysis. Often the formulation gets written reasonably well and falls at the last hurdle as the therapist

Table 8.1   Criteria Used for Writing a Functional Analysis of Individual Cases

1. A word limit of 250 words.
2. A *brief*, demographic and psychiatric description of problem, e.g., 'A four-year-old child was referred for fecal incontinence. The family consisted of mother (divorced) and two other children.'
3. *At least* one operationalized target 'behavior' which might be an overt behavior (e.g., 'crying'), cognitive (e.g., 'recurrent thoughts of worthlessness'), or physiological (e.g., 'feelings of tension').
4. At least one operationalized antecedent which must include examples, e.g., 'feelings of worthlessness' most often happened when alone (early morning/late at night) and after failures to assert herself (giving in to her husband), *or* state 'antecedents unknown'.
5. At least one operationalized consequence which must include examples, e.g., 'The pain behavior appeared to be maintained by both positive reinforcers, primarily social in nature (e.g., frequent visits to GP, attention from family) and negative reinforcers (excessive use of anxiolytics such as minor tranquilizers, alcohol and analgesics, avoidance of driving in certain cases and certain social activities described as stressful', *or* state 'consequences unknown'.
6. A stated distinction between onset and maintenance which may or may not require separate functional analyses, e.g., 'No clear onset could be identified, although the problem got considerably worse after he changed his job.'
7. A brief history to include (a) the onset (traumatic/insidious) e.g., 'this problem began about 15 years ago, but with no clear point of onset'; and (b) factors which have been associated with an increase or decrease in the severity of the problem during its development, e.g., 'this person's control of his temper has always been poor, but has got considerably worse following the loss of his job and moving house.'
8. Describe the secondary gains that may often be relevant and important for design of treatment, e.g., 'The adoption of the role of a person with an incurable and mysterious illness gained the person considerable status in her family and neighborhood.'
9. Describe the functions of the behaviors in terms of the purposes that they serve for the subject, e.g., 'The agoraphobic symptoms appeared to keep her husband at home more often than otherwise might have happened.'
10. State a treatment, either planned or implemented, which is explicitly linked to (3), (4), or (5) e.g., 'Rational emotive therapy was selected to modify the dysfunctional cognitions which maintain the depression', or 'A Patterson-style behavior management program was implemented in order to change the patterns of instructions given to the child *and* to increase parental use of praise.'

reflexly recommends their favorite kind of therapy. The example above contains some clear examples of this. (In this situation the choice of therapy is more closely linked to the behavior of the clinician than to the behavior of the client!) In the next section developing links between formulation and treatments is discussed in more detail.

As part of several training exercises these criteria have been used to teach participants to discriminate between 'good' and 'bad' formulations. Participants have been asked to score up descriptive case emphasis and their own initial attempts to write a functional analysis of a current case. They are then asked to write their initial functional analysis using the above criteria as guidelines. The example above could be written as follows.

A 30-year-old lady was referred for a simple phobia of using stairs, assertiveness difficulties with her elderly parents, and an unresolved grief relating to the death of her fiancé a year ago. She frequently avoided stairs. When she did attempt them she would become highly aroused and fearful, become sweaty, cry and solicit help from members of the public. A hierarchy of antecedents relates to the height and gradient of the stairs and whether or not the stairs were open-sided. Important consequences appeared to be fear reduction through passive avoidance and soliciting help from other people. Assertive difficulties with her elderly parents were shown through speaking quietly and submissively to them, avoiding certain 'difficult' topics, and reacting to their angry criticism by running to her room and crying. Typical antecedents have included talking about her difficulties with stairs, her boyfriend and anything to do with an independent, adult role. Finally, her unresolved grief over her boyfriend was shown through long periods of reminiscing about him, looking at photos, and crying. She could not visit his grave. These episodes were most likely to happen on certain anniversary dates, but also during evenings and weekends when she was alone and inactive. Again avoidance of discussing topics related to this matter was thought to be a key maintaining variable. Since avoidance and lack of assertiveness appeared to be key elements in all three, apparently independent problems, she could be trained in a general strategy to deal assertively with difficulties. This could include developing hierarchies of difficult situations, rehearsing assertive strategies in her head, and gradually systematically reducing passive avoidance, and learning relaxation and assertion in fearful situations.

This example is less than perfect; it is slightly overlength due to the multiple problems presented, and does not discuss secondary gains. However, when compared to the first example it is clearly more analytical, more treatment-oriented and attempts to identify a common function across three different kinds of problems.

Comment

Teaching clinicians to write a formulation which accurately conforms to the criteria in Table 8.1 is relatively simple. Although such a summary of the information is useful, it is not a guarantee of an adequate functional analysis. It is clearly dependent upon the quality of the assessment information available, the ability of the clinician to abstract commonalities across different problems, and to link the assessment information to an intervention. It should also be noted that these criteria fit only relatively simple kinds of functional analyses. The role of setting events, the possibility that target behaviors have multiple functions or that the relationships between multiple target behaviors are complex, are not explicitly addressed in these criteria. Despite these limitations these criteria encourage clinicians to become more focused in their writing of functional analyses and can be a useful intermediate step in shaping up clinicians towards making more subtle and complex functional analyses.

In order to improve the quality of a functional analysis and test its validity two important considerations can be made. First, testing the functional analysis can be carried out to validate and develop it further. Second, a number of strategies can be used to develop a treatment strategy from the foundation. The next two sections discuss these issues.

TESTING A FUNCTIONAL ANALYSIS

Several authors have emphasized that a functional analysis must not be merely conjecture. Rather, as with scientific hypotheses, clinical hypotheses must be tested in order to assess their validity (Cullen, 1983). Shapiro (1970, p. 651) put it this way: 'If one or more hypotheses are suggested by an observation, then steps must be taken to test them. In this way further observations are accumulated in a systematic manner.'

In previous chapters we have seen that competing clinical hypotheses guide the collection of information (Turkat, 1988). The process of evaluating competing clinical hypotheses is inherent in collecting and evaluating information in this way. Competing clinical hypotheses guide the collection of assessment information by highlighting potential models of behavior. As one model becomes untenable then it is modified or discarded.

One important method of testing competing clinical hypotheses is to make predictions. Of course, it is easy to make sense of presenting information retrospectively since most humans have self-serving biases in the evaluation of their own performance. It is more difficult to honestly and explicitly predict behavior prospectively.

This approach can be illustrated by Turkat's (1988) transcript of hypothesis-driven interviewing. Following an initial 30 seconds of interviewing a young adult client with a needle phobia Turkat's formulation can be paraphrased as follows: 'Charles is angry about insulin injections because they make him appear weak. . . . His overconcern with appearing weak or dependent leads him to view things generally in a combative manner. . . . He acts 'tough' in the interview to 'prove his independence'. From this hypothesis Turkat makes six predictions. Two of them are: (1) 'Charles will not permit himself to appear weak or dependent . . . he will not disclose much, particularly if it involves emotional expression other than anger.' (2) 'Charles will not have many, if any friends.' Clearly, close friendships are incompatible with always being 'tough'. Thus, even from a very modest amount of information predictions—which may well prove to be wrong—can be made.

Consider the following referral letter:

Will you please see this man who has suffered a severe grief reaction following the death of his son in a police car chase and accident. He has recently separated from his wife.

Using this information some of the following hypotheses could be evaluated.

1. Abnormal grief reactions are often associated with ambivalent, emotionally laden relationships. The police chase related to the son's death suggests the possibility that the son had some kind of police contact which could be related to an ambivalent, emotionally laden father–son relationship.
2. The separation from his wife might be a traumatic life event involving either loss of reinforcement, massive punishment or loss of support for adaptive behavior.

Of course, either or both of these hypotheses might be wrong, but they provide several areas for exploration early during assessment interviews.

Another method of hypothesis testing is to make predictions and test them with 'mini-experiments'. Here is one example.

After interviewing staff and making informed observations on a man with moderate/severe developmental disabilities there were some clear hints that the behavior problems were motivated by escape from demands. A brief mini-experiment was planned to test the following predictions. (1) If left alone he would show no behavior problems since no demands would be present. (2) In the presence of a staff member he would show no behavior problems so long as demands were not presented. (3) When demands or related requests were presented behavior problems would begin. (4) Behavior problems would escalate if demands were presented repeatedly. (5) If given an opportunity to remove demands he would do so. The following sequence was captured on videotape. (1) When James was left alone for 2 minutes he was calm, showed no behavior (confirming hypothesis 1). (2) When initially approached he was friendly and smiled. This confirms hypothesis (2). Even when a simple demand was presented he initially said 'yes'. (3) After a demand was presented for more than one or two seconds his behaviors gradually began and rapidly escalated in frequency and intensity. This confirms hypotheses (3) and (4). (4) At the end of the tape presentation James was asked 'Do you want to be left alone?' He immediately replied 'yes', smiled and visibly relaxed, confirming hypothesis (5). The entire procedure was repeated once more. The entire experiment took less than 5 minutes.

Conducting mini-experiments such as these can be a very quick way of testing a clinical hypothesis. There are no hard and fast rules as how to conduct such procedures. One component to mini-experiments is to attempt to positively identify key antecedents and consequences from other assessment information and systematically present them. Thus, one component to a mini-experiment is a good analysis of the information already available. Here is a second example of developing 'mini-experiments' to test clinical hypotheses.

A client presented with a severe and disabling phobia of social situations and crowds. Although presenting with numerous signs and symptoms of anxiety the predominant ones were related to breathing difficulties. One hypothesis was that this phobia was a fear of asphyxiation. The therapist tested this possibility by seeing if he could attempt to hold the client down in his chair by holding him across his shoulders and chest. This immediately precipitated a panic attack. Interestingly, interacting with the therapist, a stranger who might prove highly evaluative, evoked only mild apprehension. Treatment could thus be directed at fear of asphyxiation, rather than fear of crowding or social evaluation.

Cullen (1983) highlights the importance of empirically testing the relationships which are hypothesized to exist amongst variables in a functional analysis rather than simply leaving them as speculation. Many hypotheses derived from initial interviews do not have data to support them. Analyzing baseline data to confirm hypotheses derived from initial interviews is another form of hypothesis testing.

An example of this kind of analysis of baseline data comes from Schlundt, Johnson and Jarrell (1985) who analyzed data from clients who kept diaries of eating behaviors. In order to empirically derive functional relationships between potential antecedents and vomiting behavior they calculated the overall average probability of vomiting (0.142). They then calculated the conditional probabilities of vomiting of five certain antecedents. They found that the overall probability of vomiting was not related to location (home vs away), presence of people, or activity (e.g., exercise, work, recreation, etc.). However, the probability of vomiting was greatly affected by feelings of fullness, time of day, and mood. For example the conditional possibilities of vomiting for location were 0.16 for alone and 0.13 for social. Thus, these differed from the overall probability (0.142). Whereas for mood the conditional probabilities of vomiting were 0.31 for negative, 0.13 for neutral, and 0.04 for positive. Thus, mood greatly affected the likelihood of the target behavior. This form of analyzing baseline data can give a more rigorous test of hypothesis derived during initial interviews.

A final method of testing a functional analysis is a full single case experimental design. A single case experimental design is a mini-experiment but more thorough and yields less ambiguous results due to the use of an experimental design. An example of this kind of testing of a functional analysis comes from Kerwin, Ahearn, Eicker and Burd (1995). Kerwin *et al.* were interested in developing an effective treatment for food refusal in three children aged two through five years with a variety of medical problems and related food refusal. In the first part of the study they evaluated the pattern of the children's refusal of food from spoons that were empty, dipped in food, quarter, half and level with food. Using a multi-element design for each child they showed orderly generalization gradients of food refusal across amount of food on the spoon. For example, Linda only accepted the spoon in her mouth for 2 of seven trials when there was no food on it, and did not accept the spoon in her mouth at any time when there was food on the spoon. Gary, on the other hand, accepted the empty spoon 100% of trials and the level spoon 75% of trials. All three children showed orderly generalization of gradients of food refusal.

Two types of interventions were used, either *non-removal of the spoon* or *physical guidance*. After eating the amount of food on the spoon the child had access to preferred reinforcers such as toys. Each intervention began at the lowest amount of food that the child would eat at. The results showed that these interventions were effective and produced some generalization to non-treated food amounts.

Comment

Testing a functional analysis is a key element of good clinical practice. Without testing a functional analysis remains merely unconfirmed speculation. There is obviously a cost in conducting an evaluation of a functional analysis, namely, the additional time between conducting the evaluation and the delay in implementing treatment. However, without at least some cursory evaluation of a functional analysis the danger exists that the treatment is founded upon unsafe grounds and will be unsuccessful. Of course, evaluation of a functional analysis is not a one-off thing; it is a recursive process. The initial formulation is made; it is evaluated; initial treatment is implemented which casts further light on the current formulation; the current formulation is revised again and the treatment is revised in the new light, and so on. It is quite likely in difficult cases or in cases where the full information is not available that initial formulations will be incorrect or substantially incomplete. In other circumstances it may take extensive clinical detective work to begin to approximate to a reasonably valid formulation.

Some authors have suggested that an effective treatment outcome is a good confirmation of a clinical hypothesis. However, such reasoning is complex. First, successful treatments do occur that are not related to the functions of the target behavior. Aspirin can successfully abolish a headache caused by a blow to the head rather than by aspirin deprivation. Electric shock will suppress self-injurious behavior maintained by all kinds of different variables. Second, a treatment may be unsuccessful for reasons other than an incorrect or inadequate functional analysis. A treatment may not work because it has not been implemented faithfully or because the link between the formulation and treatment is incorrect. Thus, successful treatment outcome will only provide ambivalent evidence that the formulation is correct.

DERIVING A TREATMENT

The process of deriving a treatment is sometimes seen as a dark and mysterious process. There have been few explicit guidelines to help the clinician translate a functional analysis into a treatment. In discussions of Nelson's (1988) Keystone strategy with students a common reaction has been 'Great! So how do you find the Keystone?' In this section a number of strategies will be highlighted that can be used to translate a formulation into a treatment which is explicitly based upon that formulation. They will be organized into six strategies: response-based strategies, consequence-based strategies, antecedent-based strategies, history-related strategies, modifying current coping strategies, and taxonomic strategies.

Response-based Strategies

An adequate functional analysis should tell the clinician how different forms of behavior are organized, how they relate to each other and if they all have the same or different functions. We saw in the previous chapter that hierarchical models of symptom organization (Evans, 1985) and response chains (Frankel, 1975) are useful models of the structure of responses since these models have different implications for how and when to intervene. If one has a hierarchical model of a set of presenting problems (see Figures 7.1, 7.2 and 7.4) then the model should indicate superordinate functions or targets for intervention. Simply targeting some other responses may lead to a laborious picking off of individual responses one by one, or to response substitution as the superordinate problem is not directly treated. In the case study generated early in this chapter several apparently unrelated problems—fear of climbing on stairs, relationship problems with parents, and unresolved grieving— were related by a common factor, or superordinate problem, namely lack of assertiveness in fear-provoking situations. In this formulation a very simple hierarchical model such as that illustrated in Figure 7.4(a) would suggest that intervention targeting the superordinate problem would be not efficient and/or effective.

The use of the response chain model (Frankel, 1975) indicates that intervention should aim to eliminate all the behaviors in a response chain, not just the terminal, most problematic response. This should be done by reducing the frequency of the earliest members of the response chain rather than the last.

A young woman presented with partly severe bulimia. Typically she would not eat during the day or at work. However, on her way home she would buy several candy bars at successive corner stores. This was especially true if she had had a bad day and was tired, irritated or tense. This would typically lead to extended snacking while preparing family meals. The chain would culminate in binging and vomiting early in the evening after which she would feel relatively relieved at the prospect of not having consumed excess calories. This chain of behavior was broken up in several ways. First, regular small meals were scheduled with small snacks from time to time. This took several weeks of shaping up appropriate eating. Second, since tension was clearly a component in the chain relaxation skills were also taught to break the response chain. Finally, a number of activities in the early evening (e.g. keep fit classes) were scheduled to break up the rather stereotyped sequence of travelling home, evening meals and lack of activity.

Analyzing response–response relationships using correlograms (Sturmey, Newton & Crisp, 1991; Wahler, 1975) can be used to identify groups of responses which are known to be incompatible with problematic target behaviors. Thus, if we know from baseline data that toy play, positive affect, and positive social interactions tend to be negatively correlated with siblings fighting, then increasing the first set of behaviors should decrease the second set. Rather than arbitrarily selecting any other behaviors to increase such a strategy will capitalize on the existing relationships between responses.

Consequence-based Strategies

Consequences that have maintained behaviors that are maladaptive, distressing and highly disruptive to a person's life are likely to be highly motivating. If these consequences can be reprogrammed to support adaptive rather than maladaptive behaviors then these programs might be very powerful. Some of the best examples of this approach come from Durand *et al.* (1989) and Repp, Felce and Barton (1988) who used a functional analysis to identify the reinforcers maintaining self-injury, stereotypy and other maladaptive behaviors in persons with developmental disabilities. The reprogramming of reinforcers involved removing them as a reliable consequence of maladaptive behaviors and reliably presenting them for adaptive behaviors. For example, if the behavior was motivated by escape from task demands then the person would be physically guided through the task, thus removing task avoidance as a reinforcer. The person would then be given short breaks as a reinforcer for compliance and other adaptive behaviors.

More generally, the consequences maintaining maladaptive behavior can highlight major issues of concern for the client. For example, if an agoraphobic client is repeatedly vigilant regarding criticism from others relating to achievement at work then this might indicate that achievement at work is of central concern to the person. This information could be explored further during initial evaluation and potentially identify gains that would be empirically important to the client.

Finally, the delivery of consequences may be associated with certain individuals. In such cases the management of the behavior of such persons is likely to be a crucial component to the intervention. These significant others may need to be educated and trained as change agents. If the behaviors of these significant others cannot be modified then their behavior may undermine any other intervention. The management of significant others in contingency management can be complex and subtle. Many programs involving the retraining of teachers, parents and care staff revolve around their potential to maintain maladaptive behavior.

A 14-year-old boy was referred for a school phobia of recent onset. He performed well at school generally and was described as a well-motivated, if somewhat anxious, pupil. After graduating to the next school year after summer recess he had a rather vague physical illness on and off for 4 weeks and then refused to return to school without saying why. Interviews with the home class teacher and analysis of the days not attended revealed that the boy had just begun a new class with a male teacher generally regarded as highly punitive. The early days off from school were all days when he would have been taught by this teacher. It was arranged for the boy to be transferred to a different group for that class. In this way the major punisher for attending the school was removed. With a little encouragement for attending the boy soon attended school regularly. Only one minor relapse occurred some months later associated with a temporary substitute male teacher.

Antecedent-based Strategies

A knowledge of the antecedents related to the target behaviors can be used to translate the functional analysis into a treatment program in a number of ways. At the most simple level a knowledge of antecedents can be used to focus attention on times when the problem is very likely and very unlikely to happen and evaluate those situations that prevent or precipitate the problems (see Figure 8.1).

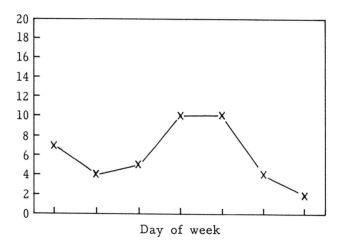

Figure 8.1 The Frequency of Behavior Incidents Plotted by Time of Day Over a Six Month Period

During a staff training exercise staff were discussing when, where, and why fecal smearing occurred. Two situations were identified. These were (a) in the training room when a peer took the person's favorite rocking chair; and (b) when training occurred. Scoring up the previous month's scatterplot by day of week showed a clear effect of day of the week confirming this hypothesis.

Stimuli which predict increases or decreases in the probability of behaviors are useful in planning generalization. It is rare for any problem to be present continuously and for no competing behaviors to exist. A key component to many interventions is the reprogramming of antecedent stimuli. Procedures such as graded exposure, desensitization, shaping and chaining all involve gradual changes, the value of antecedent stimuli as predictors of reinforcers and punishers.

History-related Strategies

Although the emphasis within a behavioral framework is usually on the current environment there are times when the problem history can play a key role in designing intervention. The most obvious examples are those relating to conditioning events and phobias, although other uses of a problem history are possible. A problem history might well be useful in identifying strategies dealing with the problem, previously reinforcing activities, interests and hobbies and previously evident islands of adaptive behavior. This history of a problem can also reveal recurrent areas of concern over a long period of time, such as relationship with authority figures, performance anxieties or vigilance for certain kinds of fears.

Modifying Current Coping Strategies

Many individuals or carers will have developed their own coping strategies for managing the presenting problem. Some of these may be partly effective. Some may inadvertently contribute to the maintenance of the problem. In either case, these management strategies can be understood within the framework of functional analysis. Such coping strategies can sometimes be early modified to approximate closely to the treatments implied by the functional analysis.

A relative's son shows modest tantrums and grizzling on numerous occasions. After extended threats and promises from his parents he is often sent to bed early, only to be comforted later by other family members. During one weekend stay at my brother's house he began whining. After one promise to be good he began crying. My brother, a great believer in functional analysis, immediately placed him in the corner of the room until he was quiet for 2 minutes. When coming out of the corner time out he was not comforted, rather he was warned that the contingencies were in effect all weekend. The weekend continued blissfully until Sunday evening. At the sight of his mother in the driveway the boy's face fell and his chin wobbled; the new stimulus indicated that the old contingencies were back. By the time his mother was in arm's reach he was vigorously crying. (This is a neat example of a generalization across distance from Mom.) Naturally, he received a cuddle, his present and candy. (He had obviously missed his mom!) The old contingencies, readily modifiable, had been reinstated.

Taxonomic Strategies

Much of the emphasis within functional analysis has been placed upon highly idiographic assessments and interventions. This arose partly as a reaction against structural-medical models where all people with the same diagnosis were given the same treatment or a selection from a menu of treatments available for that diagnosis. However, such a highly idiographic approach can be very time-consuming and may tax the skills of the clinician to the extreme. As a reaction to this problem, and in order to develop a heuristic device to help clinicians some researchers have developed taxonomic approaches (Repp & Karsh, 1994) or behavioral diagnostics (Pyles & Bailey, 1990) approaches. A similar model has been developed for school non-attendance (Kearney & Silverman, 1990). These approaches attempt to simplify the deviation of treatment from a functional analysis by limiting treatment choices to a small number of options ahead of time. In this way the options available to the clinician are limited and clinical choices are simplified (see Figure 8.2).

In Kearney and Silverman's (1990) treatment model for school non-attendance there is a mapping from behavioral diagnosis to treatment similar to those proposed by Pyles and Bailey (1990) and Repp and Karsh (1994). In this model there are four possible functions of school non-attendance each with its own prescription for treatment. School non-attendance due to fear and over-anxiety is treated with imaginal or *in vivo* desensitization and relaxation training. Avoidance of aversive social situations is treated by cognitive behavior therapy and/or modelling to improve social skills and academic performance. School non-attendance maintained by parental attention at home was treated with shaping up of school attendance and removal of verbal and physical attention for being at home during school hours. School non-attendance maintained by tangible reinforcers (watching TV, access to toys, etc.) is treated with contingency contracting using the reinforcers identified during the functional analysis.

Comment

There are now several strategies for translating a functional analysis into treatment. Until recently there have been no explicit guidelines for doing so. The development of taxonomic approaches is one solution to this problem. Yet, translating a functional analysis into a treatment can be subtle and complex. The processes by which clinicians do this are obscure and require further study. Some issues related to this matter are discussed in the final chapter. The use of behavioral diagnostics again raises new issues. First, the reliability with which regular clinicians can make accurate behavioral diagnoses is as yet unknown. As

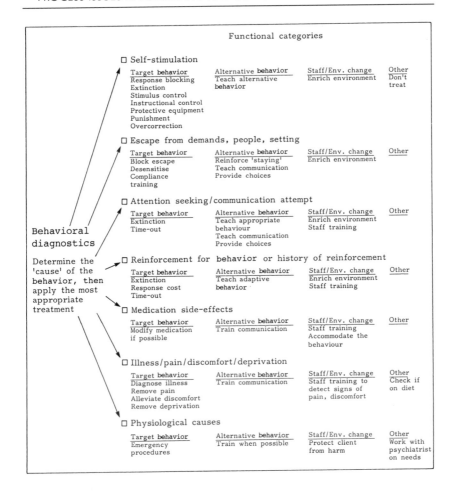

Figure 8.2 The Behavioral Diagnostic Model

Reproduced by permission of Sycamore Publishing Co. from Pyles, D. A. M. & Bailey, J. S. (1990). Diagnosing severe behavior problems. In A. C. Repp & N. N. Singh (Eds) *Perspectives on the Use of Non-aversive and Aversive Interventions for Persons with Developmental Disabilities*, p. 389, Figure 3

we have seen in Chapter 6, psychometric instruments used to assess the functions of target behaviors have mixed reliability at best. Accurate behavioral diagnoses are a fundamental requirement of this approach. Second, the prescriptions made for treatment need to be robust across diverse problems. That is, once a behavioral diagnosis is made then a substantial proportion of the individuals with this diagnosis must respond to the prescribed treatment to a clinically significant extent.

REFORMULATING A FUNCTIONAL ANALYSIS

On many occasions the intervention that is tried first will not be effective to a clinically significant degree, may be ineffective, or may even produce an undesirable outcome. This issue of treatment failures has generally been neglected, but is a fertile area for the development treatment. A full account of treatment failures can be found in the excellent book by Foa and Emmelkamp (1983). When intervention fails it may be necessary to consider whether or not the initial functional analysis was a valid one, and if not, whether a reformulation of the problem should be made. The reformulated functional analysis can then form the basis of a new intervention made on the basis of this new formulation.

Determining Whether a Reformulation is Appropriate

Evaluating an intervention failure

The first reaction to an intervention failure might be to make a reformulation of the problem. However, on many occasions this may not be appropriate. Intervention may fail for many reasons other than an inappropriate initial functional analysis. These reasons should be fully explored before a reformulation is made. If this is not done an initial functional analysis which was actually valid may be rejected incorrectly. Subsequently, a reformulation may be made in which the clinician is forced into errors of judgement based on an incorrect belief that the initial formulation was incorrect. This incorrect belief may then lead to a cascade of judgement errors on the part of the clinician as the belief that the initial functional analysis was wrong may color the way that many pieces of evidence are perceived.

When an initial intervention fails there are a number of alternative explanations that need to be evaluated before a reformulation is considered. One of the most common causes for an initial intervention to fail is that the treatment was incorrectly implemented. This issue is sometimes referred to the integrity of the independent variable (Peterson, Homer & Wonderlich, 1982). For some forms of intervention assessing this issue is relatively concrete. For example, a clinician might assess how many practice sessions of predetermined walking outside a person with agoraphobia and panic attacks conducted. However, assessing even such a concrete aspect of treatment integrity is not always easy. If the clinician depends simply on self-report, then clients are subject to self-serving biases and may exaggerate their efforts at implementation. They may simply fail to remember accurately if the time period is very long, or they may have difficulties in recalling their performance because the task was completed under conditions of extreme anxiety. If, in this example, the clinician depends on written records then these may be incomplete, lost, or forged. In either case it may be difficult to assess treatment integrity accurately. Interviewing clients after treatment may also suffer from similar problems.

A 35-year-old woman with agoraphobia and panic attacks had completed an initial evaluation. The initial functional analysis indicated that avoidance of aversive bodily sensations associated with walking outside was an important function of her problems. As part of the initial evaluation interviews her husband had been present at the interviews and subsequently agreed to help in intervention in any way that he could. Part of the initial treatment sessions was for the client to begin taking short walks from her home on the way to the local stores although not to go in the stores.

After the first week of treatment both client and husband returned to the clinician very despondent. They reported that the intervention had not worked and had made the client very much worse and very upset. Rather than reject the initial formulation the clinician interviewed both parties to ascertain exactly what had happened. Several breaches in the integrity of the treatment were noted. First, the husband reported that he was concerned that his wife was unable to travel alone at all. In order to help her he had accompanied her on every trip out of the home, even the short ones. Thus, no independent travel had actually occurred. Second, the client reported that on each occasion she was determined to overcome the problem. She pushed herself as much as she could stand until the anxiety became unbearable and was then forced to return home in a state of terror. Thus, instead of ending each exposure session with a success each exposure trial had led to a further strengthening of the negative reinforcing value of avoidance of aversive bodily sensations.

In this example future efforts should focus on implementing the current treatment accurately. This might involve more careful education of the client and husband as to the exact procedure that they should be following or perhaps much more careful supervision of the implementation of the treatment, for example, daily supervision by phone by the therapist. An alternative strategy might be to develop a second, more acceptable intervention that is still based upon the initial functional analysis. For example, it might be necessary for the exposure sessions to take the form of exposure to the aversive bodily sensations via hyperventilating whilst remaining indoors, rather than *in vivo* exposure. However, at this point in time there is no evidence that the initial functional analysis is incorrect. Thus, at this point there is no justification for a reformulation to be made.

Evaluating the integrity of relatively simple intervention procedures is not necessarily easy. However, assessing the integrity of cognitive therapies presents the therapist with many additional challenges. In many cognitive therapies there can be confusion between the independent and the dependent variable. For example, a variety of interventions might be implemented to change the strength of the client's belief in apparently maladaptive thoughts. In cognitive therapy the change in the strength of the beliefs is supposed to be the basis for subsequent behavior change. Thus, in cognitive therapy the key independent variable is the strength of the client's maladaptive beliefs. Conducting exercises to challenge the strength of the client's current belief, or asking them to evaluate the evidence for maladaptive belief, would not actually constitute the independent variable. Rather, it is a mechanism to change the person's core beliefs. Thus, documenting that all the exercises with the client and homework exercises were implemented and performed correctly would not constitute a measure of treatment integrity. Rather, it would be necessary to show that the strength of the client's beliefs had changed.

One aspect of treatment integrity that may be important to check on is the number or amount of treatment sessions implemented and the amount of associated homework completed by the client. In many treatments implemented in regular clinical sessions the therapist attempts to replicate procedures reported in the research literature. Careful review of those articles often reveals that for treatment to be correctly implemented many treatment sessions may be needed. Further, in research they are typically implemented by highly motivated therapists whose resumés and reputations are at stake, rather than by tired, overworked therapists who are planning their family's evening meal in the middle of a therapy session. Initial treatments may be ineffective simply because an insufficient quantity of treatment has been implemented, or because of poor compliance with implementation of the therapy on the part of the therapist, or poor compliance with treatment and/or homework on the part of the client. Before a reformulation is to be seriously considered the therapist should check carefully as to what exactly constitutes the procedure that is being implemented and evaluate if what has been done corresponds to the actual treatment procedure. Only when it is clear that the original procedure has been faithfully replicated can one consider whether the treatment failed because the initial functional analysis was incorrect.

Making a Reformulation

Making a reformulation is a clinical activity, yet this is rarely discussed in the research literature. Such reformulations are commonly made and should be addressed more vigorously by research. Below are some examples of reformulations that can occur at a variety of stages during assessment and intervention.

Reformulating during the course of successful intervention

As intervention proceeds it is possible that a functional analysis may need revision, even when treatment is very successful. Significant refinement in a functional analysis can occur at any point in working with a client. This may occur simply because, as treatment proceeds, new information comes to light that was not previously available or the client reveals information that previously was not revealed. If the initial formulation was based on incomplete or inaccurate information then treatment may need further refinement.

A 47-year-old woman with agoraphobia had been assessed during three initial interviews. On the second interview her husband was also present as informant. The initial functional analysis was that she was so highly avoidant of situations that she believed that she should be evaluated negatively by other people. She reported that she avoided crowds because of the embarrassment of making eye contact with strangers and brief interactions when bumping into others. She was very shy and unassertive, but appeared to have good social skills, although she did report making social blunders when she was overly anxious, even with friends and relatives.

During the first session of flooding, which was focused on going into crowded stores, talking to strangers, and deliberately bumping into other people, additional information became available. After the first hour she took out a tranquilizer from her purse and swallowed it quickly. She appeared embarrassed. She told the therapist that she could not leave the house without one as she did not feel safe. If she had one with her she always knew that she could calm herself down if she got into real panic. The formulation could now be revised to include abuse of minor tranquilizers as another form of avoidance of anxiety in embarrassing situations.

This is a relatively minor revision in the functional analysis. However, it had some important implications for treatment. In consultation with her primary physician her medication was switched from a rapid acting minor tranquilizer with a short half-life to a slow acting minor tranquilizer with a long half-life. In this way the abuse of medications was unlikely as there would be no short-term avoidance of anxiety by using them in situations that were very tense. Further, the new medication was more likely to lead to a more even level of anxiety, rather than many peaks and valleys in anxiety.

Treatment proceeded very successfully. After two months she was able to find herself a new job. This was the first time she had been able to work for two years. During the exit interview she let it be known that she no longer needed to take alcoholic drinks in the evening to sleep because of her anxiety. This additional avoidance of abuse of substances that gave a short-term relief of anxiety was, in retrospect, an important component of her formulation which had not been a part of her initial functional analysis. Important information had not been presented to the therapist. This was either because of reluctance on the part of the client to reveal the information to a stranger, who might evaluate her negatively for being so apparently weak, or in the case of medication abuse, because the client had failed to make the connection between these problems.

Reformulating in mid-treatment

A substantial reformulation may be necessary in mid-treatment. The need for a reformulation may arise because the function of the behavior may change as the person learns. Alternatively, a reformulation may occur because the person is exposed to new situations that either provoke new functions of the target behavior that have not hitherto been observed, or that cause the reemergence of behavior that has not been observed during the current time period.

Chuck was a 20-year-old man with Downe syndrome who had been referred for treatment for severe self-injury. The initial functional analysis was a very simple one. When he was left alone he did not self-injure. Rather, he engaged in more or less constant restraint. When staff approached him and attempted to take him out of restraint to interact with him, train him, or engage him in even very easy daily living skills he would self-injure, vocalize loudly and aversively, pull away from them, or occasionally slap them. When staff persisted or attempted to engage him in tasks that were difficult or did not have a high density of reinforcement associated with them then his behavior would intensify dramatically.

The initial functional analysis was not a difficult one to make. This was behavior that occurred almost exclusively in response to a specific antecedent—being taken out of restraint—associated with an aversive consequence—various kinds of demands. The behavior appeared to be reinforced by removal of these demands. The behavior was too dangerous for an experimental functional analysis to be conducted. However, systematic comparison of periods of time when he was left alone and taking him out of restraints for very brief periods of training revealed a very consistent relationship between removal of restraint and self-injury.

The implications for treatment of the initial functional analysis were also very simple, although very difficult to implement. The functional analysis identified access to restraint and removal of demands as very powerful reinforcers. Initially, Chuck was taken out of restraints for periods of approximately two minutes to work on easy tasks that were as highly reinforcing as could be found, such as eating a favorite breakfast cereal. Access to restraint was made contingent upon completing the task and after a brief period of no self-injury. Initial success in this and other, similar tasks was followed by very gradual generalization by, (a) increasing the length of time working, (b) gradually increasing the range of tasks to be worked on, (c) following non-preferred tasks with preferred tasks and breaks, and (d) shaping up walking for progressively longer periods of time and to more locations.

This procedure was very successful. After a few months Chuck was engaging in many tasks with little prompting, self-restraint was rarely observed at work, and self-injury was less frequent and intense. Only minor medical care was needed for injuries. Further, Chuck had gone from being miserable, clingy and distressed to being fairly happy and sociable at times.

As treatment proceeded all forms of social behavior were encouraged, including playing soccer with staff, hugs, smiling, and playing about. Within a couple of months a new problem began to emerge. Staff began to report that he was aggressive to staff. Sometimes a playful interaction would gradually turn from chasing to trying to hit staff or from giving a hug to sliding his hand over their head to poke their eye. None of these new problems, except perhaps some of the aggression, occurred in demand situations. Rather, they appeared to be social behaviors which were part of a response chain beginning with some appropriate social interactions. It was believed that they were maintained by staff reaction. The procedure was revised in order to address the new social operant function of the behavior by continuing to strengthen and reinforce appropriate behavior. However, precursor behaviors early in the chain such as beginning to chase staff would lead to calm interactions from staff and promoting of other behaviors such as going to work.

At another point during Chuck's treatment staff reported that he had begun spitting at them. This typically was in demand situations. This was addressed by staff not backing away from him and by immediately redirecting him to work.

At a later point the frequency and severity of the behaviors had greatly subsided. However, there was still residual non-compliance and self-injury. Some was certainly made worse during periods of minor illness and could be addressed to some extent by careful monitoring of health and prompt inter-vention for health problems. Some may have been untreated demand-related behavior and due to staff not picking up subtle cues or being tolerant of what was now behavior of low intensity. However, sometimes there were increases in behavior when no reason could be determined.

In this example three reformulations were necessary. The first reformu-lation addressed the emergence of a new function, the second reformu-lation addressed the emergence of a new topography, and the third reformulation addressed the functions of residual behavior problems. One observation that can be made from this example is that when a problem has several functions, then all the functions may not be apparent initially if one function predominates during the initial assess-ment. In such a situation the initial intervention might be highly appro-priate. When it has been implemented and effective it will reduce those behaviors related to that function. At that point the primary function will no longer predominate and other, unaddressed functions will become much more important. Because of this, when intervening with a multi-function behavior an intervention that was initially both appropri-ate and effective will become inappropriate and less effective. This is illustrated in Figure 8.3.

Reformulating after a treatment failure

An initial intervention has failed, or failed to have a significant impact on, the presenting problem. As discussed earlier this may be for many reasons other than an incorrect functional analysis. If there has been a careful elimination of the alternative explanations for treatment failure then a reformulation may be necessary.

A woman with obsessive compulsive hand washing had been placed in a relaxation training group. After the end of the group she reported that she

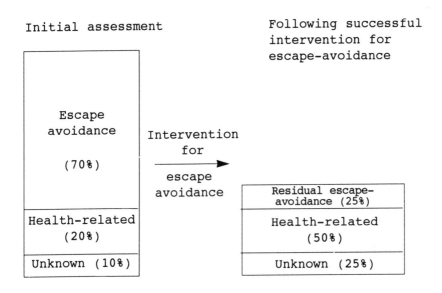

Figure 8.3 The Effect of an Initial Intervention for a Target Behavior with Several Functions (see text for discussion)

had learned to relax well and had received some benefit from this. However, the primary problem was unaffected.

A review of the case with the psychologist revealed that his initial hypothesis was that since she was unable to control her anxiety in response to contamination relaxation training would help her do that. Further, in evaluating the initial treatment it does appear that the intervention was carried out with reasonable integrity. The client had attended nearly all sessions, had learned to relax, and reported that she did use relaxation outside of therapy sessions. A reformulation was therefore justified.

In retrospect this initial functional analysis could be viewed as deficient in several ways. First, it failed to analyze the antecedents for anxiety in any detail. A more complete functional analysis would have included a hierarchy of stimuli that provoked anxiety. Second, it did not address the issue of avoidance of anxiety-provoking situations, a likely component of any anxiety-based problem. Third, obsessive compulsive rituals are very time-consuming and disruptive to others. It seemed that the functional analysis was incomplete in that it did not address the reactions of family members and friends to the problem. The failure to respond to intervention now makes sense. Relaxation would not address any of these three issues.

At this point the clinician was advised to collect more information related to these three issues by (a) interviewing the client in much more detail to establish a hierarchy of fearful stimuli, (b) interviewing the client about the reaction of others to her rituals and associated problems, and (c) interviewing one or two key family members about the problem to ascertain their reactions to her problems. This reformulation could then be used as the basis for a new plan of intervention that would be appropriate to the functions of the problem.

CONCLUDING COMMENTS

A functional analysis is a tool for a clinician to use both to understand the presenting problems and to derive a treatment based upon a knowledge of the individual circumstances and motivations of a client's problems. The functional analysis should be written down. Without doing so a clinician's work is imprecise and possibly sloppy. Explicit predictions can be made from the functional analysis in a way that can be disproved. Almost anyone can convince themselves that events make sense in retrospect. If necessary more than one functional analysis should be entertained at the same time. From each formulation different predictions can be derived and the evidence for or against each formulation be evaluated.

When interventions fail, as they often do, the clinician must carefully evaluate the reasons behind treatment failure. Reformulations should only be made after alternative explanations have been ruled out or when alternative interventions from the first functional analysis have also been tried.

Clinical Process: a Neglected Issue

This and the preceding chapter both illustrate the importance of understanding the clinical process of functional analysis. Research has focused on the tools that could be used to conduct a functional analysis. The importance of this effort should not be dismissed. There are now many methods of collecting assessment information that were not available to the clinician in the past. Also, we have a better understanding of the value of some of these methods.

Future research should focus on investigating the way clinicians behave when making a functional analysis. We need to know what methods they typically use and how they determine in which order to use these methods. We need to know if clinicians can correctly determine when low cost assessments are adequate and valid, and when high cost methods are justified. We need to know what clinicians do when faced with the demands of an entire caseload, rather than an individual client, how they assign priorities to cases. We need to know if they are able to make appropriate judgements as to when and where to focus the extra investment of resources required for some forms of functional analysis.

The judgements that clinicians make do not occur in a vacuum. The behavior of clinicians is highly responsive to the environments they work in. In some settings clinicians languish with few consequences for doing either a good or a bad job. Sometimes there are so many demands placed on them that it may not be possible to meet all those demands effectively or they may not be able to take time to plan their priorities effectively, responding to each request moment by moment. In some settings clinicians can be assisted in appropriate clinical judgement through good supervision practices, effective external monitoring, and training. The environmental support for appropriate clinical skills has not been studied extensively and directly impacts the clinician's use or misuse of functional analysis skills.

Part IV

CRITICAL ISSUES

Chapter 9

CRITICAL ISSUES IN FUNCTIONAL ANALYSIS

The preceding chapters have touched upon a wide range of conceptual and practical issues relating to functional analysis. These have included the conceptual basis of functional analysis, the use of functional analysis for assessing a presenting problem, and translating assessment into intervention. In this final chapter a number of remaining issues will be reviewed in this area of importance to both theoreticians and practitioners alike.

Like any other approach, functional analysis raises a number of critical issues. In the enthusiasm to support a position one believes in, which can advance our understanding further, and can generate effective treatments for recalcitrant problems, limitations are not attended to explicitly and sufficiently in research publications. These limitations and areas for future development are often apparent to clinicians on a day to day basis and are frequently informally acknowledged by researchers. However, in the hyperbole of early publications in a new area there can be little room for question and qualification.

A more explicitly critical evaluation of functional analysis is beginning to be found in the literature both on the limitations of particular methodologies (Sturmey, 1995a, b, c) as well as on some of the limitations in attempting to implement assessments and interventions based on functional analyses (Oliver, 1994). This review of these issues addresses four major concerns. In the first two sections we review issues of reliability and validity in functional analysis. In the third section we review issues relating to the efficacy of interventions based on functional analysis. Here we present a brief review of outcome studies based on functional analysis. In the fourth section we present a review of some of the resource implications of functional analysis.

RELIABILITY AND FUNCTIONAL ANALYSIS

In the early days of behavior analysis it was assumed that the issue of reliability had been sidestepped as we moved away from the amorphous, abstract concepts of psychoanalysis to the concrete, self-evidently valid world of behaviorism. However, comparing the behaviorism of the 1960s with that of the 1990s, one is struck by how the abstract has returned. Determining the structure of response classes, the function or multiple functions of target behaviors, piecing together a formulation, determining and evaluating a test of the formulation, and translating the formulation into a treatment, which might include changing how people think and feel, are redolent of abstraction and complexity. If reliability ever left as an issue it is back to stay.

Identifying and Operationalizing Target Behaviors

A fundamental issue in functional analysis is determining the target behaviors to be evaluated and treated. Reliability of target behavior identification is a necessary condition for the reliability of all other aspects of a functional analysis. Yet, it is surprising how little this matter has been attended to. As we saw in Chapter 7, a wide range of potentially conflicting guidelines are available to the clinician. These conflicting guidelines and the contingencies operating on the clinician could easily form the basis for problems in identifying and agreeing target behaviors.

Determining target behaviors is a social process whereby the clinician and other people attempt to reach consensus on the target behavior. At times the actual cause of a problem cannot be directly addressed. For example, in Malatesta's (1990) functional analysis of a tic the behavioral process involved a punishing father and an acquiescent mother. In this case a systems analysis might correctly address the patterns of interaction between family members as the target behaviors to change. One might target teaching the father to reinforce the son's appropriate behavior more frequently. However, making such a process explicit might completely undermine the possibility of being able to intervene. Thus, Malatesta selected the son's tic as the target behavior and intervened with the father to change his behavior in an oblique fashion. Similar issues are commonly apparent when working with teachers and residential staff. Directly addressing the issues of staff incompetence, provocative staff practices, and ineffective management practices that support incompetence in staff can be very counter-productive. There are many occasions when making the child's or resident's target behavior the apparent center of clinical concern is necessary initially in order to teach skills to staff or managers. In such situations it is not clear whether one should consider the behavior of the client or of the staff and managers to be the target behavior.

Selecting and operationalizing a target behavior is a social process with a variety of contingencies operating on the clinician. The clinician may have limited training to initially acquire good clinical skills to identify or operationalize target behaviors and the trained clinician may have poor environmental support for appropriate clinical skills. Thus, selecting and operationalizing a target behavior may be a fragile skill in functional analysis.

Reliability of identifying target behaviors

Wilson and Evans (1983) conducted an analog study of target behavior selection. They mailed written clinical vignettes to 118 members of the American Association of Behavior Therapy (AABT). The three case studies related to each of three childhood disorders—anxiety, conduct disorder, and withdrawal. Half of the subjects received vignettes relating to three problems, and half received vignettes relating to six problems. Subjects were posed for open-ended questions: (a) whether treatment was warranted; (b) to describe the child's major difficulty; (c) state treatment goals; and (d) specify and rank order treatment targets.

The results were perturbing. First, references to intra-psychic processes (e.g., 'internalized hostility'), use of diagnostic summary labels instead of operationalized target behavior, and inferred situational factors not present in the case material were all relatively common. Only approximately 20% of responses referred to specific target behaviors. Psychodynamic explanations were more likely in complex problems. Target behaviors could be rank ordered in terms of how likely raters were to nominate them as target behaviors. Shyness was nominated by over 80% of raters, whereas daydreaming was nominated by only approximately 20% of raters. Agreement on target behaviors between raters was only 39% (range 18% to 73%). Agreement was significantly poorer for the conduct disorder vignette. Agreement was not affected by complexity.

This study is very worrisome for advocates of functional analysis. If its results are valid it indicates poor agreement between raters on the apparently simple task of identifying target behaviors. This becomes even more acute given that the raters were all AABT members and presumably more knowledgeable and skilled in behavior therapy than clinicians generally. Of course, analog studies such as this, which use written case vignettes rather than free access to the child, informants, and other clinical materials may be limited. Perhaps if raters were allowed access to the full range of clinical material normally available in clinical practice agreement might be higher. Or the converse might also be true. Clinicians might be confused by the additional complexity. They might simply use the additional information to support poor clinical practice rather than develop an accurate and appropriate operationalized target behavior.

Reliability of operationalizing a target behavior

As we saw in Chapter 7 there are often many ways to operationalize a target behavior. Thus, the issue of the reliability of target behaviors refers to at least two separate processes: selecting a target behavior and subsequently operationalizing it. Even if different clinicians agree on the broad area of behavior to target they may subsequently operationalize and measure very different aspects of behavior.

In the experience of this author this issue can cause considerable consternation among clinicians. Apparently minor modifications to behavior definitions and methods of collecting data can have major implications for what is measured and for intervention. Further, the operationalization of a target behavior usually takes place early on in therapy. Future changes in behavior that have important implications for the operationalization of a target behavior, such as the emergence of a new topography, cannot always be anticipated early on.

The issue of the reliability of operationalizing a target behavior is clearly important but has many subtleties. For example, agreeing on the same target behavior may not be important for reliability if both behaviors correlate closely with each other as in the case of different members of a response class. For example, suppose a child is treated for temper tantrums. If the response class 'temper tantrums' includes both screaming and stomping feet and both responses continue to correlate with each other throughout the course of assessment and intervention, then if two independent clinicians selected these two apparently different target behaviors they would probably both produce the same results, during both the assessment and the intervention phases. On the other hand a slight difference in operationalizing a target behavior might have a major impact on reliability. For example if, when assessing and intervening with a child with daytime incontinence, one clinician selected the number of correct voidings and another selected the time in between accidents substantially different results might ensue. Although this is clearly important no published studies on this issue were located in the literature. This is clearly a neglected aspect of functional analysis.

Reliability of Identifying Functions

Most reports of the reliability of functional analysis have been focused narrowly on the reliability of certain types of data such as the reliability of items and scales on questionnaire measures or the reliability of a target behavior in an observational measure of the functions of a target behavior. Surprisingly little attention has been given to the reliability of identifying the function of the target behavior.

Interview methods

No studies were identified that assessed the reliability of interviews in assessing the functions of target behaviors. There is a literature on the procedural reliability of semi-structured interviews (Barrios, 1988). However, this addresses whether or not the interviewer correctly followed the interview procedure rather than the reliability of the conclusions drawn from the content of the interview. The effects of the quality of information from different informants, and the effects of informants who observe the person in different environments may all affect the reliability of interviews in reliably identifying the functions of target behaviors.

Unstructured, hypothesis-testing interviewing requires a considerable amount of skill, rapid thinking and judgement on the part of the clinician, and of course a certain amount of good luck. The difficulty of specifying what constitutes a hypothesis-testing interview makes it more difficult to train clinicians in this style of interviewing than in semi-structured interviewing. This may also mean that some clinicians are able to conduct this style of interview and correctly draw conclusions about the functions of a target behavior. Other clinicians may not be able to conduct this style of interviewing accurately. If this is the case then one might predict relatively poor agreement across clinicians using semi-structured interviewing.

Questionnaire measures

In Chapter 6 we reviewed the use of psychometric instruments to determine the functions of target behaviors. The results were equivocal at best. Whereas it may be possible to reliably identify the functions of behaviors through questionnaire measures, under some circumstances these circumstances may be limited.

On the other hand it should be remembered that even when the overall data are unreliable there may still be examples of individuals within the sample where there is agreement at least for those individuals (Sigafoos, Kerr & Roberts, 1994). One could still go on to correctly point out that reliability for these individuals is no guarantee of the validity of the results. However, in routine services these initial data might be a good start to a functional analysis for a proportion of cases.

Reliability of naturalistic observational measures

Much attention has been paid in observational studies to the reliability of measuring the target behavior. Generally, published observational studies report acceptably to very high reliability in measuring the target behavior. However, little attention has been paid to the issue of the reliability of observational methods to identify functions of target behaviors.

There are several aspects of observational studies which could contribute to the possible unreliability of observational measures in identifying the functions of target behaviors. First, minor procedural variations in how clinicians and researchers use the observational protocols could cause significant differences in results. Second, since there are several different observational protocols to identify the functions of target behaviors for some problems, such as self-injury, the selection of alternative observational protocols might contribute to unreliability in observational methods in identifying the functions of target behaviors in some cases. Third, the interpretation of the data might also be unreliable in some cases, especially if combined with ambiguous data from other sources.

Reliability of experimental, observational measures

There is little evidence that experimental, observational analyses of behavior are unreliable. Since, by definition, they involve turning the behavior on and off repeatedly they are, in at least one sense, reliable. However, in certain circumstances it is not always clear if the results of experimental analysis of behavior can be said to be reliable.

First, in some circumstances repeated assessments have revealed different functions on different occasions. For example, Lerman et al. (1994)

reported reassessment of four cases of self-injury in persons with developmental disabilities, using analog baselines. Four subjects were all referred following relapse after their initial treatment based on their first analog baseline assessment. In one of the four cases reassessment with analog baselines revealed that the function of the behavior was the same as on the first occasion. However, in the first analysis with this subject the results of the functional analysis were not apparent in sessions 1 through 30. Only during sessions 30 through 50 did the function become apparent. In this case there is ambiguity as to whether the results should be regarded as reliable since the ability to turn the behavior on and off was not present during the early sessions. If the analysis had stopped at session 30 one might conclude that the behavior was motivated by sensory reinforcement or other variables not addressed in the analog baselines. Thus, it is unclear if one could regard this experimental analysis of behavior as truly reliable. In all of the three remaining cases reassessment with analog baselines revealed that a new function of the behavior had apparently emerged. These reassessments took place between two months and two years after the initial assessment. So far we have few examples of repeating experimental analyses of behavior a short time after they have been conducted. It might be interesting to see if the same results are obtained. Although this is fairly likely to be the case, it might be interesting to see if this is so and to evaluate under which conditions the results are unreliable.

A second source of unreliability of experimental analysis of behavior is the graphical presentation of data. Results can be unreliable if data are difficult to interpret. Graphs can produce unreliable interpretation if the variance is high, if there are trends in the data, or if the data are not stable.

Third, there are certain procedural aspects of experimental analyses of behavior which might generate unreliability. Taking the example of Lerman *et al.* (1994) again we can note that different experimental designs were used in some cases when the traditional analog baseline multi-element design failed to yield reliable results. Again it is unclear how clinician behavior such as the choice of an experimental design might contribute to the reliability of conclusions regarding the functions of target behaviors.

Reliability and private events

Functional analysis has recently begun to take a renewed interest in private events as part of clinical practice in areas traditionally left to cognitive therapists, such as depression (Dougher & Hackbert, 1994), and to biological psychiatrists, such as psychoses (Layng & Adonis, 1984). In the field of developmental disabilities greater attention is being given to private events such as medical conditions or feeling tired as components of a functional analysis. This renewed interest in private events has not yet been accompanied by any methodological advances in the evaluation of private events. For example, although Kohlenberg and Tsai (1994) illustrate some examples of case material on how to elicit information on private events the issue of reliability of this process is noticeably absent.

Reliability of translating assessment into intervention

When a functional analysis has reliably identified the function of a target behavior the clinician still has to develop a treatment plan on the basis of those results. As we saw in Chapter 8 there are several strategies that can be used to generate interventions from the results of a functional analysis. However, there is no simple relation between the results of a functional analysis and intervention. We do not know how clinicians and treatment teams respond to these results. For example, I have observed clinicians and treatment teams develop intervention strategies that are directly contra-indicated, even though a good functional analysis was available to them.

One of the processes that can contribute to the potential unreliability of the process of translating the results of a functional analysis into intervention is that a functional analysis can indicate several interventions. For example, in the functional analysis of tics presented by Malatesta (1990) the experimental functional analysis only indicated that the boy's tic rate was reliably higher in the presence of his father compared to other persons. By combining this finding with the results of interviews with the family, Malatesta concluded that the father was insecure, perfectionistic and intolerant of minor imperfections in the boy's behavior. Such a functional analysis could suggest several interventions. For example legitimate interventions might include: (a) teach the father to be more tolerant of imperfections; (b) teach the boy to do better at school; (c) use systematic desensitization with the boy to the presence of the father and/or to his criticisms, and so on. In fact the successful intervention included none of these elements even though they were indicated by the functional analysis.

Thus, one complication in evaluating the reliability of translating a functional analysis into a treatment plan is that there is no simple one-to-one correspondence between a functional analysis and intervention. Although some interventions may be indicated and some may be contra-indicated there is considerable room for choice on the part of the clinician, and hence for error.

Functional analysis is an assessment procedure that produces stimuli for the clinician to respond to differentially. This is a complex clinical task. It is a clinical skill that is not easily learned and not easily maintained. A clinician responds to many factors other than the results of the assessment of the functions of the behavior when designing an intervention. These other factors may influence the clinician to design interventions that are contra-indicated by the functional analysis. So far we do not have any empirical studies of how clinicians respond to the results of different functional analyses while designing interventions.

Comment

Issues relating to the reliability of functional analysis are not simple. One cannot simply declare functional analysis to be reliable or unreliable. Those evaluations of the reliability of functional analysis have hitherto focused upon components of the process of functional analysis, such as the reliability of identifying a target behavior. Currently we do not have any evaluations of the reliability of the entire process of functional analysis from initial referral through to discharge. Evaluating the reliability of the entire clinical process of functional analysis from intake to discharge would be hard to conceptualize and formidable to undertake.

Some of the elements of such an undertaking are illustrated in Figure 9.1, which shows functional analysis to incorporate many stages and many decisions. Any of these steps could generate problems with reliability. Equally it may be possible for clinicians to compensate for early errors at a later stage. For example, important information missed by choosing an inappropriate assessment method might become apparent during an unsuccessful initial treatment. A skillful clinician might quickly detect this and then come to the same conclusion as would have been reached at an earlier stage, if a more appropriate assessment method had been selected. In such a situation evaluation of the reliability of certain sub-components of the process, such as selection of assessment methods, initial evaluation of the functions of the target behaviors, and selecting an intervention appropriate to the functions of the target behavior, would indicate poor reliability. However, if clinicians come to the same valid conclusion, but at different points in the clinical process, and eventually implement a treatment appropriate to the function of the target behavior would we say their overall results were reliable?

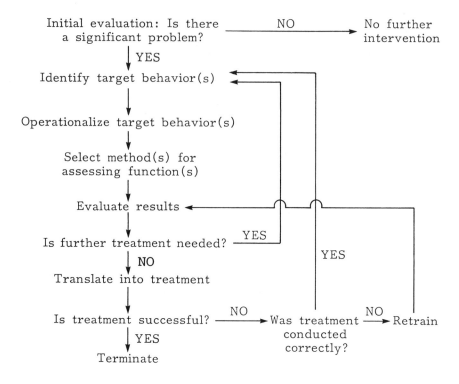

Figure 9.1 The Various Stages of a Functional Analysis that can Affect Reliability

VALIDITY

Validity, like reliability, has returned to the field of functional analysis as a major issue. Two questions regarding the validity of functional analysis are especially important. What constitutes an adequate functional analysis? and, When are the clinician's judgements valid during functional analysis?

Criteria for an Adequate Functional Analysis

Surprisingly few authors have explicitly set forth operationalized criteria for functional analysis. In this section we will review those proposed by Horner, O'Neill and Flannery (1992), Oliver and Head (1993), and by Sturmey (Chapter 8, this volume).

Horner, O'Neill and Flannery (1992) have suggested that all of four criteria must be met for a functional analysis to be adequate. First, an operational definition of the behavior(s) must be made. Second, variables that predict the occurrence and non-occurrence of the problem behaviors should be identified. This should include both immediate antecedents and more temporally distant establishing and abolishing operations. Third, the maintaining consequences of the behavior should be identified. Finally, verification, or testing of the clinical hypotheses, is a necessary criterion for an adequate formulation (Baer, Wolf & Risley, 1968; Skinner, 1953). Horner, O'Neill and Flannery's criteria require that both behaviors and current environmental events are clearly specified, and that the hypothesis is verified through environmental manipulation.

Oliver and Head (1993) reviewed criteria for an adequate functional analysis suggested by earlier reviews (Blackman, 1985; Kiernan, 1973). They suggest that three criteria must be met. These were 'that behavior (B) is considered in terms of the influence of events preceding the behavior, or its antecedents (A), and the events consequent (C) upon it . . . That the influences of antecedents and consequences should be empirically demonstrated . . . That all necessary and sufficient conditions for a behavior to occur should be considered' (Oliver & Head, 1993, p. 14). Although this definition shares certain features with Horner, O'Neill and Flannery's definition the third criterion is a stringent sting in the tail. In order to demonstrate 'all the necessary and sufficient conditions for a behavior to occur' is indeed a tall order. While this definition indeed anticipates the importance of establishing and disestablishing operations on a simple ABC relationship it is hard to imagine such a very comprehensive analysis of behavior being performed routinely. A further criticism is that this definition is somewhat vague as it only requires that these criteria are 'considered'. It does not state what would constitute an adequate consideration of these factors.

In Table 8.1 ten criteria for an adequate written functional analysis were specified. Although broadly similar to those proposed by Horner, O'Neill and Flannery there are some important differences. These criteria are more detailed than those proposed by Horner and colleagues and may be of greater assistance in training new clinicians. The criteria also require additional information such as details relating to development of the problem, possible secondary gains, and the implications for intervention. However, these criteria do not require an experimental validation as the Horner, O'Neill and Flannery criteria do.

So far we do not have validation data on different sets of criteria for a functional analysis. Clinicians, students and teachers would probably find major differences between written functional analyses that score low versus those that score high on any of the three sets of criteria reviewed above. It is likely that functional analyses with similar scores on one of these sets of criteria would probably get similar scores on the other two sets of criteria. Those clinicians and researchers who are closely wedded to the experimental analysis of behavior would probably find anything other than an experimental manipulation of observable behavior unacceptable.

The principal difference between these two approaches is the status of verifying a written, functional analysis based on correlational data. Without this information a functional analysis is generally on weaker ground. The information in correlation may contain confounds between variables, and may be complex, and thus lead to errors of clinical judgement. On the other hand correlational approaches are generally easier to conduct, and can also be applied to a very wide range of problems, that may not readily lend themselves to experimental manipulation.

Having information from an experimental analysis of behavior is clearly desirable. It places the functional analysis on a firm footing that a descriptive analysis of behavior does not. However, the experimental analysis of behavior is costly in terms of time and specialized clinical skills. It does not match up with current office-based clinical practice. Further, the manipulation of the target behavior may be unethical, if the target behavior is very dangerous, such as suicide threats and attempts (Sturmey, 1995a), or very difficult to conduct if the behavior is infrequent (Sturmey, 1995b). The differences between descriptive and experimental functional analyses can be viewed as a cost-benefit issue. Generally descriptive approaches are cheaper, but may lead to lower quality information. Generally, experimental approaches are more costly but may lead to better quality information. There are, of course, exceptions to both of these generalizations.

Convergent Validity

If different methods of assessing the functions of target behaviors are valid then assessment with different methodologies should converge on similar conclusions. There have been few evaluations of the convergent validity of different methods of functional analysis outside of the field of developmental disabilities. Those reports that have been made have been rather disappointing. Poor agreement was reported between questionnaire and observational measures used to assess the functions of stereotyped behavior by Crawford, Brockel, Schauss and Miltenberger (1993). Oliver (1991) found very poor agreement across questionnaire, interview, and analog baseline measures in assessing the functions of self-injury.

These results may be explicable in part by the generally poor reliability of questionnaire measures (Sturmey, 1994). Thus, if other methods are valid there would be poor agreement between valid and invalid measures. Oliver and Head (1993) suggest that the ability of different methods to adequately identify the functions of target behaviors reflects their ability to meet the three requirements they suggest are necessary for an adequate functional analysis (see the discussion above). They suggest that clinical interviews can assess ABCs and can identify necessary and sufficient conditions for a behavior, but cannot manipulate variables experimentally. Naturalistic observations, including ABC diaries, are limited because they do not manipulate the environment and may not identify all the necessary and sufficient conditions for a behavior. Experimental studies, such as analog baselines, meet the second criterion, but are limited in the range of variables considered and therefore only meet the first two, but not the third criterion.

Clinical Judgement and Treatment Validity

The role of clinical judgement in conducting a functional analysis has not been sufficiently acknowledged. However, clinical judgement issues can be found at every juncture in the process of functional analysis. Reviews of clinical judgement typically reveal a rather pessimistic view of the clinician's abilities to make complex decisions (Rock et al., 1987, 1988). Rock et al. suggest that clinicians are often unreliable in complex decision making such as that involved in diagnosis, fail to combine information from multiple sources well, fail to learn from experience if there is no explicit feedback on their performance, do no better in clinical prediction than lay judges, and are unjustifiably overconfident in the validity of their performance. Although this literature has typically been in the context of making decisions such as diagnosis it can be taken as one example of human complex decision making. Thus, some of these findings may well apply to the behavior of clinicians attempting to process the complex information and decision making involved in functional analysis.

Variables affecting clinical judgement

Several variables have been shown to affect clinical judgement—unfortunately, informing clinicians about their likely biases is not one of them. Giving clinicians more information can make them more confident, but not necessarily more accurate. Several studies have showed that professional training does not yield better clinical predictions, or at most only marginally small improvements. Training does not affect strategies used during hypothesis testing. This latter conclusion could be especially pertinent to functional analysis, a process that is explicitly driven by clinical hypotheses (Rock *et al.*, 1987, 1988).

The tetrahedron model

Rock *et al.* (1987, 1988) argue that the literature in this area is limited due to its lack of ecological validity. For example, clinicians in these studies may have been so constrained that the tasks and decisions were too unlike real life decision making to accurately reflect their day to day behavior. In defense of this ecological approach they note that under some circumstances clinicians do outperform naïve judges in some complex tasks. They propose that the ecological validity of clinical judgement should be considered from a tetrahedron model which considers therapist characteristics, the clinical judgement task, the kinds of clinical materials available to the therapist, and the learning activities included in the task (Jenkins, 1979).

These four aspects of the tetrahedron model can be readily applied to the processes involved in developing a functional analysis. Therapist characteristics include more than years of experience. Also relevant are their skills in using the methods of functional analysis, and their clinical knowledge, proficiency and experience in using the methods of functional analysis. Criterial tasks include the kinds of tasks to be conducted such as selection of assessment methods, making a formulation, testing the formulation, translating it into a treatment, and evaluating the intervention. Clinical material again is highly relevant since it refers to the range of information available to the clinician. Under certain circumstances a clinician may only be able to work from information available from one source, such as third party informants at a case conference, or from observation when walking through a classroom. In other situations a wide range of clinical materials may be available for use during a functional analysis. Finally, learning activities refers to the opportunities for feedback and the kind of feedback available to clinicians on their performance as well as the opportunity to correct apparent errors. Given the possibility that interventions can be successful when a functional analysis is incorrect, or that a functional analysis can be correct, but intervention fail for a variety of reasons (Lerman *et al.*, 1994) the relationship between the clinician's performance and the outcome of intervention may be an indirect one.

Judgement prostheses for clinicians

The area of clinical judgement in functional analysis has hitherto been underplayed, yet its importance may have been implicitly acknowledged in a number of ways. Several technological developments can be viewed as developing decision-making prostheses to assist clinicians in appropriate clinical decision making during functional analysis. The use of behavioral diagnostics can be seen as a way to limit the number of choices that a clinician may have as to the possible functions of behavior. This limited number of options is then used to direct the selection of interventions by indicating those interventions that are appropriate and those that are contra-indicated. In this way the behavior of the clinician is restricted and supported in the right direction. Clinical workbooks such as that by O'Neill *et al.* (1991) guide the clinician through the maze of decisions to be made by laying out a number of stages to work through and a number of clinical tools for the clinician to use at each stage. So far, the value of these devices in assisting clinicians in appropriate decision making, and in developing treatments that are more effective than those that otherwise would have been implemented, has yet to be evaluated. Other methods of supporting appropriate clinical skills such as feedback mechanisms or supervision practices have not yet been developed or evaluated for use in functional analysis.

TREATMENT OUTCOME AND FUNCTIONAL ANALYSIS

Part of the central dogma of functional analysis is that treatments based on an individualized functional analysis will be superior to those based on other approaches. Thus, interventions based on a functional analysis should be more effective than behavioral treatments that are not based upon a functional analysis, the most effective treatment for a particular diagnostic category as indicated by a systematic review of the literature, or by a randomly selected, but very plausible intervention. This dogma is a direct reflection of a functionalist rather than a structuralist approach. The outcome of treatments based on functional analysis relates not only to the usual questions relating to the efficacy, efficiency, and ethics of treatment selection. It also addresses questions fundamental to the validity of functional analysis.

The number of published case studies and case series using functional analysis is very large and a comprehensive review will not be attempted. Rather, a selective approach will be used to illustrate some of the issues at hand. For the sake of convenience the studies will be organized into four groups: uncontrolled, descriptive case studies; experimental case studies; experimental case studies involving comparison of treatments; and, finally, group studies.

Uncontrolled, Descriptive Case Studies

A large number of uncontrolled descriptive case studies have been published which provide some general description of treatment outcome. Some examples of these are summarized in Table 9.1. For a large number of illustrations of case studies based on functional analysis the interested reader is referred to West and Spinks (1988).

Redd and Rusch (1985) present a number of case studies of behavior problems associated with cancer and its treatment. They present two patients who had acute leukemia. During part of their treatment they had to be isolated for over three weeks due to compromised immune function. Thus, following a period of free access to frequent social contact they were suddenly placed in an environment with very little social contact. The first patient developed a raspy cough and the second patient developed itching which did not clear up following the resolution of an initial physical cause. Analysis of an observational baseline revealed that symptoms were strongly associated with the presence of staff for both patients. Redd and Rusch hypothesized that the presence of staff was exerting stimulus control over the problem and that staff were inadvertently reinforcing the symptoms. On the basis of this assumption they implemented a simple program of extinction and differential reinforcement. This intervention was highly effective. Comparison of pre- and post-data on symptom frequency revealed a statistically and clinically significant difference in the symptom frequency for both patients.

This study and those listed in Table 9.1 reveal some of the advantages and disadvantages of uncontrolled case studies. They are clinically very rich. They often illustrate quirky and ingenious clinical practice. However, they do not address the key question being considered here. Even when such case studies are supported by data the results remain

Table 9.1 A Summary of some Case Studies Using Functional Analysis with some Description of Outcome

Reference	Population and clinical area
Bergman (1976)	Childhood insomnia/hyperactivity
Frankel (1975)	Childhood behavior problems
Kearney & Silverman (1990)	School refusal
Layng & Andronis (1984)	Delusional speech and hallucinatory behavior
McKinley, Kelly & Collum (1977)	Conversion reaction in adolescence
Redd and Rusch (1985)	Behavior problems in cancer patients
West & Spinks (1988)	Wide range of clinical cases
De Seixas Queiroz, Motta, Madi et al. (1981)	Obsessive-compulsive disorders
Wolpe (1989)	Adult neuroses

ambiguous since change could be due to such causes as spontaneous remission or non-specific effects of therapy, rather than the treatment itself. In particular, uncontrolled case studies do not directly compare treatments based upon functional analysis with other treatments. A further comment is warranted. In the cases discussed, the functional analysis was not directly tested during assessment. It remained a hypothesis. Such testing of functional analysis prior to treatment is seen as a necessary requirement to confirm the validity of the functional analysis and thus treatment failures might simply be explained by the initial assessment not being complete.

Experimental, Single Case Studies

A wide range of experimental, single case studies have been published. Some examples of these are listed in Table 9.2. As an example let us consider Mace *et al.* (1988) who evaluated a treatment based upon a functional analysis of bizarre, psychotic speech. The subject was a 29-year-old woman diagnosed as schizophrenic with mildly developmental disabilities. The initial functional analysis was conducted using informal observations, interviews with staff and analog baseline conditions (Iwata *et al.*, 1982). This revealed that bizarre speech was greatest during demand conditions. Based on this formulation, treatment consisted of guided compliance through task demands and ignoring bizarre speech. The treatment was evaluated using an ABAB experimental design. The respective rates of bizarre speech were 3.0, 1.3, 7.7 and 1.4 per minute, and for task completion were 0.5, 1.3, 0.7 and 1.5.

Table 9.2   Experimental, Single Case Studies which Evaluate Functional
Analysis

Reference	Participant	Behaviors
Mace *et al.* (1988)	Adult with developmental disabilities and schizophrenia	Bizarre speech; compliance
Malatesta (1990)	Child	Eye tic
McNight *et al.* (1984)	Adults	Depression
Repp *et al.* (1989)	Children with developmental delays	Stereotypy and self-injury
Day *et al.* (1986, 1988)	Children with developmental disabilities	Self-injury
Parrish *et al.* (1985)	Children with developmental delays	Self injury and stereotypy
Carr & Durand (1985)	Children	Behavior problems
Goren, Romanczk & Harris (1977)	Children with autism	Echolalia

Thus, experimental control clearly indicated that the behavior could be effectively reduced by the treatment. A further experimental study in the client's home group replicated these results.

There are a wide range of studies such as this, which have reported the outcome of treatments based upon a functional analysis. (See Iwata, Vollmer & Zarcone, 1990, for a review of those studies in persons with developmental disabilities.) However, this research strategy does not answer the question at hand here. Although they demonstrate that treatments derived from a function analysis can be highly effective, they do not demonstrate the superiority of treatments based upon a functional analysis over those which are not since no direct comparison between them is made.

Comparative Studies

A number of studies, again almost all of which are single case studies, have attempted to compare treatments derived from an initial functional analysis with alternate treatments. These studies are important because they begin to address the important issue at hand—comparing treatments derived from a functional analysis with other treatments.

McNight *et al.* (1984) evaluated treatments for depression. The subjects were nine adult out-patients selected from a group of 72 women volunteers. Subjects had to be over 18 years old, not under any current professional care, and had to meet research diagnostic and psychometric criteria for depression. The nine subjects were constituted by meeting criteria for three different functional types of depression: social skills deficits, irrational cognition, or both. Subjects were classified on the basis of a battery of assessments used to develop a functional analysis of their depression. All subjects received eight weeks of therapy in an alternating treatment design. The interventions were social skills training or rational-emotive therapy. Outcome was assessed using multiple measures of affect, social behavior and global self-ratings of depression. In general, treatments based upon the initial assessment were the most effective. Thus, depressed subjects with social skills deficits improved most when they received social skills training on measures of social skills and depression. Depressed subjects with irrational cognition improved most after receiving cognitive therapy or measures of cognition and depression. Thus, this study supports the hypothesis that intervention based on a functional analysis is more effective than other, plausible interventions.

There are many such studies in the developmental disabilities field. For example, Repp, Felce and Barton (1988) implemented treatments for stereotypy and self-injury on the basis of an initial observational assessment of the functions of self-injury. Observations of subject 2 revealed that this subject showed very little engaged behavior and had few opportunities presented to him during the baseline. Thus, the self-stimulation hypotheses was supported. Treatment based on this hypothesis was experimentally compared with treatment based upon the positive reinforcement hypothesis. Treatment based upon the self-stimulation hypothesis consisted of compliance training, presenting many opportunities for engagement, and training in groups. Treatment based on the positive reinforcement hypothesis was extinction. This consisted of removing all the consequences of the behavior identified during baseline observations. Using a multiple baseline design across settings Repp, Felce and Barton showed that only treatment based on the self-stimulation hypothesis was effective. Furthermore, this finding was replicated across two other subjects. There are numerous other comparative treatment studies producing similar results in favor of treatments based on functional analysis in persons with developmental disabilities (Iwata, Vollmer & Zarcone, 1990).

At first sight these studies provide strong support for the efficiency of treatments based on a functional analysis. Although a detailed review of such papers would reveal the usual litany of methodological problems in this field—lack of long-term follow-up, lack of measures of treatment integrity, poor subject description, and so on—it would still be true that these papers fairly uniformly show the superiority of treatments based on functional analysis. However, careful examination of this strategy reveals a fundamental problem. In this strategy the treatment selected as a control is *directly contra-indicated* by the functional analysis. That is, the control treatment selected is one which is particularly likely to fail. The most appropriate control treatment would be one that is likely to be effective, but not based upon the functional analysis of the individual case. Thus, an appropriate control treatment for the McNight *et al.* (1984) study might have been the most effective anti-depressant medication combined with the most effective package of cognitive-behavioral treatments for depression based upon a literature review. Similarly, in treating maladaptive behaviors in persons with developmental disabilities the most appropriate control treatment might be differential reinforcement of incompatible behavior with some aversive consequence for the target behavior. Such a strategy would clearly be a conservative one, but if treatments based on a functional analysis are superior to best alternatives, then the case for treatments based upon functional analysis is strong. If the results of such comparisons are equivalent how can the extra resources required to conduct a functional analysis be justified?

Analog baselines: Iwata's series

Iwata *et al.* (1994) present a retrospective analysis of 152 cases of self-injury in persons with developmental disabilities evaluated using analog baselines accumulated over ten years of work. This is an amazing piece of work!

The results strongly supported the efficacy of interventions based on functional analysis and the lack of effectiveness of those treatments that were contra-indicated by a functional analysis. Single functions were identified for 90% of cases. More than one function was identified for a further 5% of cases. Strong interactions between the results of the functional analysis and the response to treatment were found. For example, in self-injury motivated by social-positive reinforcement, attention-extinction was effective in almost all applications whereas response interruption was never associated with effective treatment. For behavior motivated by social-negative reinforcement (task avoidance) attention-extinction and time out were never effective whereas escape-extinction was nearly always effective. These, and other similar findings, strongly support the efficacy of interventions based on analog baselines.

The current status of analog baselines is controversial (Oliver, 1991; Oliver & Head, 1993; Sturmey, 1995c). Analog baselines have been criticized because they focus on a narrow range of variables, do not yield a complete functional analysis (Oliver & Head, 1993), and are appropriate for only a relatively narrow range of problems (Sturmey, 1995c). Further, the role of other concurrent treatments such as psychotropic medications was not discussed (Sturmey, 1995c). The most telling criticism for the current review is again that the control treatment used in analog baselines is one that is especially likely to fail. It would be interesting for future research to compare treatments indicated by analog baselines with a treatment that is especially likely to be effective based on a literature review.

The Bochum Anxiety-Therapy Project

The Bochum Anxiety-Therapy Project directly evaluated interventions based on functional analysis with a plausible, best behavioral treatment for anxiety disorders (Schulte, Kunzel, Pepping & Scholte-Bahrenbert, 1992). The subjects all met DSM-III criteria for phobia and met no other diagnostic criteria, such as depression, although some had multiple phobias. The most common diagnosis was agoraphobia (78%). The subject's average age was 39 years, 64% were female, and the average duration of the phobia was over 17 years. Most had received previous treatments: 85% had received previous pharmacological treatments and 58% had received previous psychological treatments. Thus, this sample appears to be a real, clinical sample rather than an analog sample with mild problems.

A sample of 120 patients were assigned randomly to three groups. Group one received individualized therapy. This consisted of an individual treatment plan based upon a behavior-diagnostic interview schedule. The treatment could be revised as sessions went on. Group two received a standardized therapy: exposure and retraining of self-verbalizations. The therapy was standardized in a manual. The yoked control group received an individualized tailored therapy developed for a subject in group one. Thus, although the therapy is individually tailored it should be irrelevant to the function of the subject's problem in group three who received it. Outcome was assessed by questionnaire measures completed by the patient, goal attainment scaling, a method of rating outcomes on individually set goals prior to the beginning of treatment, and global ratings by the patient and therapist.

From the perspective of functional analysis the results were very disappointing. *All* treatments led to statistically significant improvements. Comparison of progress of the three groups across time showed that patients receiving standardized treatment made the most rapid progress during treatment. As treatment progressed these differences between the three groups gradually reduced until no significant differ-ences were left at six-month follow-up. Thus, at six-month follow up the group receiving intervention based on functional analysis were doing no better than the standardized exposure and cognitive therapy group or even the yoked control group who were receiving treatments irrelevant to the functions of their phobias. Since it appeared that the *in vivo* exposure might have been a key element which accounted for the difference between the standardized and individualized treatment groups, subjects within the individualized treatment groups were compared who did and did not receive exposure treatment. As expected, subjects who received exposure treatment did better than those who did not in the individualized treatment groups.

The results of this study seriously question the treatment validity of functional analysis. However, a number of features of the study might contribute to its validity being limited. First, the therapists in the study were relatively inexperienced. The median number of patients treated prior to this project was only 9 patients (range 0 to over 200). Although therapists with a better experience of clinical work may have had better success no such correlation was found within this sample of therapists. Second, better therapist training in functional analysis may have been able to assist therapists to conduct both functional analyses and therapy more effectively. This may be especially true for those therapists who were very inexperienced. Third, since the therapists used the standar-dized form of therapy on a third of all the subjects the therapists would be more practiced with the standardized form of therapy. Fourth, as noted earlier in this volume, the difficulties in defining what constitutes an adequate functional analysis can make it difficult to say with cer-tainty that a functional analysis was truly conducted. Whereas it is possible for the therapists to follow a predetermined assessment schedule correctly, this may not adequately constitute a valid functional analysis. Thus, although at first sight the Bochum Anxiety-Therapy Project appears to be a serious challenge to the belief that a functional analysis yields interventions that are more effective than treatments that are not based on a functional analysis, this study has some limitations that may seriously mitigate such a conclusion. Nevertheless, it clearly throws down the gauntlet to those who strongly believe that functional analysis yields interventions that are more effective than other approaches to clearly substantiate this hypothesis with data.

Functional Analysis as Treatment

As noted in Chapter 1, one of the connotations of functional analysis is that of functional analysis as treatment. Thus, in many treatment packages such as anger management, anxiety management, and cognitive-behavioral treatments for alcohol and substance misuse, functional analysis is included as one treatment component. This may take the form of simply sharing the functional analysis with the client and explaining the rationale for treatment. In some cases it may involve the client collecting data, coming to understand the functions of their problematic behaviors, and participating in the development of their own treatment plan on the basis of a shared understanding of the functional analysis.

A comprehensive review of the outcome literature in this area is beyond the scope of this chapter. However, the most important point in this regard is that no studies were located in which the functional analysis component was isolated from other elements of the treatment package. Thus, it is unclear if working with the client on the functional analysis is an effective treatment component. It would be an interesting question to see if getting a client to work out a functional analysis of their own problem would be superior to any other treatments which involve active participation in therapy.

Functional Analysis, Reinforcement and Punishment

A functional analysis can imply several intervention strategies and the clinician is free to select from a variety of implied treatments when translating the results of the functional analysis into an intervention. For example if, using Kearney and Silverman's (1990) assessment battery to evaluate school refusal, the clinician determines that school refusal is maintained by positive reinforcement for remaining at home by access to preferred leisure activities and through negative reinforcement by avoidance of school work, what intervention should the clinician use?

One option is to reschedule access to leisure activities by only permitting access contingent on attending school. A second option is to add on additional school work for every hour spent at home. Strategy three would be to consequate every day at home with additional school work and not to alter access to the leisure activity. Which strategy should the clinician use? Strategy one may be more acceptable than strategies two and three since it does not involve punishment. However, intervention strategies that use reinforcement only are less likely to be effective than interventions and punishment. Strategy two is more likely to change behavior quickly than either of the other strategies because it reschedules the reinforcer maintaining behavior, and includes contingent punishment. Strategy three is least likely to be effective because it does not reschedule a reinforcer maintaining school refusal, although a powerful punisher will change behavior in the face of reinforcement of the target behavior if the punisher is powerful and the reinforcer is only moderately effective. Also, the third strategy may be least acceptable because of lack of positive elements.

In some situations the strategies that are indicated by a functional analysis may be only weak and behavior may only change slowly if at all. In other circumstances where a quick behavior is needed, for example when a client may pose a severe danger to themselves or others, inclusion of punishers indicated by a functional analysis may be an effective strategy. However, the issue then arises as to whether an intervention based on rescheduling the reinforcers and punishers indicated by the functional analysis would be any more effective than an intervention based on introducing reinforcers and punishers that are derived empirically rather than through a functional analysis (Fisher, Piazza, Bowman, 1994a, b).

Comment

As with so many other intervention strategies, the outcome literature on functional analysis is ambiguous. It is clear that treatments based upon functional analysis can be highly effective. However, there is as yet no unequivocal evidence or consensus that conducting a functional analysis yields additional treatment validity above and beyond other, valid treatment alternatives. This may seem unduly pessimistic a condition to some. However, it may reflect the relative youth of this field. Most studies have aimed to establish that treatments based upon functional analysis can be effective rather than tackling the more fundamental question of relative treatment efficacy.

The literature on treatment outcome also highlights other important issues. The evaluation of interventions based on functional analysis may be somewhat more complex than evaluating a specific treatment. A functional analysis may indicate a wide range of different therapies to be appropriate, rather than any specific treatment. The integrity of treatments based on a functional analysis can only be shown if there is clear evidence that the functional analysis was conducted in a valid manner and that the treatments implemented are clearly indicated by the functional analysis. These are key requirements for the evaluation of treatments based on functional analysis without which we cannot evaluate the incremental treatment validity of functional analysis. Because we do not have clear criteria by which to evaluate the selection of target behaviors, the analysis of the controlling variables, and the conversion of such an analysis into a treatment, the evaluation of treatments based on functional analysis remains difficult.

Finally, we noted that little attention has been focused on engaging clients to conduct a functional analysis of their own problems. There are few training materials for clients to use and little information on how best to train clients in this key activity. Future research could attend to this matter.

RESOURCE IMPLICATIONS

Services need to be efficient and economic in the balance between resources invested into additional assessments and the likely benefits to be accrued by the client needing to be assessed. Resources invested in the assessment of one client are resources which are not allocated to their treatment or to the care of other clients. If conducting a functional analysis consumes resources beyond that of other assessment and treatment methods then there should be an overall benefit to all parties concerned beyond that which would have been accrued through using other interventions.

Concerns related to resource issues can be seen constantly in the literature on functional analysis. For example, analog baselines, which were developed in the early 1980s (Iwata et al., 1982), are relatively expensive in terms of expertise needed to conduct them, the cost in staff time to conduct them and subsequently analyze the data. It was partly in reaction to this problem that psychometric instruments were developed. In this section we review three aspects of the costs and benefits to functional analysis: the development of cheaper functional analyses, the costs of assessment failure, and the merits and limitations of simple versus complex formulations.

Towards Cheaper, Effective Functional Analysis

One example of a recent development of observational methods has been the development of relatively rapidly performed functional analyses based in an out-patient clinic (Steege, Wacker, Berg et al., 1989). In this approach to conducting relatively rapid functional analyses of severe behavior problems Steege et al. (1989) combined direct assessment of reinforcer preferences and analog baseline-like observational assessments of the functions of these behaviors. In their first study Steege *et al.* worked with an 8-year-old boy who was non-verbal and non-ambulatory and displayed chronic hand mouthing which had produced skin irritation and damage. During baseline sessions two responses were recorded: self-injury (SIB) and pressing a microswitch. During baseline assessment they found that both a fan and a radio were highly reinforcing stimuli and that activation of the microswitch was associated with major decreases in SIB. Observation of three naturally occurring conditions showed that the rate of SIB varied dramatically as a function of the task available. SIB was observed during 68% of intervals while toileting, during 57% while positioning and during 0% of intervals during vocational training. On the basis of this information it was hypothesized that the behavior was maintained by self-stimulation since it occurred when reinforcement and activity were not available. Therefore, treatment of self-injurious behavior consisted of making the microswitch and reinforcers available during the two conditions when SIB was frequent. Data showed that clinically significant gains were achieved and maintained at 6-month follow-up.

In order to extend this methodology further Northup *et al.* (1991) developed an out-patient service to conduct a functional analysis in approximately 90 minutes. An extensive questionnaire is used prior to appointment to develop probable target behaviors, select reinforcers for use during assessment and develop possible clinical analog experiments, hypotheses for testing during assessment. For each client three classes of responses were recorded. These were (a) aggression, (b) appropriate behavior, and (c) an alternative behavior, such as recognizable speech, sign or gesture. Only relevant conditions are selected from analog baselines and are administered only once. On the basis of this initial data a hypothesis about the maintaining conditions is made and a treatment is developed from that hypothesis. The treatment is evaluated by a single reversal design. For example, Curtis was assessed with only the Alone and Escape analog conditions. He displayed aggression during 23% and 12% of intervals during the Escape condition, and none during the Alone condition. He was never observed to sign. During the treatment evaluation escape from task demands was used as a reinforcer and signing 'please' was prompted as a demand for escape. Although he never completed the set tasks his aggression reduced to 3% and 8%, became very mild—light taps, rather than bruising the experimenter—and was generally less resistant to prompting. Thus, Northup *et al.* developed a method of conducting a functional analysis on an out-patient basis which was rapid and resulted in treatment proposals being made and evaluated following 90 minutes of observational assessment.

A second example of the development of economic approaches to conducting functional analyses was the development and evaluation of a technical assistance model, by Northup, Wacker, Berg *et al.* (1994). The work took place in a school for children with severe disabilities. The technical assistance model consisted of a two-day workshop, and an initial project in which staff worked in teams to develop a functional analysis with the author acting as model for the first functional analysis. Further supervision was available through supervision half a day a week over an 18-month period. Over this period of time staff were able to independently conduct functional analyses and implement successful interventions based on them. One criticism of this study is that the exact process of consultation and training is not well defined in the article (Milne, 1986). Nevertheless, this study acts as a model for developing the functional analysis skills of other staff in a variety of settings and populations.

One final example of a more economic approach to functional analysis comes from a study by Paisey, Whitney and Hislop (1991) who modified analog baseline into direct assessment conducted during mealtimes. In this way there was less disruption to the person's life and there could be additional benefits in terms of increased validity, since the conditions were conducted with real tasks with the regular staff conducting the procedure.

The Cost of Assessment Failure

The importance of weighing the costs of functional analysis has recently been highlighted by reports that sometimes functional analysis does not yield results (Sturmey, 1995b; Vollmer, Marcus & LeBlanc, 1994). Sturmey (1995b) reported a case in which extensive efforts were made at a functional analysis of self-injury. These methods included questionnaires, informal observations, analog baselines, individually tailored experimental analyses of behavior, and analysis of the behavior rate with pollen counts. These analyses were all unsuccessful in identifying a function for the behavior. It was estimated that during the course of this extensive period of evaluation the subject exhibited several million acts of self-injury. Vollmer, Marcus and LeBlanc (1994) were able to successfully intervene with self-injury and hand mouthing after analog baselines failed to yield results as to the function of the behavior. Intervention consisted of fairly simple strategies such as environmental enrichment and contingent reinforcement. Such interventions could have been implemented earlier without any functional analysis.

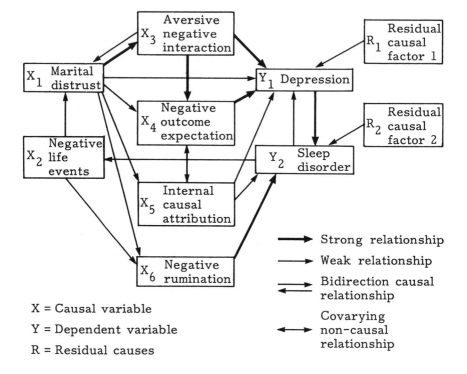

Figure 9.2 Functional Analytic Causal Model of Client Whose Primary Presenting Complaints were Sleep Onset, Insomnia and Behavioral Depression (e.g., decreased social interaction, decreased recreational behaviors)

Reproduced with permission from: Haynes, S. W. and O'Brien, W. H. (1990). Functional analysis in behavior therapy. *Clinical Psychology Review*, **10**, 649–668. Copyright © Pergamon Press

Simple and Complex Formulations

Some methodologies which could be used in functional analysis are complex and potentially expensive in terms of collecting data, analysis, and interpretation. Haynes has published several papers on causal models as functional analyses of presenting problems in clinical psychology (Haynes & O'Brien, 1990). An example is reproduced in Figure 9.2. This model illustrates bi-directional relationships, multiple causal pathways, the strengths of causal pathways, relationships that are medicated by other variables, and causal and non-causal functional relationships between variables.

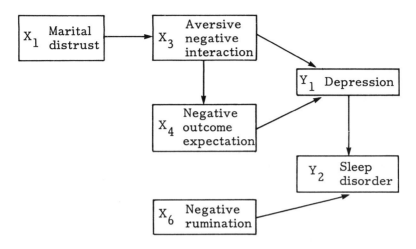

Figure 9.3   A Simplified Version of Figure 9.2

Such models appear to be relatively complete accounts of the clinical problems. They do, however, present a range of resource issues. First, the difficulties in establishing truly causal relationships are enormous in routine clinical practice. The development of a model, such as that in Figure 9.2, requires assessment of 10 variables and 20 relationships between variables. Second, such a model is complex. It is unclear if there is any additional incremental treatment validity from the additional complexity. Indeed, the additional complexity may confuse the clinician. For example, Figure 9.3 represents a highly simplified version of Figure 9.2. In this simplified model only strong relationships have been drawn and variables X3 and X4 have been combined to one variable. From such a simplified formulation points of intervention are clarified—marital distrust and negative rumination. The robustness of such an approach depends on how strong the causal relationships are, and how much of the variability in the problems relates only to these major relationships. It is unclear when and where the additional time and energy in delineating all the existing relationships pays off in terms of treatments which are more effective.

As well as the cost in time, extensive assessment might involve other costs. These include the cost of delay in treatment implementation to the client. Extensive assessment might result in personal distress and discomfort, or in some cases, more extreme risks when a problem goes untreated. Also, in some cases, the assessment procedure itself might be dangerous. For example, in Iwata *et al.*'s (1982) work on analog base-lines to assess self-injury nursing staff were available if needed. Thus, functional analysis, like all treatment and assessment methods, continues to raise numerous, unresolved issues relating to resources.

CONCLUDING COMMENTS

Functional analysis has become a major force within clinical practice (Dougher, 1994; Neef, 1994; West & Spinks, 1988). Within certain sub-groups of behavioral practitioners it is the major influence on their clinical work (Milne, 1994; Shook, 1993). The influence of functional analysis has been most markedly felt in the field of developmental disabilities (Iwata, Vollmer & Zarcone, 1990) although its application can also be seen in a wide variety of populations in both research and clinical practice (Milne, 1994; Milne & Ridley, 1994). Research can be found on such diverse problems as childhood behavior disorders, depression, eating disorders, criminological psychology (Hollin, 1990), chronic mental health problems (Scotti, McMorrow & Trawitz, 1993) and behavioral geriatrics (Bakke, Kvale, Burns *et al.*, 1994). In a national survey of behavior therapists in the United Kingdom the majority of practitioners reported that the most common problems they worked with were anxiety, depression, and behavior problems (Milne, 1994). Recently several behavioral journals which were primarily interested in theoretical issues have published special issues or sections on applications of theory to practice (Dougher, 1994). This rapid expansion is indicative of a new, healthy, growing area of research and practice.

The critical issues raised in this final chapter should stimulate further developments and critical debate which eventually will lead to improved understanding and interventions for the clients we serve. Behavioral research has been characterized by relatively rigorous empirical evaluation research and critical review. This should be taken in the spirit in which it is intended. Namely, the more important the issues and the more promising the methodology, the more thorough the critical review should be in order to stimulate further research in the area. To review a field critically is not to damn it, but rather to compliment it as worthy of attention.

Future Directions

The last 15 years have seen a rapid expansion of the methodologies available to use to assist the clinician and researcher develop a functional analysis. This line of research can be expanded in a number of ways. These methodologies need further refinement and development (Sturmey, 1994, 1995c). Existing methods can be developed for use in other populations and new problems (Bakke *et al.*, 1994; Kearney & Silverman, 1990; Munck & Repp, 1994; Pace, Iwata, Cowdery *et al.*, 1994). It would be especially helpful to clinicians if the strategy described as 'mini-experiments' could be developed further. There is a need for the development of methodologies that are brief, economic and meet the requirements of experimental control.

Certain areas such as long-term care for people with continuing psychiatric disorders have been very neglected (Scotti, McMorrow & Trawitz, 1993) although significant impact can be seen in some settings on assessment and case management (Hall & Baker, 1994). This relative neglect is ironic since some of the earliest work on functional analysis was done with this population (Ayllon, Haughton & Hughes, 1965). Further, some chronic psychiatric problems which are refractory to psychotropic medication may be responsive to environmental assessment and manipulation (e.g., Haddock, Benthall & Slade, 1994; Morrison, 1994).

Although expansion and refinement of existing methodologies is important, a broader expansion of functional analysis methodologies is also called for. Most important is that greater attention should be paid to the process of functional analysis. Methodologies that are reliable will not by themselves assist a clinician who is unable to make appropriate decisions, who misses important clues, or who fails to develop and evaluate an intervention appropriately. An important area of future development will be the development of methodologies that can train and support clinicians through the process of developing and using a functional analysis. One part of this would be research into current clinical practice. It would be useful to know how clinicians make decisions while undertaking a functional analysis, how they respond to various inputs from clients and team members, how they assign priorities to the use of their time in order to determine which cases need little investment of resources and which cases need heavy investment of resources. In order to achieve this aim better training materials and methods of monitoring clinician performance are needed.

In certain services some form of functional analysis is routine. In many American services for persons with developmental disabilities some form of written functional analysis is required either through funding regulations, court orders, or the fear of litigation. In services for other populations there are no such requirements for functional analysis and so treatments based on functional analysis are rarely found. In services for people with developmental disabilities in other countries there is no such regulation that directs services and consequently functional analyses and treatment based upon them are very rare. In some states in the USA there is a vigorous behavioral culture among clinicians, in other states behaviorists languish in isolation. Future research should attend to those factors that foster and support a professional culture that supports this field.

One of the major developments over the last ten years has been that functional analysis methodologies have brought us back to our experimental roots (Horner, 1994). The behavioral interventions in the 1970s are now often criticized because they became mechanical and non-analytic. However, a similar danger may be occurring with the methodologies of functional analysis. Slavishly following the existing assessment methodologies of functional analysis may not be a guarantee of conducting an experimental analysis of a clinically important problem. There is a danger that if we reflexively follow current assessment methodologies, we may fail to conduct a comprehensive assessment of the environment and behavior, and could miss what may be readily apparent, but is not assessed by current popular methodologies.

REFERENCES

Altmann, J. (1974) Observational study of behaviour: Sampling methods. *Behaviour*, **49**, 227–265.

American Psychiatric Association (1994) *Diagnostic and Statistical Manual* (4th edn) (DSM-IV) Washington DC: American Psychiatric Association.

Axelrod, S. & Apsche, J. (Eds) (1983) *The Effects of Punishment on Human Behavior*. New York: Academic Press.

Ayllon, T. & Azrin, N. (1968) *The Token Economy. A Motivational System for Therapy and Rehabilitation*. New York: Appleton-Century-Croft.

Ayllon, T., Haughton, E. & Hughes, H. B. (1965) Interpretation of symptoms: Fact or fiction? *Behaviour, Research and Therapy*, **3**, 1–7.

Baer, D. M., Wolf, M. M. & Risley, T. R. (1968) Some current dimensions of applied behavior analysis. *Journal of Applied Behavior Analysis*, **1**, 91–97.

Bakke, B. I., Kvale, S., Burns, T., McCarten, R., Wilson, L., Maddox, M. & Cleary, J. (1994) Multi-component for agitated behavior in a person with Alzheimer's disease. *Journal of Applied Behavior Analysis*, **27**, 175–176.

Balsom, P. D. & Bondy, A. S. (1988) The negative side effects of reward. *Journal of Applied Behavior Analysis*, **16**, 283–296.

Barnett, P. A. & Gottlieb, I. H. (1988) Psychosocial functioning and depression: Distinguishing among antecedents, concomitants, and consequences. *Psychological Bulletin*, **104**, 97–126.

Barrios, B. A. (1988) On the changing nature of behavioral assessment. In A. S. Bellack & M. Hersen (Eds) *Behavioral Assessment. A Practical Handbook* (3rd edn) (pp. 3–41). New York: Pergamon Press.

Barrios, B. A. & Hartmann, D. P. (1986) The contribution of traditional assessment: Concepts, issues and methodologies. In R. O. Nelson & S. C. Haynes (Eds) *Conceptual Foundation of Behavioral Assessment* (pp. 156–200). New York: Guilford Press.

Bellack, A. S. & Hersen, M. (1988) (Eds) *Behavioral Assessment. A Practical Handbook* (3rd edn) New York: Pergamon Press.

Bergman, R. L. (1976) Treatment of childhood insomnia diagnosed as 'hyperactivity'. *Journal of Behavior Therapy and Experimental Psychiatry*, **6**, 199.

Biglan, A., Metzler, C. W. & Ary, D. V. (1994) The social context for risky sexual behavior among adolescents. *Journal of Behavioral Medecine*, **17**, 419–438.

Bijou, S. W. (1963) Theory and research in mental (developmental) retardation. *Psychological Record*, **13**, 95–110.

Bijou, S. W. (1966) A functional analysis of retarded behavior. In R. Ellis (Ed.) *International Review of Research in Mental Retardation*, Vol. 1 (pp. 1–19). New York: Academic Press.

Bijou, S. W. & Baer, D. M. (1961) *Child Development. The Universal Stage of Infancy*. New York: Appleton.

Bijou, S. W. & Baer, D. M. (1965) *Child Development. A Systematic and Empirical Theory*. New York: Appleton.

Bijou, S. W. & Dunitz-Johnson, E. (1981) Inter-behavioral analysis of developmental retardation. *The Psychological Record*, **31**, 305–329.

Blackman, D. E. (1985) Contemporary behaviourism: A brief overview. In C. F. Lowe, M. Richelle & D. E. Blackman (Eds), *Behaviour Analysis and Contemporary Psychology*. London: Lawrence Erlbaum.

Brady, J. V. (1986) Invited case transcript. Behavioral analysis of a case of psychogenic nausea and vomiting. *Journal of Behavior Therapy and Experimental Psychiatry*, **17**, 271–274.

Brady, J. V. (1990) Toward applied behavior analysis of life aloft. *Behavioral Science*, **35**, 11–23.

Brophy, J. (1981) Teacher praise: A functional analysis. *Review of Educational Research*, **51**, 5–32.

Brown, D. K., Kratochwill, T. R. & Bergan, J. R. (1982) Teaching interview skills for problem identification: An analogue study. *Behavioral Assessment*, **4**, 63–73.

Burke, A. E. & Silverman, W. K. (1987) The prescriptive treatment of school refusal. *Clinical Psychology Review*, **7**, 353–362.

Carbone, V. & Lynch, R. (1983) The functional analysis of behavior in a juvenile detention facility. *Journal of Offender Counseling Services and Rehabilitation*, **6**, 21–41.

Carr, E. G. (1977) The motivation of self-injurious behavior: A review of some hypotheses. *Psychological Bulletin*, **84**, 800–816.

Carr, E. G. & Durand, V. M. (1985a) The social-communicative basis of severe behavior problems in children. In S. Reiss & R. R. Bootzin (Eds) *Theoretical Issues in Behavior Therapy*. New York: Academic.

Carr, E. G. & Durand, V. M. (1985b) Reducing behavior problems through functional communication training. *Journal of Applied Behavior Analysis*, **18**, 111–126.

Carr, E. G., Newsom, C. D. & Binkoff, J. A. (1976) Stimulus control of self-destructive behavior in a psychotic child. *Journal of Abnormal Child Psychology*, **4**, 139–153.

Chapman, S., Fisher, W., Piazza, C. C. & Kurtz, P. F. (1993) Functional assessment and treatment of life-threatening drug ingestion in a dually diagnosed youth. *Journal of Applied Behavior Analysis*, **26**, 155–156.

Chioda, J. (1987) Invited case transcript. Bulimia: an individual behavioral analysis. *Journal of Behavior Therapy and Experimental Psychiatry*, **18**, 41–49.

Cimenero, A. R., Calhoun, S. & Adams, H. E. (1977) (Eds) *Handbook of Behavioral Assessment*. New York: Wiley.

Clark, C. D. (1984) Reasoning about hallucinations. *The Behavior Analyst*, **7**, 215–216.

Coggins, T. E. & Frederickson, R. (1988) Brief report: The communicative role of a highly frequent repeated utterance in the conversations of an autistic boy. *Journal of Autism and Developmental Disorders*, **18**, 687–694.

Cohen, J. (1960) A coefficient for nominal scales. *Educational and Psychological Measurement*, **68**, 409–412.

Crawford, J., Brockel, B., Schauss, S. & Miltenberger, R. G. (1992) A comparison of methods for the functional assessment of stereotyped behavior in persons with mental retardation. *Journal of the Association for Persons with Severe Handicaps*, **17**, 77–86.

Cullen, C. (1983) Implications of functional analysis. *British Journal of Clinical Psychology*, **22**, 137–138.

Day, R. M., Johnson, W. L. & Schussler, N. G. (1986) Determining the communicative properties of self-injury: Research, assessment, and treatment implications. *Advances in Learning and Behavioral Disabilities*, **5**, 117–139.

Day, R. M., Rea, J. A., Schussler, N. G., Larsen, S. E. & Johnson, W. L. (1988) A functionally based approach to the treatment of self-injurious behavior. *Behavior Modification* **12**, 565–589.

De Seixas Queiroz, L. O., Motta, M. A., Madi, M. B. B. P., Sossai, D. L. & Boren, J. J. (1981) A functional analysis of obsessive compulsive problems with related therapeutic procedures. *Behaviour Research and Therapy*, **19**, 377–388.

Delprato, D. J. & McGlynn, F. D. (1988) Interactions of response patterns and their implications for behavior therapy. *Journal of Behavior Therapy and Experimental Psychiatry*, **19**, 199–205.

Donnellan, A. M., Mirenda, P. L., Mesaros, R. A. & Fassbender, L. L. (1984) Analyzing the communicative functions of aberrant behavior. *Journal of the Association for Persons with Severe Handicaps*, **9**, 201–212.

Dougher, M. J. (1993, September) On the advantages and implications of a radical behavioral treatment of private events. *The Behavior Therapist*, 204–206.

Dougher, M. J. (1994) Introduction. *The Behavior Analyst*, **17**, 261.

Dougher, M. J. & Hackbert, L. (1994) A behavior-analytic account of depression and a case report using acceptance-based procedures. *The Behavior Analyst*, **17**, 231–333.

Durand, V. M. & Crimmins, D. B. (1988) Identifying the variables maintaining self-injurious behavior. *Journal of Autism and Developmental Disorders*, **18**, 99–117.

Durand, V. M., Crimmins, D. B., Caulfield, M. & Taylor, J. (1989) Reinforcer assessment I. Using problem behaviors to select reinforcers. *Journal of Autism and Developmental Disabilities*, **18**, 99–117.

Evans, I. M. (1985) Building systems models as a strategy for target behavior selection in clinical assessment. *Behavioral Assessment*, **7**, 21–32.

Eyberg, S. M. & Johnson, S. M. (1974) Multiple assessment of behavior modification with families: Effects of contingency contracting and order of treatment problems. *Journal of Consulting and Clinical Psychology*, **42**, 594–606.

Ferster, C. B. (1973) A functional analysis of depression. *American Psychologist*, **28**, 857–870.

Fisher, W., Piazza, C. C., Bowman, L. G., Hagopian, L. P. & Langdon, N. A. (1994a) Empirically derived consequences: A data-based method for prescribing treatments for destructive behaviors. *Research in Developmental Disabilities*, **15**, 133–149.

Fisher, W., Piazza, C. C., Bowman, L. G., Kurtz, P. F., Sherer, M. R. & Lachman, S. R. (1994b) A preliminary evaluation of empirically derived consequences for the treatment of pica. *Journal of Applied Behavior Analysis*, **27**, 447–458.

Fleece, L., Gross, A., O'Brien, T., Kistner, J., Rothblum, E. & Drabman, R. (1981) Elevation of voice volume in young developmentally delayed children via an operant shaping procedure. *Journal of Applied Behavior Analysis*, **14**, 351–355.

Foa, E. B. & Emmelkamp, P. M. G. (1983) *Failures in Behavior Therapy*. New York: Wiley.

Frankel, A. J. (1975) Beyond the simple functional analysis—The chain: A conceptual framework for assessment with a case example. *Behavior Therapy*, **6**, 254–260.

Fremouw, W. J. & Brown, J. P. (1980) The reactivity of addictive behaviors to self-monitoring: A functional analysis. *Addictive Behaviors*, **5**, 209–217.

Garb, H. N. (1988) Comment on 'The study of clinical judgement: An ecological approach.' *Clinical Psychology Review*, **8**, 411–416.

Glenn, S. S., Ellis, J. & Greenspoon, J. (1992) On the revolutionary nature of the operant as a unit of behavioral selections. *American Psychologist*, **47**, 1329–1336.

Glenn, S. S. & Field (1994) Functions of the environment in behavioral evolution. *The Behavior Analyst*, **17**, 241–159.

Goldiamond, I. (1974) Toward a constructional approach to social problems. Ethical and constitutional issues raised by applied behavior analysis. *Behaviorism*, **2**, 1–84.

Goldiamond, I. (1975a) Alternate sets as a framework for behavioral formulation and research. *Behaviorism*, **3**, 49–86.

Goldiamond, I. (1975b) Insider-outsider problems: A constructional approach. *Rehabilitation Psychology*, **22**, 103–116.

Goodall, E. & Murphy G. (1980) Measurement error in direct observation: A comparison of common recording methods. *Behaviour Research and Therapy*, **18**, 147–150.

Goren, E. R., Romanczk, R. G. & Harris, S. L. (1977) A functional analysis of echolalic speech. The antecedent and consequent events. *Behavior Modification*, **1**, 481–498.

Gottman, J. M. (1985) Observation measures of behavior therapy outcome: A reply to Jacobson. *Behavioral Assessment*, **7**, 317–321.

Green, C. W., Reid, D. H., White, L. K., Halford, R. C., Brittain, D. P. & Gardner, S. M. (1988) Identifying reinforcers for persons with profound handicaps. *Journal of Applied Behavior Analysis*, **21**, 431–443.

Greenwood, C. R., Delguardi, J. C., Stanley, S. O., Terry, B. & Hall, R. V. (1985) Assessment of ecobehavioral interaction in school setting. *Behavioral Assessment*, **7**, 331–347.

Gresham, F. M. (1985) Behavior disorder assessment: Conceptual, definitional, and practical connotations. *School Psychology Review*, **14**, 495–509.

Gresswell, D. M. & Hollin, C. R. (1992) Toward a new methodology of making sense of case material: An illustrative case involving attempted multiple murder. *Clinical Behaviour and Mental Health*, **2**, 329–341.

Groden, G. (1989) A guide for conducting a comprehensive behavioral analysis of a target behavior. *Journal of Behavior Therapy and Experimental Psychiatry*, **20**, 163–169.

Haddock, G., Bentall, R. P. & Slade, P. (1994) Psychological treatment of chronic auditory hallucinations: Two case studies. *Behavioural and Cognitive Psychotherapy*, **22**, 335–346.

Hall, R. & Baker, J. (1994) A review of the applications of the REHAB scale. *Behavioral Psychotherapy*, **22**, 211–231.

Harrop, A. & Daniels, M. (1986) Methods of time sampling: A reappraisal. *Journal of Applied Behavior Analysis*, **19**, 73–77.

Harrop, A. & Daniels, M. (1993) Further reappraisal of momentary time sampling and partial interval recording. *Journal of Applied Behavior Analysis*, **26**, 277–278.

Harrop, A., Faulkes, C. & Daniels, M. (1989) Observer agreement calculations: The role of primary data in reducing obfuscation. *British Journal of Psychology*, **80**, 181–189.

Hartmann, D. P., Roper, B. L. & Bradford, D. C. (1979) Some relations between behavioral and traditional assessment. *Journal of Behavioral Assessment*, **1**, 3–23.

Hartup, W. W. (1974) Aggression in childhood. Developmental perspectives. *American Psychologist*, **29**, 336–341.

Hay, W. M., Hay, I. R. & Nelson, R. O. (1977) Direct and collateral changes in on-task and academic behavior resulting from on-task and academic contingencies. *Behavioural Therapy*, **8**, 431–441.

Hayes, S. C., Strosahl, K. & Wilson, K. G. (in press) *Acceptance and Commitment Therapy*. New York: Guilford.

Hayes, S. C. & Wilson, K. G. (1994) Acceptance and Commitment therapy: Altering the verbal support for experiential avoidance. *The Behavior Analyst*, **17**, 289–303.

Haynes, S. N. (1986) A behavioral model of paranoid behaviors. *Behavior Therapy*, **17**, 266–287.

Haynes, S. N. (1988) Current models and the assessment–treatment relationship in behavior therapy. *Journal of Psychopathology and Behavioral Assessment*, **10**, 171–183.

Haynes, S. N., Nelson, R. O. & Jarrett, R. B. (1987) The treatment utility of assessment. A functional approach to evaluating assessment quality. *American Psychologist*, **42**, 963–974.

Haynes, S. N. & O'Brien, W. H. (1990) Functional analysis in behavior therapy. *Clinical Psychology Review*, **10**, 649–668.

Hersen, M. (1988) Behavioral assessment and psychiatric diagnosis. *Behavioral Assessment*, **10**, 107–121.

Hollin, C. R. (1990) *Cognitive-Behavioural Interventions with Young Offenders*. New York: Pergamon Press.

Horner, R. H. (1994) Functional assessment: Contributions and future directions. *Journal of Applied Behavior Analysis*, **27**, 401–404.

Horner, R. H., O'Neill, R. E. & Flannery, K. B. (1992) Building effective behavior support plans from functional assessment. In M. Snell (Ed.), *Instruction of Persons with Severe Handicaps* (4th edn) (pp. 184–214). Columbus, OH: Merrill.

Hughes, J. N. & Sullivan, K. A. (1988) Outcome assessment in social skills training with children. *Journal of School Psychology*, **26**, 167–183.

Iwata, B. A., Dorsey, M. F., Slifer, K. J., Bauman, K. E. & Richman G. S. (1982) Toward a functional analysis of self injury. *Analysis and Intervention in Developmental Disabilities*, **2**, 3–20.

Iwata, B. A., Pace, G. M., Dorsey, M. F., Zarcone, J. F., Vollmer, T. R., Smith, R. G. *et al.* (1994) The functions of self-injurious behavior: An experimental-epidemiological analysis. *Journal of Applied Behavior Analysis*, **26**, 215–239.

Iwata, B. A., Vollmer, T. R. & Zarcone, J. R. (1990) The experimental (functional) analysis of behavior disorders: Methodology, application and limitations. In A. C. Repp & N. N. Singh (Eds) *Perspectives on the Use of Non-aversive and Aversive Interventions for Persons with Developmental Disabilities* (pp. 301–330). Sycamore, IL: Sycamore Publications.

Jackson, H. F., Glass, C. & Hope, S. (1987) A functional analysis of recidivist arson. *British Journal of Clinical Psychology*, **26**, 175–185.

Jacobson, N. S. (1985a) The role of observational measures of behavior therapy outcome. *Behavioral Assessment*, **7**, 297–308.

Jacobson, N. S. (1985b) Uses versus abuses of observational measures. *Behavioral Assessment*, **7**, 323–330.

Jenkins, J. J. (1979) Four points to remember. A tetrahedron model of memory experiments. In L. S. Cermak & I. M. Craik (Eds) *Levels of Processing in Human Memory* (pp. 429–446). New York: Erlbaum.

Jones, R. S. P. (1983) Functional analysis: Some cautionary notes. *Bulletin of the British Psychological Society*, **36**, 237–238.

Jones, R. S. P. & Heskin, K. J. (1988) Toward a functional analysis of delinquent behavior: A pilot study. *Counselling Psychology Quarterly*, **1**, 33–42.

Jones, R. S. P. & Owens, R. G. (1992) Applying functional analysis: A reply to Samson & McDonnell. *Behavioural Psychotherapy*, **20**, 37–40.

Kanfer, F. H. & Grimm, L. G. (1977) Behavior analysis. Selecting target behaviors in the interview. *Behavior Modification*, **1**, 7–28.

Kanfer, F. H. & Phillips, J. S. (1970) *Learning Foundations of Behavior Therapy*. New York: Wiley.

Kazdin, A. E. (1977) Artefact, Bias and Complexity of Assessment: The ABCs of Reliability. *Journal of Applied Behavior Analysis*, **10**, 141–150.

Kazdin, A. E. (1985) Selection of target behaviors: The relationship of the treatment focus to clinical dysfunction. *Behavioral Assessment*, **7**, 33–47.

Kazdin, A. E., Matson, J. L. & Esveldt-Dawson, K. (1981) Social skill performance among normal and psychiatric inpatient children as a function of assessment conditions. *Behaviour, Research and Therapy*, **19**, 145–152.

Keane, T. M., Fairbank, J. A., Cadell, J. M., Zimering, R. T. & Bender, M. T. (1985) A behavioral approach to assessing and treating post-traumatic stress disorder in Vietnam veterans. In C. R. Cregley (Ed.), *Trauma and its Wake: The Study and Treatment of Post-traumatic Stress Disorder* (pp. 257–294). New York: Bruner/Mazel.

Kearney, C. A. (1994) Inter-rater reliability of the Motivation Assessment Scale: Another, closer look. *Journal of the Association for Persons with Severe Handicaps*, **19**, 139–142.

Kearney, C. A. & Silverman, W. K. (1990) A preliminary analysis of a functional model of assessment and treatment for school refusal behavior. *Behavior Modification*, **14**, 340–366.

Kennedy, P., Fisher, K. & Pearson, E. (1988) Ecological evaluation of a rehabilitation environment for spinal cord injured people: Behavioural mapping and feedback. *British Journal of Clinical Psychology*, **27**, 239–246.

Kerwin, M. L. E., Ahearn, W. H., Eicher, P. S. & Burd, D. M. (1995). The costs of eating: A behavioral economic analysis of food refusal. *Journal of Applied Behavior Analysis*, **28**, 245–259.

Kiernan, C. C. (1973) Functional analysis. In P. Mittler (Ed.), *Assessment for Learning in the Mentally Handicapped*. London: Churchill Livingstone.

Kohlenberg, R. J. & Tsai, M. (1994) Improving cognitive therapy for depression with functional analytic psychotherapy: Theory and case study. *The Behavior Analyst*, **17**, 305–319.

Kratochwill T. R. (1985) Selection of target behaviors: Issues and directions. *Behavioral Assessment*, **7**, 3–5.

Lalli, J. S., Browder, D. M., Mace, F. C. & Brown, D. K. (1993) Teacher descriptive analysis data to implement interventions to decrease student problem behaviors. *Journal of Applied Behavior Analysis*, **26**, 227–238.

Lawrenson, H. J. (1993) *Concurrent validity and inter-rater reliability of the Motivation Assessment Scale*. University of Manchester, UK: unpublished MSc thesis in clinical psychology.

Layng, T. V. J. & Andronis, P. T. (1984) Toward a functional analysis of delusional speech and hallucinatory behavior. *The Behavior Analyst*, **7**, 139–156.

Lerman, D. C., Iwata, B. A., Smith, R. G., Zarcone, J. R. & Vollmer, J. R. (1994) Transfer of behavioral function as a contributing factor in treatment relapse. *Journal of Behavior Analysis*, **27**, 357–370.

Leve, R. M. & Burdick, L. (1977) A functional analysis of reinforcement within a social system. *Behavior Therapy*, **8**, 456–459.

Levine, B. A. (1987) Invited case transcript. The importance of checking the assumptions of the professional referral source. *Journal of Behavior Therapy and Experimental Psychiatry*, **18**, 241–244.

Lewinsohn, P. M., Hoberman, H. M., Teri, L. & Hantsinger, M. (1988) An integrated theory of depression. In S. Reiss and R. R. Bootzin (Eds), *Theoretical Issues in Behavior Therapy* (pp. 331–359). New York: Academic Press.

Loro, A. D. & Orleans, C. S. (1981) Binge eating in obesity: Preliminary findings and guidelines for behavioral analysis and treatment. *Addictive Behaviors*, **6**, 155–166.

Lyons, J. A. & Scotti, J. R. (in press) Behavioral treatment of post-traumatic stress disorder: An illustrative case of direct therapeutic exposure. *Journal of Traumatic Stress*.

Mace, F. C., Browder, D. M. & Lin, Y. (1987) Analysis of demand conditions associated with stereotypy. *Journal of Behavior Therapy and Experimental Psychiatry*, **18**, 25–31.

Mace, F. C., Lalli, J. C. & Lalli, E. P. (1991) Functional analysis and the treatment of aberrant behavior. *Research in Developmental Disabilities*, **12**, 155–180.

Mace, F. C., Webb, M. E., Sharkey, R. W., Mattson, D. M. & Rosen, H. S. (1988) Functional analysis and treatment of bizarre speech. *Journal of Behavior Therapy and Experimental Psychiatry*, **19**, 289–296.

Mace, F. C. & West, B. J. (1986) Analysis of demand characteristics associated with reluctant speech. *Journal of Behavior Therapy and Experimental Psychiatry*, **17**, 285–294.

Malatesta, V. J. (1990) Behavioral case formulation: An experimental assessment study of transient tic disorder. *Journal of Psychopathy and Behavioral Assessment*, **3**, 219–232.

Martens, B. K. & Witt, J. C. (1988) Expanding the scope of behavioral consultation: A systems approach to classroom behavior problems. *Professional School Psychology*, **3**, 271–281.

Mash, E. J. (1985) Some comments on target selection in behavior therapy. *Behavioral Assessment* **7**, 63–78.

Mash, E. J. & Terdal, L. (Eds) (1976) *Behavioral Assessment of Childhood Disorders*. New York: Guilford Press.

McCuller, W. R. & Salzberg, C. L. (1982) The functional analysis of imitation. In N. R. Ellis (Ed.) *International Review of Research*, Vol. 11 (pp.285–320). New York: Academic Press.

McDonnell, A. & Samson, D. (1992) Explanation and prediction in functional analysis: A reply to Jones & Owens. *Behavioural Psychotherapy*, **20**, 41–43.

McEvoy, R. E., Loveland, K. A. & Landry, S. H. (1988) The functions of immediate echolalia in autistic children: A developmental perspective. *Journal of Autism and Developmental Disorders*, **18**, 657–668.

McKinlay, T., Kelly, J. A. & Collum, J. M. (1977) The multi-modal treatment of conversion reaction in adolescence: A case study. *Journal of Clinical Child Psychology*, **6**, 66–68.

McNight, D. L., Nelson, R. O., Haynes, S. C. & Jarrett, R. B. (1984) The importance of treating individually assessed response classes in the amelioration of depression. *Behavior Therapy*, **15**, 315–335.

Merluzzi, T. V. & Biever, J. (1987) Role-playing procedures for the behavioral assessment of social skills: A validity study. *Behavioral Assessment*, **9**, 362–377.

Michael, J. (1982) Distinguishing between the discriminative and motivational functions of stimuli. *Journal of the Experimental Analysis of Behavior*, **37**, 149–158.

Miller, W. R. (1978) Behavioral treatment of problem drinkers: A comparative outcome study of three controlled drinking therapies. *Journal of Clinical and Consulting Psychology*, **46**, 74–86.

Milne, D. (1986) *Training of Behaviour Therapists: Methods, Evaluation and Implementation with Parents, Nurses and Teachers*. London: Croom Helm.

Milne, D. (1994) Behavioural psychotherapists in practice: A survey of UK practitioners. *Behavioral and Cognitive Psychotherapy*, **22**, 247–257.

Milne, D. & Ridley, N. (1994) A review of Behavioural Psychotherapy in the 1980s. On course? *Behavioural and Cognitive Psychotherapy*, **22**, 75–85.

Miltenberger, R. G. & Fuqua, R. W. (1985) Evaluating a training manual for the acquisition of behavioral assessment interviewing skills. *Journal of Applied Behavior Analysis*, **18**, 323–327.

Miltenberger, R. G. & Veltum, L. G. (1988) Evaluation of an instructions and modelling procedure for training behavioral assessment interviewing. *Journal of Behavior Therapy and Experimental Psychiatry*, **19**, 31–41.

Morganstern, I. P. (1988) Behavioral interviewing: The initial stages of assessment. In M. Hersen and A. S. Bellack (Eds) *Behavioral Assessment: A Practical Handbook* (3rd edn). Oxford: Pergamon Press.

Morrison, A. P. (1994) Cognitive behaviour therapy for auditory hallucinations without concurrent medication: A single case study. *Behavioural and Cognitive Psychotherapy*, **22**, 259–264.

Munck, D. D. & Repp, A. C. (1994) Behavioral assessment of feeding problems of individuals with severe disabilities. *Journal of Applied Behavior Analysis*, **27**, 241–250.

Neef, N. A. (1994) Editor's note. *Journal of Applied Behavior Analysis*, **26**, 196.

Nelson, R. O. (1977) Assessment and therapeutic functions of self-monitoring. In M. Hersen, M. Eiseler & R. M. Miller (Eds) *Progress in Behavior Modification*, Vol. 5. New York: Academic Press.

Nelson, R. O. (1988) Relationship between assessment and treatment within a behavioral perspective. *Journal of Psychopathology*, **10**, 155–170.

Newton, T. & Sturmey, P. (1991) The Motivation Assessment Scale: Inter-rater reliability and internal consistency in a British sample. *Journal of Mental Deficiency Research*, **35**, 372–374.

Northup, J., Wacker, D., Berg, W. K., Kelly, L., Sasso, G. & DeRaad, A. (1994) The treatment of severe behavior problems in school settings using a technical assistance model. *Journal of Applied Behavior Analysis*, **27**, 33–47.

Northup, J., Wacker, D., Sasso, G., Steege, M., Cigrand, K., Cook, J. & DeRaad, A. (1991) A brief functional analysis of aggressive and alternative behavior in an out-patient clinic setting. *Journal of Applied Behavior Analysis*, **24**, 509–522.

Norton, G. R. & Nielson, W. R. (1976) Headaches: The importance of consequent events. *Behavior Therapy*, **8**, 504–506.

Oliver, C. (1991) The application of analogue methodology to the functional analysis of challenging behaviour. In B. Remington (Ed.) *The Challenge of Severe Mental Handicap. A Behaviour Analytic Approach* (pp. 97–117). New York: Wiley.

Oliver, C. (1993) Self-injurious behaviour: From response to strategy. In C. Kiernan (Ed.) *Research to Practice? Implications of the Challenging Behavior of People with Learning Disability* (pp. 136–188). Clevedon, UK: BILD Publications.

Oliver, C. & Head, D. (1993) Self-injurious behaviour: Functional analysis and interventions. In R. S. P. Jones and C. B. Eyeres (Eds) *Challenging Behaviour and Intellectual Disability: A Psychological Perspective*. Clevedon, UK: BILD Publications.

Ollendick, T. H. & Hersen, M. (Eds) (1984) *Child Behavioural Assessment: Principles and Procedures*. New York: Pergamon Press.

O'Leary, D. (1972) The assessment of psychopathology in children. In H. C. Quay & J. S. Werry (Eds) *Psychopathological Disorders of Childhood* (pp. 234–274). New York: Wiley.

O'Neill, R. E., Horner, R. H., Albin, R. W., Storey, K. & Sprague, J. R. (1991) *Functional Analysis of Problem Behavior; A Practical Assessment Guide*. Sycamore, IL: Sycamore Publications.

Owens, R. G. & Ashcroft, J. B. (1982) Functional analysis in clinical psychology. *British Journal of Clinical Psychology*, **21**, 181–189.

Owens, R. G. & Jones, R. S. V. (1992) Extending the role of functional analysis in challenging behaviours. *Behavioural Psychotherapy*, **20**, 45–46.

Pace, G. M., Ivancic, M. T., Edwards, G. L., Iwata, B. & Page, T. J. (1985) Assessment of stimulus preference and reinforcer value with profoundly retarded individuals. *Journal of Applied Behavior Analysis*, **18**, 249–255.

Pace, G. M., Iwata, B. A., Cowdery, G. E. Andree, P. J. & McIntyre, T. (1994) Stimulus (instructional) fading during extinction of self-injurious escape behavior. *Journal of Applied Behavior Analysis*, **26**, 205–212.

Paisey, T. J. H., Whitney, R. B. & Hislop, P. M. (1991) Brief report: Non-intrusive operant analysis of aggressive behavior in persons with mental retardation. *Behavioral Residential Treatment*, **6**, 51–64.

Parrish, J. M., Iwata, B. A., Dorsey, M. F., Bunck, T. J. & Slifer, K. J. (1985) Behavior analysis, program development and transfer of control in self-injury. *Journal of Behavior Therapy and Experimental Psychiatry*, **16**, 159–168.

Peterson, L., Homer, A. L. & Wonderlich, S. A. (1982) The integrity of the independent variable. *Journal of Applied Behavior Analysis*, **15**, 477–492.

Prizant, B. M. & Duchan, J. F. (1981) The functions of immediate echolalia in autistic children. *Journal of Speech and Hearing Disorders*, **25**, 241–249.

Proshansky, H., Ittleson, W. & Rivlin, L. (1975) (Eds) *Environmental Psychology*. New York: Holt, Reinhart & Winston.

Pyles, D. A. M. & Bailey, J. S. (1990) Diagnosing severe behavior problems. In A. C. Repp & N. N. Singh (Eds) *Perspectives on the Use of Non-aversive and Aversive Interventions for Persons with Developmental Disabilities* (pp. 381–401). Sycamore, IL: Sycamore Publications.

Quay, H. C. (1986) Classification. In H. C. Quay & J. S. Werry (Eds) *Psychopathological Disorders of Childhood* (3rd edn) (pp. 1–34). New York: Wiley.

Rachman, S. (1981) The primacy of affect: Some theoretical formulations. *Behaviour, Research, and Therapy*, **19**, 279–290.

Redd, W. H. (1980) Stimulus control and extinction of psychosomatic symptoms in cancer patients in protective isolation. *Journal of Consulting and Clinical Psychology*, **48**, 448–455.

Redd, W. H. & Rusch (1985) Behavioral analysis in behavioral medicine. *Behavior Modification*, **18**, 131–154.

Repp, A. C., Felce, D. & Barton, L. E. (1988) Basing the treatment of stereotypic and self-injurious behaviors on hypotheses of their causes. *Journal of Applied Behavior Analysis*, **21**, 281–289.

Repp, A. C., Harman, M. L., Felce, D., Acker, R. V. & Karsh, K. G. (1989) Conducting behavioral assessments on computer-collected data. *Behavioral Assessment*, **11**, 249–268.

Repp, A. C. & Karsh, K. G. (1994) Hypothesis-based intervention for tantrum behaviors of persons with developmental disabilities in school settings. *Journal of Applied Behavior Analysis*, **27**, 21–31.

Rickland, K. M. & Titley, R. W. (1988) The hypothesis-testing game: A training tool for the graduate interviewing skills course. *Teaching of Psychology*, **15**, 139–141.

Rock, D. L., Bransford, J. D., Maisto, S. A. & Morey, L. (1987) The study of clinical judgement: An ecological approach. *Clinical Psychology Review*, **7**, 645–661.

Rock, D. L., Bransford, J. D., Morey, L. C. & Maisto, S. A. (1988) The study of clinical judgement: Some clarifications. *Clinical Psychology Review*, **8**, 411–416.

Rosen, E., Fox, R. E. & Gregory, I. (1972) *Abnormal Psychology* (2nd edn). Philadelphia, PA: W. B. Saunders.

Ross, S. M. & Schwartz, C. W. (1974) State dependent learning and its implications for treatment of drug abuses. *Psychiatric Quarterly*, **48**, 368–373.

Sackett, G. O. (1978) *Observing Behavior*, Vol. II. Baltimore, MD: University Park Press.

Samson, D. M. & McDonnell, A. A. (1990) Functional analysis and challenging behaviours. *Behavioural Psychotherapy*, **18**, 259–271.

Schlundt, D. G., Johnson, W. G. & Jarrell, M. P. (1985) A naturalistic functional analysis of eating behavior in bulimia and obesity. *Advances in Behaviour Research and Therapy*, **7**, 149–162.

Schulte, D., Kunzel, R., Pepping, G. & Scholte-Bahrenbert, T. (1992) Tailor-made versus standardized therapy of phobic patients. *Advances in Behaviour Research and Therapy*, **24**, 67–92.

Schuster, R. H. (1969) A functional analysis of conditioned reinforcement. In D. P. Hendry (Ed.) *Conditioned Reinforcement*. Homewood, IL: Dorsey Press.

Scotti, J. R., Evans, I. M., Meyer, L. H. & Walker, P. (1991) A meta-analysis of intervention research with problem behavior: Treatment validity and standards of practice. *American Journal of Mental Retardation*, **96**, 233–256.

Scotti, J. R., McMorrow, M. J. & Trawitz, A. L. (1993) Behavioral treatment of chronic psychiatric disorders: Publication trends and future directions. *Behavior Therapy*, **24**, 527–550.

Shapiro, M. (1966) The single case in clinical-psychological research. *The Journal of General Psychology*, **74**, 3–23.

Shapiro, M. (1970) Intensive assessment of the single case: An inductive-deductive approach. In P. Mittler (Ed.) *The Psychological Assessment of Mental and Physical Handicap* (pp. 645–666). London: Methuen.

Shook, J. (1993) The professional credentialling of behavior analysts. *The Behavior Analyst*, **16**, 87–101.

Sigafoos, J., Kerr, M. & Roberts, D. (1994) Interrater reliability of the Motivation Assessment Scale: Failure to replicate with aggressive behavior. *Research in Developmental Disabilities*, **15**, 333–342.

Singh, N. N., Donatelli, L. S., Best, A., Williams, E. E., Barrera, F. J., Lenz, M. W. et al. (1992) Factor structure of the Motivation Assessment Scale. *Journal of Intellectual Disabilities Research*, **37**, 65–74.

Skinner, B. F. (1953) *Science and Human Behavior*. New York: Macmillan.

Skinner, B. F. (1989) *Recent Issues in the Analysis of Behavior*. Columbus, OH: Merrill.

Slade, P. (1982) Toward a functional analysis of Anorexia Nervosa and Bulimia Nervosa. *British Journal of Clinical Psychology*, **21**, 167–179.

Sobell, M. B., Sobell, L. C. & Sheahan, D. B. (1976) Functional analysis of drinking problems as an aid in developing individual treatment strategies. *Addictive Behaviors*, **1**, 127–132.

Staats, A. W. & Burns, G. L. (1992) The psychological behaviorism theory of personality. In G. Caprara & G. L. Van Heck (Eds) *Modern Personality Theory: Critical Reviews and New Directions* (pp. 161–199). New York: Harvester Wheatsheaf.

Staats, A. W. & Heilby, E. M. (1985) Paradigmatic theory of depression: Unified, explanatory, and heuristic. In S. Reiss & R. Bootzin (Eds) *Theoretical Issues in Behavior Therapy* (pp. 277–330). New York: Academic Press.

Steege, M., Wacker, D., Berg, W., Cigrand, K. C. & Cooper, L. (1989) The use of behavioral assessment to prescribe and evaluate treatments for severely handicapped children. *Journal of Applied Behavior Analysis*, **22**, 23–33.

Stevenson, H. C. & Fantuzzo, J. W. (1984) Application of the 'generalization map' to a self-control intervention with school-aged children. *Journal of Applied Behavior Analysis*, **17**, 203–212.

Street, R. L. & Butler, D. B. (1987) Nonverbal response patterns in physician-patient interactions: a functional analysis. *Journal of Nonverbal Behavior*, **11**, 234–253.

Sturmey, P. (1991) Case transcript: Assessment of challenging behaviour by semi-structured, behavioural interview. *Mental Handicap*, **19**, 56–60.

Sturmey, P. (1993) The use of DSM and ICD diagnostic criteria in people with mental retardation. A review of empirical studies. *The Journal of Nervous and Mental Disease*, **181**, 39–42.

Sturmey, P. (1994) Assessing the functions of aberrant behavior: A review of psychometric instruments. *Journal of Autism and Developmental Disabilities*, **24**, 293–304.

Sturmey, P. & Crisp, A. G. (1994) Group engagement: A conceptual analysis. *Journal of Intellectual Disabilities Research*, **38**, 455–468.

Sturmey, P. (1995a) Assessing the functions of self-injurious behavior: A case of assessment failure. *Journal of Behavior Therapy and Experimental Psychology*.

Sturmey, P. (1995b) Suicidal threats and behavior in a person with developmental disabilities: Effective psychiatric monitoring based on functional assessment. *Behavioral Interventions: Theory and Practice in Residential and Community-based Programs*, **9**, 235–245.

Sturmey, P. (1995c) Analog baselines: A critical review of the methodology. *Research in Developmental Disabilities*, **16**, 269–284.

Sturmey, P. (1995d) Diagnostic-based pharmacological treatment of behavior disorders in persons with developmental disabilities: A review and decision-making typology. *Research in Developmental Disabilities*.

Sturmey, P. & Bertman, L. J. (1992) *The Functional Analysis Checklist: Inter-rater and test-retest reliability*. Unpublished manuscript.

Sturmey, P., Carlton, A., Crisp, A. G. & Newton, J. T. (1987) A functional analysis of multiple aberrant responses: A refinement and extension of Iwata *et al.* (1982) *Journal of Mental Deficiency Research*, **32**, 31–46.

Sturmey, P., Newton, T. & Crisp, A. G. (1991) Validation of the Pethna toy through changes in collateral behaviours. *Journal of Mental Deficiency Research*, **35**, 459–471.

Taplin, P. S. & Reid, J. B. (1973) Effect of instructional set and experimenter influence on observer reliability. *Child Development*, **44**, 547–554.

Tarnowski, K. J., Rasnake, L., Linscheid, T. R. & Mulick, J. A. (1989) Ecobehavioral characteristics of a pediatric burn injury unit. *Journal of Applied Behavior Analysis*, **22**, 101–109.

Taylor, J. C. & Romancyk, R. G. (1994) Generating hypotheses about the functions of student problems behaviors by observing teacher behavior. *Journal of Applied Behavior Analysis*, **27**, 251–265.

Thompson, S. & Emerson, E. (in press) Inter-informant agreement of the Motivation Assessment Scale. *Mental Handicap Research*.

Tinbergen, N. (1963) On the aims and methods of ethology. *Zeitschrift für Tierpsychologie*, **20**, 410–432.

Touchette, P. E., MacDonald, R. F. & Langer, S. N. (1985) A scatter plot for identifying stimulus control of problem behavior. *Journal of Applied Behavior Analysis*, **18**, 343–351.

Trower, P., Yardley, K., Bryant, B. M. & Shaw, P. (1978) The treatment of social failure: A comparison of anxiety reduction and skill acquisition procedures on two social problems. *Behavior Modification*, **2**, 41–60.

Turkat, I. D. (1988) Invited case transcript. The initial clinical hypothesis. *Journal of Behavior Therapy and Experimental Psychiatry*, **18**, 349–356.

Turkat, I. D. & Maisto, S. A. (1985) Application of the experimental method to the formulation and modification of personality disorders. In D. H. Barlow (Ed.) *Clinical Handbook of Psychological Disorders* (pp. 503–570). New York: Guilford Press.

Upper, D., Livingstone, L., Connors, G. J. & Olans, J. (1982) Evaluating a social and coping skill training group for psychiatric day hospital patients. *International Journal of Partial Hospitalization*, **1**, 203–211.

Van Houten, R. & Rolider, A. (1991) Applied behavior analysis. In J. L. Matson & J. A. Mulick (Eds) *Handbook of Mental Retardation* (2nd edn) (pp. 569–585). New York: Pergamon Press.

Van Houten, R., Rolider, A. & Ikowitz, O. (1989) *The Functional Analysis Checklist*. Unpublished manuscript.

Vandereycken, W. & Meerman, R. (1988) Chronic illness behavior and noncompliance with treatment: Pathways to an interactional approach. *Psychotherapy and Psychosomatics*, **50**, 182–191.

Vollmer, T. R., Marcus, B. A. & LeBlanc, L. (1994) Treatment of self-injury and hand mouthing following inconclusive functional analysis. *Journal of Applied Behavior Analysis*, **27**, 331–344.

Wahler, R. G. (1975) Some structural aspects of deviant child behavior. *Journal of Applied Behavior Analysis*, **8**, 27–42.

Weiseler, N. A., Janson, R. H., Chamberlain, T. P. & Thompson, T. (1985) Functional taxonomy of stereotypic and self-injurious behavior. *Mental Retardation,* **23**, 230–234.

Weiss, R. L. & Frohman, P. E. (1985) Behavioral observation as outcome measures: Not through a glass darkly. *Behavioral Assessment,* **7**, 309–315.

Wetherby, A. M. & Pritting, C. A. (1984) Profiles of communicative and cognitive-social abilities in autistic children. *Journal of Speech and Hearing Research,* **27**, 364–377.

West, J. & Spinks, P. (1988) *Clinical Psychology in Action: A Collection of Case Studies.* London: Wright & Butterworth Scientific.

Wilkinson, W. K., Parrish, J. M. & Wilson, F. E. (1994) Training parents to observe and record: A data-based outcome evaluation of a pilot curriculum. *Research in Developmental Disabilities,* **15**, 343–354.

Wilson, F. E. & Evans, I. M. (1983) The reliability of target-behavior selection in behavioral assessment. *Behavioral Assessment,* **5**, 15–32.

Wolpe, J. (1980) Behavior analysis and therapeutic strategy. In A. Goldstein & E. A. Foa (Eds) *Handbook of Behavioral Interventions. A Clinical Guide.* New York: Wiley.

Wolpe, J. (1989) The derailment of behavior therapy: A tale of conceptual misdirection. *Journal of Behavior Therapy and Experimental Psychiatry,* **20**, 3–15.

Wolpe, J. & Turkat, I. D. (1985) Behavioral formulation of clinical cases. In I. D. Turkat, *Behavioral Case Formulation* (pp. 5–36). New York: Plenum Press.

Wulfert, E. & Biglan, A. (1994) A contextual approach to research on AIDS prevention. *The Behavior Analyst,* **17**, 353–363.

Zarcone, J. R., Rodgers, T. A., Iwata, B. A., Rourke, D. A. & Dorsey, M. F. (1991) Reliability analysis of the Motivation Assessment Scale. *Research in Developmental Disabilities,* **12**, 349–360.

Zlutnick, S., Mayville, N. J. & Moffat, S. (1975) Modification of seizure disorders: The interruption of behavior chains. *Journal of Applied Behavior Analysis,* **8**, 1–13.

Zwick, R. (1983) Assessing the psychometric properties of psychodiagnostic systems: How do research diagnostic criteria measure up? *Journal of Consulting and Clinical Psychology,* **51**, 117–131.

INDEX

The Wiley Series in

CLINICAL PSYCHOLOGY

Anthony Lavender and   Community Care in Practice: Services for the
Frank Holloway (Editors)   Continuing Care Client

J. Mark G. Williams,   Cognitive Psychology and Emotional
Fraser N. Watts,   Disorders
Colin MacLeod and
Andrew Matthews

John Clements   Severe Learning Disability and Psychological
Handicap

Related titles of interest from Wiley...

Brief Therapeutic Consultations
An Approach to Systemic Counselling
Eddy Street and **Jim Downey**

Outlines the theory and practice of brief therapeutic consultations, an approach that involves the counsellor and client in a straight-forward exchange about the nature of the problem as perceived by the client.

Wiley Series in Brief Therapy and Counselling
0471 96343 7   170pp   1996   Paperback

Research Methods in Clinical and Counselling Psychology
Chris Barker, Nancy Pistrang and **Robert Elliott**

Presents a practical description of the research process, using a chronological framework. It takes readers through the sequence of steps involved in executing a project: formulation, measurement, design, analysis and interpretation.

0471 93612 X   300pp   1994   Hardback
0471 96297 X   300pp   1995   Paperback

Stereotyped Movement Disorders
Robert S.P. Jones, Peter Walsh and **Peter Sturmey**

Brings together a wide variety of behavioural and biological research on stereotyped behaviours. It explores the major theories which attempt to account for the presence of these behaviours and examines both assessment and treatment from a broad-based psychological perspective.

Wiley Series in Clinical Psychology
0471 93903 X   250pp   1995   Hardback

The Working Alliance
Theory, Research and Practice
Edited by **Adam O. Horvath** and **Leslie S. Greenberg**

Offers a comprehensive, in-depth overview of the nature of the relationship between client and therapist, and illuminates the ways in which it promotes positive therapeutic change

0471 54640 2   316pp   1994   Hardback